# LUCY STONE

*Pioneer of Woman's Rights*

# LUCY STONE

*Pioneer of Woman's Rights*

*By* ALICE STONE BLACKWELL

WITH AN
INTRODUCTION
BY
RANDOLPH
HOLLINGSWORTH

UNIVERSITY PRESS
OF VIRGINIA
*Charlottesville and London*

THE UNIVERSITY PRESS OF VIRGINIA

Printed in the United States of America

*First University Press of Virginia edition published 2001*

♾ The paper used in this publication meets the minimum requirements of the American National Standard for Information Sciences—Permanence of Paper for Printed Library Materials, ANSI Z39.48-1984.

Library of Congress Cataloging-in-Publication Data

Blackwell, Alice Stone, 1857–1950.
Lucy Stone : pioneer of woman's rights / by Alice Stone Blackwell.
p. cm.
Originally published: Boston : Little, Brown, c1930. With new introd.
Includes index.
ISBN 0-8139-1990-8 (pbk. : alk. paper)
1. Stone, Lucy, 1818–1893. 2. Suffragists—United States—Biography. 3. Women's rights—United States—History—19th century. I. Title.

JK1899.S8 B62 2001
323.3'4'092—dc21
[B] 00-053400

"We hold in our hearts the memory of a loving and gracious presence, a voice like the music of brooks in the ear of a thirsty traveller, a smile that brightened the day, a hand ever ready to help; a young Joan of Arc, who listened to the voices in her youth, and whose fidelity to their demands kept her ever young and beautiful." — From the memorial address of Mrs. Ednah D. Cheney on Lucy Stone

*Contents*

Introduction ix

Bibliography xxv

Preface xxix

*Lucy Stone: Pioneer of Woman's Rights* 1

Appendix 299

Index 303

# *Introduction*

RANDOLPH HOLLINGSWORTH

"Justice, simple justice is what the world needs."
—Lucy Stone

The story of Lucy Stone is the story of a woman who would not be silenced. Born in 1818 on her parents' farm in central Massachusetts, Stone grew up in the heart of antebellum New England reform movements, but her worldview was far broader than that of the average farm girl. She learned early about principles of absolute racial and sexual equality from the radical orator and utopianist Frances Wright, who lectured in nearby Worcester. She heard Abby Kelley, an abolitionist who spoke in churches about the horrors of degradation in the lives of slave women. So when the sixteen-year-old Lucy Stone heard ministers thundering against women who spoke in public, she resolved to study the Bible in its Greek and Hebrew versions in order to determine for herself whether God ordained women to be quiet. Her first feminist act was to raise her hand in church to vote for Kelley's right to speak in mixed company.

When her father would not pay for her college education, Stone worked for years to earn her own tuition. Rather than stay in Massachusetts at the newly founded Mount Holyoke Female Seminary, she studied the classical program at Oberlin College in Ohio. There her independent spirit led her to read and write what many considered too radical for antebellum women; and she honed her oratorical skills in an off-campus debating club for ladies that she organized with her best friend, Antoinette "Nettie" Brown. The controversy over the debating club and her newspaper, *The Plain Speaker,* intensified with her public-speaking debut at a celebration for West Indian emancipation. At the end of her college career, she demanded the right to speak at her graduation ceremony. As one of the best scholars, she had been elected to write an essay, and she wished to read it from the podium alongside her male colleagues who had also won this distinction. The Ladies Board at Oberlin denied her request, and she refused to submit any essay at all rather than have a man read her work in her stead.

When she graduated from college in 1847 she became one of the first women in the United States to do so, and she was the first orator to establish a career in lecturing exclusively on women's rights. Whether the gathering she addressed was devoted to antislavery, temperance, or women's rights, Stone consistently drew her audience's attention to the inequities of women's lot. A small, attractive woman with a strong, charismatic voice, Stone attracted crowds of hundreds to her lectures on women's rights. Meanwhile the young Elizabeth Cady Stanton sat in the audience at Seneca Falls while men led the now-famous 1848 women's rights convention. Although many local and statewide meetings on women's rights had been held in the 1840s, including Lucretia Mott and Paulina Wright Davis's efforts in Philadelphia,[1] Stone's feminist stance was radical for her times because she insisted on speaking out for herself and because she assumed equality across race, gender, and class lines.

In 1850 Stone organized and led the First National Women's Rights convention in Worcester, Massachusetts. Participants at this meeting established standing committees to work on women's rights and resolved to meet annually thereafter. Subsequently she joined with Elizabeth Cady Stanton, Susan B. Anthony, Elizabeth Garritt Smith, and Amelia Bloomer in trying to live their principles of equality by wearing the comfortable pants and short dress of the "Bloomer" costume, but within a few years public ostracism led them all, one by one, to exchange it for their customary long dresses.

In 1855 Stone again compromised her principles when, despite her opposition to contemporary laws and customs for married women, she finally married one of her most ardent suitors, Henry B. Blackwell, a dashing entrepreneur and member of a celebrated family.[2] His sisters were the first women to become licensed American physicians, and his brother Sam married Stone's best friend, Antoinette Brown, the first woman ordained as a minister in America.

Taking a husband's name was custom and not law; Stone defied custom by retaining her own. When she and Henry Blackwell married in 1855, they published a joint statement in protest of marriage laws and customs that deprived a married woman of her legal identity and control of her own body. Newspapers all across the country published the full text of their "Marriage Protest," and Lucy Stone became famous for refusing to become "Mrs. Henry Blackwell." Their marriage protest was not the first: John Stuart and Harriet Mill had done something similar in 1851, as had Theodore and Angelina Grimké Weld in 1838. Nevertheless, Stone's refusal to adopt a "married name" was a powerful statement at the time, and is probably the act for which she is best remembered today. The Lucy Stone League was created in the 1920s to encourage women to keep their own names after marriage, and those who did were called "Lucy Stoners."

The year 1857 saw Stone's first pregnancy and the birth of her daughter Alice, but she kept up the pace of her organizational activities for the national and local conventions and maintained her speaking schedule. During that year she was the first woman to appear before the Massachusetts state legislature, where she called for woman suffrage and equal property rights for married women. She refused to pay taxes on her farm in New Jersey on the republican principle of "No taxation without representation," and her household goods were accordingly auctioned off in one wintry day.

The demands of pregnancy and child care led Stone to relinquish her leadership role to her confidante and collaborator Susan Anthony. From 1857 to 1863 Stone headed her letters to fellow activists "From the Kitchen" or "In the Little Kitchen with Mother and Baby." She raised Alice basically on her own: her husband was often away, and when Stone and Blackwell traveled together (living in boarding houses from New Jersey and New York to Cincinnati, Chicago, and Wisconsin), she usually assumed primary care for Alice. (While they were in Chicago, Stone gave birth to a premature baby boy, who died.)

At the tenth Women's Rights Convention in May 1860, a deep rift appeared among the leaders: Stanton presented twelve divorce-reform resolutions against Stone's express wish. Stone had insisted that the issue of divorce reform was not a woman's rights issue "since it concerns men just as much."[3] The convention voted down Stanton's resolutions as Stone had predicted; Antoinette Blackwell's thirteen counter-resolutions affirming the cultural importance of marriage vows passed unanimously. Mirroring the national debate over slavery and secession, the women's rights activists were divided over how best to achieve the goal of freedom and equality.

When the Civil War began, women's rights leaders agreed to suspend their May anniversary conventions until the war was over. On May 14, 1863, Lucy Stone helped organize the Woman's National Loyal League, whose goal was to collect one million signatures for an amendment to abolish slavery. When Angelina Grimké proposed at their convention that both blacks' and women's rights would need to be achieved for true national peace, however, her resolution was defeated. In 1865 the New England Anti-Slavery Society debated whether women's rights could again be taken up as a cause, with Wendell Phillips urging the women activists to accept that it was the "Negro's hour" and that the "hour of woman" had not yet come. Stone disagreed, and began barnstorming New England and New York to promote simultaneous suffrage for both blacks and women. She followed up on her lectures with her trademark reform activism: she mentored the organizing of educational cadres at the local levels, and initiated petition drives for state and national legislative changes. She also met with Senator Charles Sumner of Massachusetts to protest the inclusion of the word "male" in the proposed Fourteenth Amendment that would further define citizenship rights for black Americans.

In the spring of 1866 Stanton and Anthony led the reorganization of the traditional Woman's Rights meeting in May as an American Equal Rights Association (AERA) that would push Congress and the general public accept the idea of universal suffrage "irrespective of race, color, or sex." Stone was elected to chair the executive committee of the AERA, but did not abandon the specific cause of women's suffrage. Around this time she organized and became the president of the New Jersey Woman Suffrage Association, and she accompanied Harry Blackwell to Boston to organize the New England Woman Suffrage Association with the socialite Julia Ward Howe as president. From this point on, Stone collaborated closely at the local and state levels in hopes of securing a new amendment to the Constitution that would guarantee equal rights for women.

The May 1869 debates in the AERA over the organization's formal response to the Fourteenth and Fifteenth Amendments led Anthony, Stanton, Davis, and Ernestine Rose to leave the group. Though reformers such as William Lloyd Garrison had all along supported women's rights, they assumed that an emphasis on women's rights was incompatible with the political cause of black men's suffrage (with black women left out of the equation altogether). Stone could not envision a partitioned freedom movement. "If one has a right to say that you cannot read and cannot vote, then it may be said that you are a woman and cannot vote. We are lost if we turn away from the middle principle and argue for one class. . . . The woman has an ocean of wrong too deep for any plummet, and the Negro, too, has an ocean of wrongs that cannot be fathomed. . . . But I thank God for the Fifteenth Amendment, and hope that it will be adopted in every state. I will be thankful in my soul if *any* body can get out of this terrible pit, and if the other party can succeed better than we, let them do it."[4]

This debate over a pro-amendment (pro–"Negro's Hour") position or anti-amendment (pro–women's suffrage) position centered on what the reform coalition should take on as their first priority. After the May 1869 AERA meeting, Anthony, Stanton, Davis, and Rose separately formed their own organization, the National Woman Suffrage Association (NWSA). Stone, for her part, worked with hundreds of activists and sent out a national call, signed by 110 people from twenty-two states, to form the American Woman Suffrage Association (AWSA). In January 1870 the AWSA's organizational strategies were complemented by publication of the *Woman's Journal,* with women typographers and Mary Livermore as editor-in-chief. The two separate women's suffrage organizations clearly differed in their strategies as well as their goals. The NWSA insisted on continuing to protest the Fifteenth Amendment, which enfranchised black men, and they used flamboyant public figures such as George Train and Victoria Woodhull in order to highlight their demand for rights for educated, native-born, white women. The AWSA committed itself to a delegate structure for its conventions, and operated via integrated state societies to channel information to and from the national organization.

For example, the AWSA mentored the formation of

the South Carolina Woman's Rights Association, the first racially integrated woman's rights organization in the South. In Massachusetts, Stone organized Working Girls' Clubs to keep in touch with working-class women's attitudes toward civil rights. She developed a systematic process of petitioning legislators that thereafter became the AWSA's trademark: she polled all the candidates about their attitudes on women's rights and published the names of those who supported expansion of the franchise, encouraging others to focus in on targeted politicians for future petition drives. By the 1870s the AWSA was directly involved in work in over a dozen states from Maine to Wyoming.[5]

Meanwhile, the *Woman's Journal* became a weekly paper published in both Boston and Chicago. Stanton and Anthony's journal, *The Revolution,* had been sold in May 1870 and soon went out of business, so the *Journal* became the only widely distributed suffrage periodical in the country, and remained so until the end of the century. Together with Alice Stone Blackwell's informational newsletter, the *Woman's Column,* it served as the key to national communication for the woman suffrage movement, raising the consciousness of readers and providing supporters with data and methods to employ in local, state, and regional activism.

From 1873 to the end of the century, American reform movements in general slumped in the face of increased economic difficulties and political stagnation. At the same time, the Supreme Court issued conservative landmark decisions against universal suffrage *(Minor v Happersett)* and basic civil liberties *(Plessy v Ferguson)*. Though she fought for women's suffrage all her life, Stone would never be able to vote. Along with other suffragists she had attempted to vote illegally; but even when in 1879 Massachusetts granted women suffrage in board of education elections, Stone's attempt to register to vote was rejected: her registration form was returned since it required her to sign with her husband's name as "Mrs. Blackwell," which she refused to do. As she had written to Susan B. Anthony some years earlier: "It is clear to me, that . . . all our little skirmishing for better laws, and the right to vote, will yet be swallowed up in the real question, viz: Has a woman a right to herself? It is very little to me to have the right to vote, to own property, &c. if I may not keep my body, and its uses, in my absolute right. Not one wife in a thousand can do that now, and as long as she suffers this bondage, all other rights will not help her true position."[6]

In late March 1888, Anthony organized a "Pioneer's Day" during the first International Council of Women. One by one, the national suffrage leaders stood at the podium to disclaim the rank of "pioneer"; instead they praised Lucy Stone as their mentor. Anthony admitted that she was not present at the 1848 Seneca Falls meeting and had been persuaded to join the women's rights movement only after she read the *New York Tribune*'s coverage of Lucy Stone's speech at the 1850 Worcester convention. Frances Willard, president of the powerful National Woman's Christian Temperance Union, spoke of her "training from Lucy Stone"; Julia Ward Howe, president of the New England Suffrage Association, proclaimed that she too was "the convert of Lucy Stone." Howe had gone to her first woman's suffrage meeting in Boston "with a very rebellious heart," but upon hearing Stone she "came out very meek" and "so continued ever since."

Stone's health deteriorated in the last decade of her life, and she became increasingly reliant on her family to support her activism. When she and her daughter negotiated in 1888 with Anthony and Rachel Foster to merge the NWSA with the AWSA, she insisted that none of the three principals involved in the original split (Stanton, Stone, and Anthony) should become president of the united organization. Her demands were ignored, however, and until 1902 first Stanton and then Anthony held the reins of the combined national organization, the National American Woman Suffrage Association (NAWSA).

Even as Stone was progressively weakened by what was eventually diagnosed as stomach cancer, she continued to dictate *Journal* editorials and to mentor young women activists, in particular Carrie Chapman Catt. One of her last letters was to this young suffragist; she enclosed one hundred dollars in support of Catt's ultimately successful efforts for Colorado women's suffrage rights. In 1893, Stone died at the age of seventy-five. Her last thoughts were on how to pass along the torch of inspiration, and her final words to her daughter Alice were "Make the world better." Her legacy was the multitude of daughters she mentored and supported and who followed in her footsteps.

Alice Stone Blackwell had known that she was going to write her mother's story since she was sixteen years old. In an 1872 letter to a cousin she had exclaimed, "Did I ever tell you that I am going to write Mamma's biography when I am older, and am collecting all the facts and stories about her that I can, for that purpose? Mama objects, but she will not be able to help herself if I persist and I shall make her correct and revise it herself. I am uncommonly proud of being Lucy Stone's daughter."[7] After Stone Blackwell graduated from Boston University, she and her mother were among the first mother-daughter members of the Association of Collegiate Alumnae (now the American Association of University Women). Raised in an atmosphere of intellectual freedom, Stone Blackwell continued on the path her mother had taken a half century before at Oberlin College. She continued working with her mother as a writer and editor, first as a coeditor of the *Woman's Journal.* It was she who started the *Woman's Column* in 1887 to aid the cause by sending copy on suffrage activities to local newspapers.

Like her parents, she was active in many progressive

organizations, including the Women's Trade Union League, the NAACP, the American Peace Society, and local boards for relief of the poor. After her mother's death in 1893 and her father's in 1909, she lived alone and subsisted on her invested savings. Multilingual and an avid reader, from 1896 to 1937 she translated into English hundreds of poems by Armenian, Yiddish, Russian, Hungarian, and Spanish-American writers.[8] During this time she also worked on her mother's biography, going through a vast collection of antislavery and suffrage records, correspondence, and speeches that her mother had kept over the years. (Carrie Chapman Catt later placed many of these documents in the Library of Congress by as part of the NAWSA Collection.)

Stone Blackwell's forty-year task of building her mother's biography was truly a feminist effort, emerging from her own commitment to women's rights. The resulting narrative merges anecdote with statistical data, personal passion-filled letters with the formal rhetoric of oratory. It is informed by the daughter-author's obvious love and admiration for the complex, powerful woman she brings to life. Modern feminist critical theory informs us of the interconnectedness of subject and object, of observer and observed. The feminist biographer admits her "attachments and detachments even while maintaining a critical, scholarly stance."[9] When Lucy Stone's daughter wrote her biography, the passions of the nineteenth-century reform movement still influenced her. But Stone Blackwell's book is important to us today precisely because of the intimacy between the writer and her subject. For Stone Blackwell herself, it was the culmination of a desire she had felt even as a teenager to defend her "Mama" from any and all critics. (For example, in a journal entry dated April 5, 1872, she described how she "couldn't help answering back" when a talkative plasterer renovating Stone's house in Dorchester offended her with "his abuse of Mama's books and all."[10]) As Marlene Merrill has noted, writing a biography of her mother provided Stone Blackwell with "the deepest sense of personal satisfaction."[11]

When Stone Blackwell's biography was published in 1930, the reform impulse that had produced the Nineteenth Amendment was coming under attack. Male-dominated bureaucracies replaced women's activist networks, and women's rights efforts moved into narrowly focused policy-making arenas. The economic crises of the 1930s led to an unprecedented rise in government regulation, and maternalist reformers helped create a highly gendered welfare state. Lucy Stone's generation of civil-rights activists, who pushed for equal rights for all and in all areas of society, seemed old-fashioned. Nevertheless, Stone's work and ideas gained a new audience through her daughter's writing. Mary Beard's anthology on U.S. women's history, *America through Women's Eyes,* appeared in 1933 and included selections from Blackwell's biography, and at least two other works were published that derived from it. In 1935, Effie Margaret Heath, Stone Blackwell's cousin on her father's side, published an abridged version of the biography in England. Heath wrote in her preface that her object for doing so was to make "so notable a woman as Lucy Stone was, better known among my countrywomen on this side of the Atlantic."[12] The biography also inspired a series of short plays by Maud Park Wood, complete with set designs and notes about productions. In her foreword to this 1938 book, Stone Blackwell commended Wood for making fresh "the stirring story of the events that attended the long struggle before woman's rights were won."[13]

*Lucy Stone, Pioneer of Woman's Rights,* now reprinted, should help us answer critical questions in women's history: How free were nineteenth-century women reformers from the mechanics of power exhibited by their society, and what role did these women's individual idiosyncrasies play in the story that unfolds? Women's historians have long been asked to reinject information about our once-famous foremothers into contemporary discussions, a task that Alice Stone Blackwell also gives us as we read her biography of her mother. In reminding us of the strength of character it takes to refuse to be silenced, this biography, passionately conceived but written with a light touch, ably responds to its subject's imperative, "Make the world better."

## *Notes*

1. See "A History of the National Woman's Rights Movement."

2. For a description of the Blackwell family and their public service, see Hays, *Those Extraordinary Blackwells,* and Horn, "Family Ties." Some of the letters between Stone and her beloved "Nettie" are in Lasser and Merrill, *Friends and Sisters.* For a romantic look at the correspondence between Stone and Blackwell, see Wheeler, *Loving Warriors.*

3. Cited in Kerr, *Lucy Stone,* p. 111.

4. Lucy Stone during the May 1869 debate over the priority of women's suffrage versus black male suffrage at the regular meeting of the American Equal Rights Association; cited in the *New York Times,* May 13, 1869, and *The Revolution,* May 20, 1869.

5. See Stanton et al., *History of Woman Suffrage,* vols. 3 and 4.

6. Lucy Stone to Susan B. Anthony, January 9, 1857, Blackwell Family Papers, Library of Congress; cited in Moore, "Reclaiming Lucy Stone," p. 201.

7. Alice Stone Blackwell to Kitty Barry Blackwell, October 29, 1872, Blackwell Family Papers, Library of Congress; cited in Merrill's afterword to Blackwell, *Growing Up in Boston's Gilded Age,* p. 244. See also Blackwell's "Tribute," in which she praises her father because he handed down to her the Blackwell family tradition of public service and because he "gave me a good mother" (p. 35).

8. See Merrill, afterword to Blackwell, *Growing Up,* pp. 241–44.

9. Introduction to Alpern et al., *The Challenge of Feminist Biography,* p. 11.

10. Blackwell, *Growing Up,* pp. 57–58.

11. Merrill, afterword to Blackwell, *Growing Up,* p. 244. Linda W. Rosenzweig in *The Anchor of My Life* analyzes the relationship between Lucy Stone and her daughter. Rosenzweig points out entries in Alice's journal, written when she was fifteen years old, that disparage her mother, but concludes that the pair's conflicts "did not reflect any real estrangement" (p. 76), and that intimacy may have been more important than conflict in their relationship.

12. Heath, *Story of Lucy Stone,* p. 7.

13. Wood, *Lucy Stone,* p. 3.

# *Bibliography*

Alpern, Sara, et al. *The Challenge of Feminist Biography: Writing the Lives of Modern American Women.* Urbana: University of Illinois Press, 1992.

Aptheker, Bettina. "Abolitionism, Woman's Rights and the Battle over the Fifteenth Amendment." In *Women's Legacy: Essays on Race, Sex, and Class in American History.* Amherst: University of Massachusetts Press, 1982.

Beard, Mary R. *America through Women's Eyes.* New York: Macmillan, 1933.

Blackwell, Alice Stone. *Growing Up in Boston's Gilded Age: The Journal of Alice Stone Blackwell, 1872–1874.* Edited by Marlene Deahl Merrill. New Haven: Yale University Press, 1990.

———. "Tribute." In *What I Owe to My Father,* edited by Sydney Dix Strong. New York: The Press of the Pioneers, 1935.

Bolton, Sarah Knowles. *Famous Leaders among Women.* New York: Thomas Y. Crowell, 1895.

Catt, Carrie Chapman, and Nettie Rogers Shuler. *Woman Suffrage and Politics: The Inner Story of the Suffrage Movement.* 1923. Reprint, New York: Charles Scribner's Sons, 1926.

DuBois, Ellen Carol, ed. *Woman Suffrage and Women's Rights.* New York: New York University Press, 1998.

Hansen, Debra Gold. *Strained Sisterhood: Gender and Class in the Boston Female Anti-Slavery Society.* Amherst: University of Massachusetts Press, 1993.

Hays, Elinor Rice. *Morning Star: A Biography of Lucy Stone, 1818–1893.* New York: Harcourt, Brace & World, 1961.

———. *Those Extraordinary Blackwells: The Story of a Journey to a Better World.* New York: Harcourt, Brace & World, 1967.

Heath, Effie Margaret. *The Story of Lucy Stone: Pioneer.* London: Allenson & Co., 1935.

Hersh, Blanche Glassman. *The Slavery of Sex: Feminist-Abolitionists in America.* Urbana: University of Illinois Press, 1978.

"A History of the National Woman's Rights Movement, for Twenty Years, with the Proceedings of the Decade Meeting Held at Apollo Hall, October 20, 1870, From 1850 to 1870. With an Appendix Containing the History of the Movement during the Winter of 1871, in the National Capitol." Compiled by Paulina W. Davis. New York: Journeymen Printers' Co-operative Association, 1871.

Horn, Margo. "Family Ties: The Blackwells, a Study in the Dynamics of Family Life in Nineteenth Century America." Ph.D. diss., Tufts University, 1980.

Iles, Teresa, ed. *All Sides of the Subject: Women and Biography.* New York: Teachers College Press, 1992.

Isenberg, Nancy. *Sex and Citizenship in Antebellum America.* Chapel Hill: University of North Carolina Press, 1998.

Kerr, Andrea Moore. *Lucy Stone: Speaking Out for Equality.* New Brunswick, N.J.: Rutgers University Press, 1992.

Lasser, Carol, and Marlene Deahl Merrill, eds. *Friends and Sisters: Letters between Lucy Stone and Antoinette Brown Blackwell, 1846–1893.* Urbana: University of Illinois Press, 1987.

McKenna, Sister Jeanne. "With the Help of God and Lucy Stone." *Kansas Historical Quarterly* 36 (spring 1970): 13–26.

Moore, Dorothea McClain. "Reclaiming Lucy Stone: A Literary and Historical Appraisal." Ph.D. diss., University of Texas at Arlington, 1996.

Newman, Louise Michele. *White Women's Rights: The Racial Origins of Feminism in the United States.* New York: Oxford University Press, 1999.

Riegel, Robert. "Lucy Stone." In *American Feminists.* Lawrence: University of Kansas Press, 1963.

Rosenzweig, Linda W. *The Anchor of My Life: Middle-Class American Mothers and Daughters, 1880–1920.* New York: New York University Press, 1993.

Sarno, Katherine C. "Lucy Stone: Anti-Racist Feminist and Woman Suffrage Leader." M.A. thesis, Sarah Lawrence College, 1993.

Smith, Wilda M. "A Half Century of Struggle: Gaining Woman Suffrage in Kansas." *Kansas History* 4 (summer 1981): 74–95.

Stanton, Elizabeth Cady, with Susan B. Anthony, Matilda Joslyn Gage, Ida Husted Harper, and others. *History of Woman Suffrage.* 6 vols. New York: Fowler and Wells, 1881–1922.

Terborg-Penn, Rosalyn. "Discrimination against Afro-American Women in the Woman's Movement, 1830–1920." In *The Afro-American Woman: Struggles and Images,* edited by Sharon Harley and Rosalyn Terborg-Penn. Port Washington, N.Y.: Kennikat Press, 1978.

Wheeler, Leslie, ed. *Loving Warriors: Selected Letters of Lucy Stone and Henry B. Blackwell, 1853–1893.* New York: Dial Press, 1981.

———. "Lucy Stone: Radical Beginnings." In *Feminist Theorists: Three Centuries of Key Women Thinkers,* edited by Dale Spender. New York: Pantheon Books, 1983.

Wood, Maud Park. *Lucy Stone: A Chronicle Play.* Boston: Walter H. Baker, 1938.

Yellin, Jean Fagan. *Women and Sisters: The Antislavery Feminists in American Culture.* New Haven: Yale University Press, 1989.

Yellin, Jean Fagan, and John C. Van Horne, eds. *The Abolitionist Sisterhood: Women's Political Culture in Antebellum America.* Ithaca, N.Y.: Cornell University Press, 1994.

## *Preface*

Lucy Stone was noteworthy for many things. She was the first Massachusetts woman to take a college degree. She was "the morning star of the woman's rights movement", lecturing for it, in the ten years from 1847 to 1857, to immense audiences all up and down the country. She headed the call for the First National Woman's Rights Convention. She converted Susan B. Anthony and Julia Ward Howe. She was the first married woman to keep her own name. She organized a nation-wide association in which those suffragists could work who did not wish to have equal suffrage mixed up with free love and other extraneous questions. She founded and edited the *Woman's Journal* of Boston, which was the principal woman suffrage newspaper of the United States for almost half a century. She was a striking example of single-hearted and lifelong devotion to a great idea.

Her husband, Henry Browne Blackwell, had great ability, and was the one man in America who devoted his life to securing equal rights for women.

One of her sisters-in-law, Doctor Elizabeth Blackwell, was the first woman in modern times to take a medical degree. Another, the Reverend Doctor Antoinette Brown Blackwell, was the first woman in the world to be ordained as a minister. Lucy Stone was thus in close touch with the movement to open the learned professions to women. Her letters give a graphic picture of early American life, as different from the life of to-day as that of some remote foreign country.

Great obligations are due to a large number of friends who subscribed a sum of money to provide me with help while writing this biography. This enabled me to have the assistance of Mrs. Ida Porter-Boyer, who has given invaluable aid in collecting and arranging the material.

ALICE STONE BLACKWELL

BOSTON, MASSACHUSETTS

# LUCY STONE

*Pioneer of Woman's Rights*

## *Chapter I*

Lucy Stone was born on August 13, 1818. She was the eighth of nine children. Her mother, a farmer's wife, had milked eight cows the night before Lucy was born, a sudden shower having called all the men of the family into the hayfield to save the hay. When told of the sex of the new baby, she said sadly, "Oh, dear! I am sorry it is a girl. A woman's life is so hard!" No one then could foresee that the little girl just born was destined to make life less hard for all the generations of little girls that were to follow.

The world upon which little Lucy first opened her bright eyes was very different from that which greets the young women of to-day. No college or university admitted women. There was not a single free public high school for girls. It was the general belief that all the education a woman needed was enough to enable her to read her Bible and keep her household accounts, and that any attempt to give her more would spoil her for a wife and mother.

In most States of the Union — all those where the law was founded upon the common law of

England — a husband had the legal right to beat his wife, "with a reasonable instrument." There is a story that Judge Buller, when charging the jury in a case of wife-beating, said, "Without undertaking to define exactly what a reasonable instrument is, I hold, gentlemen of the jury, that a stick no thicker than my thumb comes clearly within that description." A committee of women waited upon him the next day to learn the exact size of the judge's thumb.

Wife-beating, unless done with uncommon brutality, was sanctioned not only by law but by public opinion. Mrs. Emily P. Collins (who organized at South Bristol, New York, in 1848, the first local woman's rights society in the world) says in her reminiscences:

"In those early days a husband's supremacy was often enforced in the rural districts by corporal chastisement, and it was considered by most people as quite right and proper — as much so as the correction of refractory children in like manner. I remember in my own neighborhood a Methodist class-leader and exhorter, esteemed a worthy citizen, who, every few weeks, gave his wife a beating with a horsewhip. He said it was necessary, in order to keep her in subjection, and because she scolded so much."

Mrs. Collins added that it was no wonder the poor woman sometimes scolded, as she had to care day and night for six or seven small children, besides cooking, cleaning, milking cows, making butter and cheese, and spinning, weaving and sewing all the clothes for the family. The United States in those days was mainly agricultural, and most farmers' wives led similar lives of excessive toil.

In the matter of legalized wife-beating, Massachusetts was a shining exception. Away back in the seventeenth century, Judge Sewall, of witchcraft fame, secured the passage of the following, among the "Liberties" adopted by the General Court:

"Every married woman shall be free from bodily correction or stripes by her husband, unless it be in his own defense, upon her assault. If there be any just cause of correction, complaint shall be made to authority assembled in some court, from which only she shall receive it."

But all a married woman's property and earnings belonged to her husband. He had the sole control of the children while he lived, and, if he died before her, he could will them away from their mother to strangers. A wife had hardly more legal rights than a minor child. She could not make a contract, could not sue or be sued, and could not make a valid will without her husband's consent, unless she left everything to him, in which case his consent was taken for granted.

When a wife died, her husband had the life use of all her real estate, if they had ever had a child born alive. When a husband died, the widow was entitled to stay only forty days in the house without paying rent, and she had the life use of only one third of his real estate.

The injustice of the laws was not due to any especial depravity on the part of men, but merely to the self-partiality of human nature. If the laws had been made by women alone, they would probably have been just as one-sided, only it would have been the other way around. Even the best men thought that the existing conditions were right. As Henry B. Blackwell said, "No governed class was ever yet without a grievance. Yet no governing class has ever been able to see that the grievance existed."

Public opinion was even harder upon women than the law. All the learned professions were closed to them. Women who had their living to earn were limited to a very few poorly-paid occupations. When a merchant first employed a saleswoman, the men boycotted his store, and the women remonstrated earnestly with him on the sin of placing a young woman in a position of such "publicity" as behind a counter.

There were no organizations of women except the church sewing circles. Public speaking by women was unknown. Even to write for publication was thought unwomanly. The gentle Charles Lamb himself said, "The woman who lets herself be known as an author invites disrespect." Law, religion and custom affirmed the inferiority of women and their duty to remain in silence and subjection; and this belief enwrapped every baby girl in her cradle, like an invisible strait-jacket.

This state of things had lasted for centuries. It did not come to an end through the general advance of civilization. It was changed by many years of hard work on the part of brave women and just men; and they had to suffer all the persecution that usually besets the pioneers of progress.

Lucy was born on a picturesque, rocky farm on the eastern side of Coy's Hill, three miles and a half from West Brookfield, Massachusetts. It was a fortunate environment for a child always keenly alive to the beauties of nature, for the top of Coy's Hill is one of the finest viewpoints in the State. There young Lucy Stone and her sisters used to go to watch the sunset; and there Lucy used to take her little daughter to watch it in after years.

She came of Revolutionary stock. Her father, Francis Stone, was descended from Gregory Stone, who came to America in 1635 in quest of religious liberty. He settled in Cambridge, Massachusetts, where he held various offices. He and his wife once testified in defence of a woman accused of witchcraft. In 1664 he was one of a committee of four who presented to the General Court a memorial from many citizens of Cambridge, protesting against the proposal to have New England governed by a Royal Commission, on the ground that it would be an arbitrary government by a Council or Parliament in which they were not represented. This was the first open stirring of the spirit that culminated in the Declaration of Independence.

Lucy's grandfather, Francis Stone, when a boy of seventeen, accompanied his father to the French and Indian War. His father was killed at the battle of Quebec, and he was sent home by General Wolfe, because he was left as the sole support of his mother. The boy shed tears at having to quit the army. He was afterwards a captain in the Revolutionary War, and later the leader of four hundred men in Shays' Rebellion.[1] Lucy's mother, Hannah Matthews, was connected with the Forbush (Forbes) and Bowman families, and came of educated and public-spirited lineage.

Lucy's father was a tanner by trade, brought up in his father's tanyard at North Brookfield. In his youth he taught school for some years. He was bright and witty, and so good a teacher that he always had the offer of more schools than he could take. But he went back to tanning and established himself in New Braintree. He was

[1] See Appendix, Note 1.

a man of strong character and of great physical and mental energy. Like all the men of his time, he believed in the divine right of a husband to rule over his wife and family. "There was only one will in our home, and that was my father's," said Lucy, long after.

Lucy's mother was an excellent Christian woman, beautiful, gentle, conscientious and kind. She too believed devoutly in a husband's right to rule. But, finding in her early married life that her children were surrounded by bad influences at the tannery, she insisted upon the removal of the family to the farm where Lucy was born, and her husband yielded to her wish. Though constantly overworked, she commanded the respect and the devoted affection of her children.

From her father Lucy inherited her courage, her sturdy physique and resolute will; from her mother, her sympathy and kindness, her clear moral perceptions and strong sense of duty.

Little Lucy grew up a healthy and vigorous child, noted for fearlessness and truthfulness, a good student at school, and a hard worker in the home and on the farm. Often she drove the cows to pasture by starlight, before the sun was up, when the dew on the grass was so cold that she would stop on a flat stone and curl one small bare foot up against the other leg to warm it. The children watched out eagerly for the first dandelion blossom, because when it appeared they were allowed to take off their stockings and shoes.

Father Stone was an early riser. The sound of his clear, sonorous voice calling the cows in the morning carried a long way and was regarded by the neighboring farmers as their rising bell. Every one on the farm worked. Even the small children were taught to creep after their father in the corn-field and plant two or three pumpkin seeds in every hill of corn.

Mother Stone wove all the cloth for the family's wearing, and little Lucy used to sit for hours together under the loom, handing up the threads to her mother, who praised her for being very accurate, and always handing them up in the right order.

Lucy and Luther, the brother next older, learned hymns as they filled the woodbox. The mother read a verse aloud, and the children repeated as much of it as they could remember, while they went in and out, bringing the armfuls of wood. Lucy always knew the verse first. She could learn more quickly than Luther, and could run faster, and he was afraid of the dark, while she was not; yet he was always given the preference over her because he was a boy, and she felt the injustice keenly.

In addition to all the usual work of an old-time farming family, Lucy and her sisters sewed coarse shoes, intended for farmers and for the slaves. Lucy was required to sew nine pairs a day, because she could work faster than the others. They received four cents a pair from the store and took their pay mainly in goods. Once, when their half-yearly account for shoe-sewing was settled, their credit showed a balance of just six cents; and they all agreed that that ought to go to Eliza, the eldest sister, because she had helped the mother so much with the housework.

Lucy's childhood in the main was happy, in spite of the hard work. After their chores were done, the children were left to their own pleasures. They had a cosset sheep named Top, and when little Lucy jumped rope, so lightly that it often seemed to her as if she had no flesh, Top would jump too, putting down its head and kicking up its heels. They also had a dog, old Bogue, who helped them herd the cows.

The children early learned to know all the wild flowers, the trees, the birds, their songs, their nests, and the color of their eggs. They knew the remarkable rock formations in the valley, called "The Rock House," all the brooks and ponds, the Hemlock Hill, and every boulder that was a good place for play.

Lucy reveled in all the beauty of the world. When she had done well in her lessons, she found it a sufficient reward to be allowed to sit on the school-room floor, where she could look up through the window and watch the flickering green leaves of the white birch trees.

If ready money was scarce, good food was plentiful. She said, in recalling her childhood:

"We had barrels of meat, and of apples; plenty of fresh milk, cream, butter, cheese and eggs; peaches, quinces, innumerable varieties of plums, and every kind of berries, and all of them fresh. We had delicious honey, more than we could eat. The bread was rye and Indian, light and dry. On gray and showery days, not good for work, the boys would go to the woods to hunt, and bring home game — squirrels, woodchucks and abundance of wild pigeons. We all worked hard, but we all worked together; and we had the feeling that everything was ours — the calves, the stock, the butter and cheese."

## *Chapter II*

The family circle in the evenings was a large one. Father Stone built magnificent fires in the great open fireplace, which stretched a long way across one side of the room; in front of it, at a safe distance, stood a large, high-backed settle that kept off the draughts. Near one end of the circle stood a small square table with a light on it, and those who were studying or sewing sat near it. The row of the others extended clear around the fire. There were Father and Mother Stone, the seven children who lived to grow up, — Francis, William Bowman, Eliza, Rhoda, Luther, Lucy and Sarah; and in the corner nearest the brick oven, old Aunt Sally, knitting. Often the neighborhood blacksmith sat there, telling stories of bears, wolves and Indians; and there was generally one or more of three old drunkards, who had been Father Stone's schoolmates, and whom he would never turn away. They often came and quartered themselves upon him for long visits. They were an affliction to Mother Stone, who had to cook for them and wash their clothes. She thought them a bad influence for the children; but the children regarded them with disgust. Once Luther and Lucy conspired secretly to break the jug of rum that one of them had hidden by a stone wall, when he came to spend a week-end.

On winter nights the children often roasted apples on the hearth, and popped corn. Two or three times in the course of the evening, one of them would be sent down cellar to bring up a quart mug of cider. It was passed from hand to hand, and they all drank from it. Tea and coffee were not used in this household.

On Sunday two wagonloads of the family were driven to church, and the rest walked. Those who rode one Sunday walked the next. The children too small to attend were gathered around the mother at home, while she read them Bible stories.

Once, as she went through the fields in summer, Lucy saw a large snake asleep upon a rock in the sun. Most little barefooted girls would have run away. Lucy picked up a heavy stone, approached softly, poised the stone exactly above the reptile's head and dropped it, crushing the head to pieces. The act was symbolic. Her whole life was, metaphorically, a bruising of the serpent's head.

Most brave men and women are courageous because they overcome their fears. Lucy was one of the very few persons who seem to have been born incapable of fear. She could feel terror for those whom she loved; but, for herself, she did not know what fear was. In her later life, in alarms arising from fire or thieves, we never saw her fluttered. She said in her old age that, during all the mobs and tumults of the antislavery time, she was never conscious of a quickened heartbeat. She laid it to the fact that she had been brought up on a farm and so had "good calm nerves." But it was not due to her bodily health. In her last illness, when her physical strength was all gone, her serene courage remained.

The overmastering purpose of her life took possession of her in childhood. She very early became indignant at the way in which she saw her mother and other women treated by their husbands and by the laws, and she silently made up her mind that those laws must be changed. Only wait until she was older! Then, one day, as she was reading the Bible, with the big book resting upon her little short legs, she came upon the words, "Thy desire shall be to thy husband, and he shall rule over thee." She was filled with horror. She knew that the laws and the customs were against the women, but it had never occurred to her that God could be against them. She went to her mother and asked, "Is there anything that will put an end to me?" Annihilation was what she craved. Seeing the child's agitation, the mother questioned her, learned the trouble, and then, stroking Lucy's hair away from her hot forehead, told her gently that it was the curse of Eve, and that it was women's duty to submit. "My mother always tried to submit. I never could," Lucy said. For a short time she was in despair. Then she made up her mind to go to college, study Greek and Hebrew, read the Bible in the original, and satisfy herself as to whether such texts were correctly translated.

When her father heard of her wish to go to college, he said to his wife, in all seriousness, "Is the child crazy?" It had not surprised him when his two elder sons wanted to go to college, but such a thing was unheard of in the case of a girl. Lucy herself had her misgivings, and asked her brother privately whether it was possible for a girl to learn Greek.

She had a keen appetite for reading matter. The stagecoach passed the schoolhouse door, and sometimes travelers would throw out a handful of tracts or other pamphlets for the children to pick up. Lucy was so eager to get them that once, nimble as a young chamois, she darted through the open window. When she came back with her prize, the teacher stood in the door and said, "You must come in as you went out," and made her climb in through the window, to her great mortification.

The only papers taken by the family were the *Massachusetts Spy* and the *Advocate of Moral Reform;* but they borrowed the *Youth's Com-*

*panion* and read it eagerly. When the children grew older, they subscribed for the *Liberator* and the *Anti-Slavery Standard.* Later, they took the *Oberlin Evangelist* for years.

They had few books. Among these, Lucy's especial delight was Guthrie's "Geographical, Historical and Commercial Grammar of the World", printed in London in 1788. They had also Fox's "Book of Martyrs", Edwards on the Affections, and a big volume gotten out by the Baptists, who were at that time intensely unpopular. It showed a certain liberality of mind on Father Stone's part that he should have bought a book setting forth the views of a denomination which was the object of so much public odium.

The only storybook in the house was "Charlotte Temple." This was said to be both true and instructive, so the children were allowed to read it. But, in general, novels were classed with cards, dancing and the theater, as utterly sinful.

The first novel Lucy ever saw was "The Children of the Abbey." Her elder sister Rhoda, teaching school in a neighboring village, read it and told Lucy about it, and, at her eager request, borrowed it for her. Lucy used to lock herself into her room to read it. While she was absorbed in the third volume, her younger sister Sarah came to the door and was refused admittance. She peeped through the keyhole and told her mother that Lucy was reading something with the door locked. The mother came up to investigate. She was shocked and distressed. Lucy begged hard for leave to finish the story. Rhoda added her assurances that it really was not a bad book, and the gentle mother, with many misgivings, consented. But it was years before Lucy read another novel.

As a child she had a high temper. Once when Sarah had angered her, and Lucy was chasing her through the house, she caught sight in a looking-glass of her own face, white with wrath. She said to herself, "That is the face of a murderer!" She went out and sat down on a stone behind the woodshed, and rocked herself to and fro, holding one bare foot in her hand and thinking how she could ever get the better of such a temper. She had an overwhelming sense that it was something which she must do alone; nobody could help her. She decided that when she was angry she must not speak; if she could refrain from breaking forth into such a flow of wrathful words, that would be the first step. She sat on the rock till it grew so dark that her mother called her in.

From that time on, she set herself seriously to conquer her temper. Luther did not make it easier. He was a tease. When he had taunted her till she grew angry, he would say, "See Luce's nose turn up! See it! See it!" Lucy's nose turned up by nature; but at this it would turn up more and more, and her face grow as red as a beet. He had no idea of the struggle going on within her. Then she would go away across the pastures to the Hemlock Hill and sit down where the sweet voice of the little brook and the soft sough of the wind in the trees helped to calm her. Those who saw her great gentleness in later life found it hard to realize that her temper had ever been so fiery.

When she was about twelve years old, she saw her mother's health giving way under the hard work, and quietly made up her mind that, if some one must be killed by overwork, she could be spared better than her mother. A strong and resolute child, she took upon herself as many as she could of her mother's burdens. The school was so far away that the children took their lunches with them and stayed till the afternoon. Now, rising very early on Monday mornings, Lucy would do the washing for the family of ten or twelve persons, hang out the clothes to dry, walk a mile to school, walk back at noon and bring the clothes in, and return for the afternoon session. She toiled early and late. Even her robust health suffered under the strain and she grew weak and pale. In those days paleness was admired. To be pale was to look "delicate." She hid her fatigue from her mother. When so tired that she could hardly stand, she would slip upstairs and lie down for a few minutes; but if she heard her mother's foot on the stair, she would at once spring up and pretend to be busy. At night, after the work was done, she sat up to study.

Things kept happening that strengthened her zeal for equal rights. Mary Lyon, the pioneer of education for women in New England, was raising money for Mount Holyoke Seminary. She spoke before the sewing circle of the West Brookfield church and told of the great lack of educational opportunities for girls. Lucy listened, her heart growing hotter and hotter within her. The sewing circle was working to educate a theological student, and Lucy was making a shirt. She thought how absurd it was for her to be working to help educate a student who could earn more money toward his own education in a week, by teaching, than she could earn toward hers in a month; and she left the shirt unfinished and hoped that no one ever would complete it.

Her father did not like to buy schoolbooks for her. He told her she could use her brother's. Once he refused to get her a necessary textbook, which he thought quite superfluous for a girl. "I went to the woods, with my little bare toes, and gathered chestnuts, and sold them for money enough to buy the book. I felt a prouder sense of triumph than I have ever known since," she said, when telling the story. After that, when she wanted books, she picked berries and nuts and sold them. She joined with other ambitious pupils to secure a college student as teacher for the school, so that they might learn more than the ordinary branches.

The teacher boarded with the Stone family. Once, when he saw Lucy go out into the pasture, catch the horses, bring them in and harness them, he told her that she ought to be a missionary's wife and live at the foot of the Rocky Mountains. This young man awakened in Lucy the first stirrings of the tender passion; but she kept her feelings strictly in her own breast. Her mind was made up never to marry.

She was not beautiful. Her father said, "Luce's face is like a blacksmith's apron; it keeps off the sparks." She told him with indignation that she did not mean to marry, and that she wished her face was even plainer. Yet, in spite of her irregular features, she was very attractive. She had a pretty figure, a beautiful rosy complexion, which remained with her through life, bright gray eyes, good teeth, a profusion of dark brown hair, unusually fine and silky, which was very little gray at her death, much personal magnetism, and a singularly sweet voice. She had also a mind as bright and swift as quicksilver, and that indescribable something which radiates from a character strong, simple and sincere. Many hearts were drawn to her. Until her marriage, which took place late in life, she never lacked wooers.

She joined the Orthodox Congregational Church of West Brookfield while still in her teens. The subject of slavery was agitating the churches more and more. William Lloyd Garrison had started his paper, the *Liberator*, in Boston, and the Governors of Virginia and Georgia had written to the Mayor of Boston, recommending that it be suppressed. They were surprised to learn that there was no law under which this could be done. The Mayor, who had never heard of the *Liberator*, sought for Garrison, and told the Governors that he and his paper were not worth notice; that his office was an obscure hole and his only visible auxiliary a Negro boy.

But the subject would not down. Soon after Lucy joined the West Brookfield church, Deacon Henshaw was expelled from it for his antislavery activities. A series of church meetings was held in regard to his case. Lucy did not know that women who were church members could not vote in church meetings, and when the first vote was taken, she held up her hand with the rest. The minister, a tall, dark man, stood watching the vote. He pointed over to her, and said to the person who was counting the votes, "Don't you count her." The man asked, "Is n't she a member?" The minister answered, "Yes, but she is not a voting member." The accent of scorn in his voice touched her to the quick. Six votes were taken in the course of that meeting, and she held up her hand every time. She held it up again, with a flash in her eyes, when she recalled the incident upon her deathbed, and thought how great the change had been since the time when "that one uncounted hand" was the only visible protest against the subjection of women in church and State.

Father Stone did not approve of Lucy's wish to go on with her studies. He thought she had had quite schooling enough for a girl. She told him that if he would lend her a small sum of money, to enable her to keep on a little longer, she would then be qualified to teach; and he agreed to do so, taking her note for the amount. As she was a minor, the note was not legally valid; but she did not know that, and, if she had, she would of course have paid the debt just the same.

At sixteen she began to teach district schools at a dollar a week, "boarding around", as was the custom. She soon became known as a successful teacher. She got larger and larger schools, until her salary reached sixteen dollars per month, which was considered very good pay for a woman.

Once she was engaged to teach the "winter term" of the school at Paxton, Massachusetts, which had been broken up by the big boys throwing the master out of the window head first into a deep snowdrift. Generally women were not thought competent to teach in the winter, because then the big boys were released from farm work and were able to attend. She soon had this difficult school in perfect order, and the big boys who had made the trouble became her most devoted lieutenants; yet she received only a fraction of the salary paid to her unsuccessful predecessor.

When Abby Kelley lectured in West Brookfield, she invited Lucy to sit in the pulpit with her. Lucy refused, partly because her hair had got all blown about on the three-mile ride from the farm to the village, and partly from a lingering traditional feeling, which she knew to be quite irrational, that the pulpit was too sacred a place for her to enter. Abby Kelley's comment was, "Oh, Lucy Stone, you are not half emancipated!"

She was teaching school in North Brookfield in 1837, when the General Association of the Congregational Ministers of Massachusetts held their Quadrennial Conference there, and issued a "Pastoral Letter" to the churches under their care, warning them against discussing slavery, and especially against letting women speak in public.

This remarkable document called attention to "the dangers which at present seem to threaten the female character with wide-spread and permanent injury." It especially deplored "the mistaken conduct of those who encourage females to bear an obtrusive and ostentatious part in measures of reform, and countenance any of that sex who so far forget themselves as to itinerate in the character of public lecturers and teachers." Such proceedings, it predicted, would open the way to "degeneracy and ruin."

In those days, the Orthodox Congregational Church was supreme in Massachusetts, and the word of its clergy carried immense weight. The Pastoral Letter was read in all the churches. At the Conference in North Brookfield the floor of the church was black with ministers, and the gallery was filled with women and laymen. While the Letter was read, the Reverend Doctor Blagden walked up and down the aisle, turning his head from side to side and looking up at the women in the gallery with an air that seemed to say, "Now! Now we have silenced you!" Lucy sat in the gallery with her cousin. She said, in after years, "I was young enough then so that my indignation blazed. My cousin said that her side was black and blue with the indignant nudges of my elbow at each aggravating sentence; and I told her afterwards that, if I ever had anything to say in public, I should say it, and all the more because of that Pastoral Letter."

This Pastoral Letter, which was satirized by Whittier in a stirring poem, was called out by the lectures of Sarah and Angelina Grimké against slavery, and the deep impression they made.

The Grimké sisters were the first American women to lecture against slavery or for woman's rights — almost the first American women to open their mouths in public at all, outside a Quaker meeting. They and Abby Kelley Foster were the three women who did the most to break down the barrier debarring women from public speech. They opened the way for Lucy, and for all who came after her. Their names should always be held in grateful remembrance.

Daughters of one of the first families of South Carolina, brought up to wealth and luxury and the service of slaves, Sarah and Angelina had become convinced that slavery was wrong, and Angelina had entered into correspondence with Garrison. In 1836 she was invited by the American Anti-Slavery Society to come and give talks against slavery, to women only. She declined the offered salary, but came and brought her sister. They spoke in New York and New Jersey, and then came to New England. It had been the intention that they should speak to women in church sewing circles and at parlor meetings, but no parlor would hold all the women who wanted to hear. Anti-slavery ministers offered the use of their session rooms. It was thought a great scandal that women should speak in so sacred a place. The interest grew. One or two men began to slip into the rear seats. At first they were turned out. Later they refused to go. Although brought up as High Church Episcopalians, the sisters had become Quakers, and did not think it wrong for a woman to speak when men were present. Before long they were lecturing to mixed audiences, largely made up of men. Then the storm broke, — a storm of tremendous violence.

The texts that were always quoted against the women were the words of St. Paul, "Let your women keep silence in the churches, for it is not permitted unto them to speak", and "I suffer not a woman to teach, nor to usurp authority over the man, but to be in silence."

The opposition to the women who spoke against slavery was due in part to the belief that their action was contrary to Scripture, in part to the usual dislike for any innovation, in part to the anger of men against any encroachment upon their exclusive privileges, and in part to the belief that the textile industries of New England could not be carried on without the slave-grown cotton of the South. The economic objection was not the least powerful.

Even while the sisters spoke only to women, their meetings had been ridiculed in the proslavery press, which included almost all the Northern newspapers. With the issuing of the Pastoral

Letter, the opposition became fiercer; but they continued to lecture to audiences that overflowed the largest halls. Angelina was beautiful, and had a calm, simple and magnetic eloquence. Wendell Phillips said, "She swept all the chords of the human heart with a power that has never been surpassed, and rarely equalled." Sarah, though an able writer, was not so good a speaker; but both sisters had the great advantage that they could tell of the facts of slavery from actual experience.

If the wrath that they aroused was great at the North, it was still greater in the South. Angelina wrote "An Appeal to Southern Women against Slavery." Many copies were mailed to South Carolina. Most of them were publicly burned by postmasters. When she wished to make a visit to her mother and sisters, the Mayor of Charleston sent her word that the police had orders to prevent her from landing or from communicating with any person while the steamer was in port; and that, if she succeeded in coming ashore, she would be put in prison. Friends warned her that she would almost certainly become the object of mob violence.

Shortly before the issuing of the Pastoral Letter, Sarah had begun to publish in the *New England Spectator* a series of articles on "The Province of Woman." She had long had the woman question very much at heart. She grieved for the sufferings not only of the slaves, but of white women and children under the unjust laws; and she had felt strongly on the subject of equal educational opportunities for women ever since, in her girlhood, her father, Judge Grimké, had refused to let her study Latin with her brother, although he declared that, if she were a boy, she would make the ablest jurist in the country.

Sarah's letters in the *Spectator* made a commotion and greatly intensified the opposition. Garrison and Phillips backed the women to the utmost; but most of the abolitionists did not yet believe in the general doctrine of equal rights for women, and, of those who did, many thought it a mistake to mix up the antislavery cause, which was intensely unpopular, with the question of woman's rights, which was more unpopular still. Angelina wrote:

"We have given great offence on account of our womanhood, which seems to be as objectionable as our abolitionism. The whole land seems aroused to discussion on the province of woman, and I am glad of it. We are willing to bear the brunt of the storm, if we can only be the means of making a breach in the wall of public opinion, which lies right in the way of woman's true dignity, honor and usefulness. Sister Sarah does preach up woman's rights most nobly and fearlessly; and we find that many of our New England sisters are prepared to receive these strange doctrines, feeling, as they do, that our whole sex needs emancipation from the thralldom of public opinion."

In reply to further remonstrances, she wrote:

"I am still glad of sister's letters, and believe they are doing great good. Some noble-minded women cheer her on, the brethren notwithstanding. I tell them that this is a part of the great doctrine of Human Rights, and can no more be separated from emancipation than the light from the heat of the sun; the rights of the slave and of woman blend like the colors of the rainbow. However, I rarely introduce this topic into my addresses, except to urge my sisters up to duty. . . . I am very glad to hear that Lucretia Mott addressed the Moral Reform Society, and am earnest in the hope that we are only pioneers, going before a host of worthy women who will come up to the help of the Lord against the mighty."

The protests were so many and so earnest, even from men who themselves believed thoroughly in equal rights, that Sarah finally discontinued her articles in the *Spectator*. They were published in pamphlet form, however, and widely circulated.

A committee of the Massachusetts Legislature was appointed in 1838 to consider the petitions that were pouring in on the subject of slavery. Hearings were held, and Angelina was among the speakers. It was the first time that a woman's voice had been heard in the Boston State House.

In the same year, she married Theodore D. Weld, a noble and valiant abolitionist. The wedding took place in Philadelphia. Three days later Angelina made what was destined to be her last public speech.

Having had great difficulty in securing halls, the Pennsylvania abolitionists and other friends of free speech had formed an association and built a beautiful hall at a cost of forty thousand dollars, to be open for free discussion on all subjects not immoral. Most of the stockholders were mechanics or working men, and many were women. Pennsylvania Hall was opened on the week of Angelina's marriage. The first three days of the dedicatory exercises included addresses on slavery, temperance, the Indians, the right of free discussion and kindred topics. On the fourth day, speeches were to be made against slavery by prominent women. The mob rose — egged on secretly, it was said, by gentlemen of property and standing — and surrounded the hall with howls and uproar. Angelina spoke for an hour, standing calm and beautiful, while the yells and execrations increased without, and missile after missile crashed through the broken windows; and the crowded audience hung upon her words. The next night the hall was burned down, without any serious effort by the city authorities to save it.

An injury received soon after her marriage

incapacitated Angelina permanently for public speaking, and her sister had already been obliged to give it up, owing to the failure of her voice.

Abby Kelley made her first public speech at the meeting where Angelina Grimké Weld made her last. Of all the pioneer women, she suffered the most persecution. She was a Quaker school-teacher, fair, comely, and of the noblest character. Born in Worcester, Massachusetts, in 1811, she studied and taught, by turns, like Lucy Stone, till she had gained the highest education then obtainable by a woman in New England. She became so deeply interested in the antislavery cause that she gave to the Anti-Slavery Society all her accumulated earnings, and her small inheritance from her father's estate, and even sold her most expensive garments in order to contribute their price. She finally resigned her position as teacher of the Quaker school in Lynn, Massachusetts, and devoted herself wholly to antislavery work. Again and again, some friend gave her a gold watch; but the gold watches always went straight into the antislavery treasury. Lucy Stone said, "She could no more have helped it than if her children had needed bread." Her path was made very hard.

She held several well-attended meetings at Washington, Connecticut, and was asked to stay and address another. Then the minister preached against her from the text, "I have a few things against thee, because thou sufferest that woman Jezebel, which calleth herself a prophetess, to teach, and to seduce my servants to commit fornication." He drew a black picture of the original Jezebel and declared that another Jezebel had arisen, making high pretensions to philanthropy and Christianity, and with fascinations exceeding even those of her Scriptural prototype. He added: "Do any of you ask for evidence of her vile character? It needs no other evidence than the fact that, in the face of the clearest commands of God, 'Let your women keep silence in the churches, for it is not permitted unto them to speak', she comes with her brazen face, a servant of Satan in the garb of an angel of light, and tramples this commandment under her feet." She went to the next prayer meeting, and stood near the door as the people passed out. With one exception, none of those who had attended her meetings, or had entertained her hospitably, gave her a word or a look. They passed her by as if she did not exist. Such things happened again and again. In 1845 she married Stephen S. Foster, a leonine abolitionist who out-Garrisoned even Garrison in his vivid and terrible denunciations of the sin of slavery and the wickedness of the clergy and the churches that countenanced it. After that, husband and wife lectured and faced the mobs together.

At the memorial exercises for Abby Kelley Foster, in 1887, Lucy Stone said:

"The open door for higher education (Oberlin) was the gray dawn of our morning. Its sure day came when the sisters Sarah and Angelina Grimké and Abby Kelley Foster began to speak publicly in behalf of the slaves. Public speaking by women was regarded as something monstrous. All the cyclones and blizzards which prejudice, bigotry and custom could raise, were let loose on these three peerless women. But they held fast to the Eternal Justice. Above the howling of the mobs, the din of the press and the thunders from the pulpit, they heard the wail of the slave and the cry of the mothers sold from their children. Literally taking their lives in their hands, they went out to speak, 'remembering those in bonds as bound with them.'

"In 1838, Angelina Grimké spoke in the House of Representatives in Massachusetts. It was packed as it probably never was before or since. The great crowd had gathered, some from their interest in the slave, more from curiosity to hear a woman, and some intent on making an uproar. But this quiet woman arose, utterly forgetful of self; with anointed lips, and with eloquence rare and wonderful she pleaded for the slave. The curious forgot their curiosity; the mobocrat dropped his brickbat before the solemn earnestness of this woman who, for the slave's sake, had braved the mob and the fagot; who could neither heed the uplifted finger that cried shame nor cease for the texts and the sermons, or the odium of the newspapers. To herself, she was not 'flying in the face of Providence.' It was no hunger for personal notoriety that had brought her there, but a great, earnest purpose that must find expression.

"How great a debt the woman's rights movement owes to her! But one such speech, or many, could not kill the hoary prejudice of ages; and circumstances soon compelled the sisters Grimké to leave the lecture field. Abby Kelley remained to bear alone the opprobrium still heaped upon the woman who so far departed from her sphere as to speak in public. Whatever of tribulation any of us have known in the advocacy of this reform, it has been play compared with the long, unrelieved moral torture endured by Abby Kelley, in the battle which finally secured the right of free speech for every woman. A sharp onset with shot and shell is no trifle; but to stand year after year, as Abby Kelley stood, in the thick of the fight, while pulpit and press, editors and clergy, poured upon her vials of bitterness and wrath, to which falsehood always resorts, required the courage of a martyr and the faith of a saint. If she had been a weak woman, she would have yielded and fled. Think what it would be to live perpetually in the midst of scorn and reproach;

to go to church and find the sermon directed against you, from the text denouncing Jezebel; and, with no chance to reply, to sit and hear all manner of lies told about you; at another time, to meet with intolerable insult under the very roof of the house where you were authorized to seek shelter, so that you fled from it, fasting for thirty-six hours. These things were actual incidents in her experience, and only a small part of what she endured. If she had been less noble, or more self-seeking, she would have abandoned the terrible pioneer's post and taken an easier way.

"The great service Abby Kelley rendered the slave is less than that by which, at such a price, she earned for us all the right of free speech. Long after this right was conceded, the effect of the old odium lingered, and she was regarded by those who did not know her as a pestilent person, no better than she should be. Even as late as the Worcester Woman's Rights Convention in 1850, the managers of the meeting conferred beforehand as to whether it was best to invite her to speak, 'She is so odious.' She was allowed to be present; and I shall never forget the thrilling voice in which she said, 'Sisters, bloody feet have worn smooth the path by which you come up here!' It was her own bleeding feet that had worn the way."

In those early days, it was considered improper not only for a woman to speak in public, but even for her to hold office in an association formed for a benevolent purpose. When Abby Kelley, in 1838, was appointed on a committee of the Massachusetts Anti-Slavery Society, it split the association in twain. Eight Congregational ministers withdrew immediately, and a new organization was formed by the seceders.

Lucy followed the controversy with the keenest interest. In 1838 she wrote to her brother Bowman:

"I would like to have you read John Q. Adams's remarks on the Misses Grimké. He says in the controversy that is begun he wishes them well; but Mr. Bartlett has 'S. M. Grimké on The Rights of Women' in pamphlet form, and if you could read that (and she says nothing but what she proves), I guess you would not think that I was too 'obstreperous.' I tell you, they are first-rate, and only help to confirm the resolution I had made before, to call no man master."

Lucy studied and taught by turns. She would teach until she had saved up a little money and then use it to study further. She was able to go for one term to the Quaboag Seminary at Warren, Massachusetts, and later, for a short time, to Wilbraham Academy. She wrote from Wilbraham to her brother on June 18, 1840:

"You ask if I am a friend of such a 'New Organization' as I find an account of in your last paper.

(This was the organization formed by the members of the Anti-Slavery Society who objected to any public work by women.) No, brother, I am not. If that is the spirit of the N. O., I am far enough from being its friend. There seems to be no feeling of Liberty about it. Its great object seems to be to crush Garrison and the women. While it pretends to endeavor to remove the yoke of bondage on account of color, it is actually summoning all its energies to rivet more firmly the chains that have always been fastened upon the neck of women. Look at the ridiculous conduct of H. G. Ludlow, at the anniversary of the Anti-Slavery Society of New Haven. If a woman would 'open her mouth for the dumb', she sha'n't. If she would let her voice speak, the cry is raised again, 'It shall not be allowed.' Thus the inalienable right that God had given is wrested from her, and the talent, or, if you please, half talent entrusted to her keeping for improvement, is violently taken away; and H. G. L., becoming the keeper of her conscience, must also answer for her at the Day of Judgment. Hear him answering to 'Where is the half talent I gave her?' 'Lord, thinking I knew better than Thou didst, and believing that might gave right, I violently took it from her, though she strove hard to maintain it. Lo, here Thou hast', etc. Must he not have an answer similar to one of whom we read, who hid his Lord's money? Yet he says, 'I have the spirit of God. I am a Christian.'

"I admire the calm and noble bearing of Abby Kelley on that occasion, and cannot but wish there were more kindred spirits.

"Only let females be educated in the same manner and with the same advantages that males have, and, as everything in nature seeks its own level, I would risk that we would find out our 'appropriate sphere.'

"I am well, and am doing well in my studies.

"Miss Adams and I walked out to Springfield last Saturday, and back again, the whole distance being nearly twenty-five miles. We do not feel any inconvenience from it.

"I have been examining the doctrine of Christian Perfection, and I cannot avoid the conclusion that it is attainable in this life.

"Will you, when you can, consistently with your other duties, write me what you think about the immortality of the spirit of beasts, and, if you think they are not, tell me how the justice of God can be reconciled with the abuse they often suffer?

"I am glad your prayer-meetings are good. Warren needs a revival. I hope you may have one. My own heart is cold as clay. I often think that I have never been a Christian, for how can one who has ever known the love of God go so far away? Will brother sometimes pray for me?

"It was decided in our Literary Society the other day that ladies ought to mingle in politics, go to Congress, etc., etc. What do you think of that?"

Lucy often said that, if women could secure education and the right to speak, they could win everything else for themselves.

She finally accumulated money enough to enter Mount Holyoke Seminary. That institution was much interested in foreign missions, and many of the teachers and students kept mite boxes in which they collected money for that work. Lucy kept, instead, one of the mite boxes of the Anti-Slavery Society, which bore a picture of a kneeling slave holding up manacled hands, with the motto, "Am I not a man and a brother?" Bowman sent her the *Liberator*, and, after reading it, she used to place it in the reading room of the Seminary. No one knew who put it there, but Lucy was suspected, because of her strong antislavery views, and, when questioned, she frankly admitted it. Mary Lyon summoned her to a private interview and talked to her very seriously. She said, "You must remember that the slavery question is a very grave question, and one upon which the best people are divided."

Lucy spent only three months at Mount Holyoke. Then her sister Rhoda died. Her mother was so heart-broken that her health failed, and Lucy went home to comfort and help her.

Meanwhile the struggle for the right of women to speak and to take part with men in antislavery work kept on. It is easy to imagine the feelings with which Lucy must have read the report of the World's Anti-Slavery Convention held in London in 1840. The Call had invited delegates from all antislavery organizations. A number of the societies in America elected women among their delegates. Despite the efforts of Wendell Phillips and many others, the convention refused to accept their credentials. Garrison had been delayed at sea. When he arrived and found that the women delegates had been rejected, he refused to take his own seat in the convention, and during the ten days of its discussions and votes upon a subject so dear to his heart, he sat in silence in the gallery, with the excluded women.

One of the delegates was the distinguished Quakeress, Lucretia Mott. Elizabeth Cady Stanton was also present, not as a delegate, but as the young wife of a delegate, Henry B. Stanton. Mrs. Mott and Mrs. Stanton took long walks together, mingling their indignation; and they determined that some day, after their return to America, they would hold a convention for woman's rights. Eight years later they carried out their plan.

## *Chapter III*

At the low wages then paid to women, it took Lucy nine years to save up money enough to enter college. There was no difficulty as to the choice of an alma mater. There was only one college that admitted women.

Oberlin College had been founded in 1833 by the Reverend John J. Shipherd, pastor of the Presbyterian Church at Elyria, Ohio, and P. P. Stewart, a returned missionary. They wished to educate ministers and teachers for the great West, and missionaries for foreign lands. They also wanted to meet the needs of poor students who were willing to work for an education. They chose Oberlin as the place because the owners of the southern part of the township of Russia, Loraine County, Ohio, had offered to give five hundred acres, on certain conditions, for educational purposes. Shipherd and Stewart made their way through the wilderness, fastened their horses to trees, and knelt down under another tree to pray for divine guidance. They had neither money nor land in possession, but both came, and the college was founded. At first it was called an Institute. It was named Oberlin after John Frederic Oberlin, a German pastor of eastern France who had devoted his life to elevating the people of his parish.

The college made no distinction of color or sex. The vote of Father Shipherd opened the door to colored students, and it was he who stated, as a prominent object of the institution, "the elevation of the female character, by bringing within the reach of the misjudged and neglected sex all the instructive privileges which have hitherto unreasonably distinguished the leading sex from theirs."

The first woman graduate of Oberlin College was Zeruiah Porter, who later married Edward Weed. She completed the Literary Course in 1838. This was not the regular college course. In 1841, three women, Mary Hosford, Elizabeth Smith Prall and Mary Caroline Rudd, were regularly graduated from the classical course, receiving the degree of Bachelor of Arts. These three were the first women in this country, and, so far as is known, the first in the world, to receive the B. A. degree on the same conditions as those prevailing in the best men's colleges of the time. In those days the course at Oberlin was fully equivalent to that at Yale.

Lucy started for Oberlin in August, 1843, with a light purse and a scanty wardrobe, but with her head full of intelligence and her heart of courage. On August 30 she wrote home:

"I am here safe in Oberlin — long-talked-of, and, to Mother, long-dreaded Oberlin. I arrived without having had a particle of trouble to myself or baggage. The whole expense of getting here, including food, was $16.65. . . . I found that the fare by the packets was $6, and by railroad $7.50; only a dollar and a half difference in the price, but three days' difference in the time; and by the packets I should have to change boats three or four times, and by the cars only once, between Albany and Buffalo; so I thought it best to go by the cars. Rode day and night. . . .

"Mother, there is not a bit of trouble about traveling. Hastings told such stories that I did not know but there might be something, but there is not a mite. I would as soon travel alone from Maine to Georgia, and from there to the Rocky Mountains, as not.

"There was an elderly gentleman rode with me from Albany to Utica. He lives in Herkimer, close to Litchfield. Knows Cousin Sam. I rode alone with the gentleman, but was not at all afraid, for he was a real gentleman."

This "real gentleman" was General Spinner, later the first Secretary of the Treasury to employ women in the Department. He had been sitting behind Lucy and looking over her shoulder. He asked her why she wanted to study Greek. She told him it was in order to find out what the Bible taught about women. He said, "Why don't you study physiology and learn about your own body?" She answered, "I have." "How many bones have you in your hand and arm?" he demanded. She answered promptly, "Nineteen." Then he thought it might do for her to study Greek. At a station he went out and brought her in some ice-cream. She found it very refreshing, as she was traveling on short rations. They had a good deal of talk together. On leaving the train at Herkimer, he pointed out his house and invited her to call upon him, if she should ever be passing that way. After she became well known, he often sent her official documents from Washington. Lucy did not describe this incident in writing home, but she often told of it in later years.

Crossing Lake Erie from Buffalo to Cleveland, she could not afford a stateroom, and slept on deck among horses and freight, with some other women who, like herself, could only pay for a "deck passage." Her letter continues:

"I was not sick at all coming over the Lake. It was a very still time, and the water was as smooth as glass, except what was disturbed by the boat. We met one steamboat, and passed about fifty schooners. They looked very grand, under full sail. At night I put my trunk beside another, and my carpet-bag at the end, and lay down and slept soundly all night. The other ladies did 'ditto', and one elderly lady, who could not sleep, kept watch. There were several men on the other side of the deck, 'camped down', but we were not disturbed at all. Saturday morning, at Cleveland, I went down on the beach and picked up a whole lot of stones for Clara and Eliza.[1] Perhaps I can't send them; but if I live to get home they shall have them. From Cleveland to Elyria (in stage), which is eight miles from Oberlin, we had a dumb set, so I slept. At Elyria we changed stages, and then four young ladies got in to go to visit Oberlin. Talk enough then; no sleep.

"We have breakfast at six, dinner at twelve, supper at half-past six. We have meat once a day, bread and milk for supper, pudding and milk, thin cakes, etc., for breakfast. We shall live well enough. My room-mate is a young lady from South Carolina, whose father is a slaveholder. She says he does not want her to talk about slavery, for fear she will be an Abolitionist; it would kill her mother, and she could never see her father. She is a good-natured little thing, sixteen years old.

"I lost nothing coming, except my gloves. I left them at the depot in Albany. They were an old pair.

[1] Her little nieces.

"Professor Finney preached last Sabbath. He is the crossest-looking man I ever saw. He said, 'Of all the reformers this side of Hell, the Come-Outers most needed reforming; forever slanging the clergy; violating the Sabbath; disturbing public assemblies, etc. We didn't know much about them here.' He said you might as well try to convert the Devil as an ambitious man.

"Thursday. I left this unfinished space yesterday so as to have room to put in the result of my examination, but I have not been examined yet, and I thought Mother would want to hear the rest, so I will not wait. After examination I will send a paper and dot it.[1]

"The water here is poor, though not so bad as in some places. I would give anything for a drink from Father's well. I don't think the land here is half as good as it is at home. It is all clay. I think I shall like it very well here. The teachers are pleasant, and the young ladies too. Colored gentlemen and ladies sit at the same table with us, and there appears to be no difference.

"With a whole lot of love,

"Lucy.

"Mother, it is your birthday. I should like to know how you get along with the work, now

[1] Letter postage at this time was twenty-five cents, so it was common to send a newspaper instead, and to dot words or letters which formed a message.

you are sixty-four. I washed Monday. Could n't help thinking how you would get along with washing and ironing and baking. Frank, you must remember and fill up the brass kettle for Mother every day, for she can't draw water.

"When you write, I want you should tell me all, — how much you get for the cheese, how you all do, and all about Chase.[1] If any inquire about me, tell them I came safe, without a bit of trouble, and find good people here."

Professor Finney was famous for his terrific brimstone sermons. The "Come-Outers" were the Garrisonian abolitionists, of whom Lucy was one. The Garrisonians were most of them unorthodox in their religious views; they severely denounced the proslavery attitude of most of the clergy and churches; they encouraged public speaking by women; they were generally nonresistants; they withheld their allegiance from the United States Constitution because it sanctioned slavery; and they advocated "No union with slaveholders." Several of the professors and a number of the students had come over to Oberlin from Lane Seminary, because its president, Doctor Lyman Beecher, forbade the discussion of slavery there. Oberlin was strongly antislavery, but its abolitionism was strictly

[1] The Reverend Moses Chase, the minister of the West Brookfield church, who persecuted the abolitionists.

orthodox and constitutional. Lucy wrote home, a little later: "There is not a single *Liberator* taken in Oberlin, nor a single *Liberator* man, woman or child here but me."

The college had a rule that students must not teach in the preparatory department till they had been at Oberlin a year, so that the faculty might judge of their mental and moral fitness. This was a great disappointment to Lucy, who had hoped to pay part of her expenses in this way. But her brother Bowman, who was now a minister, wrote a letter testifying to her good character, and to the fact that she had been for years a successful teacher; so an exception was made in her case. During her first year, she taught in the preparatory department two hours a day, for twelve and a half cents an hour, and did housework in the Ladies' Boarding Hall at three cents an hour. Some one who saw her at work in the Ladies' Boarding Hall said that she had put her Greek book up in a little rack where she could consult it, and as she wiped the dishes she stepped back and forth between the dishpan and the book, learning her Greek line by line, as she had learned the hymns in her childhood while bringing in the wood.

At this time a number of men who afterwards became famous also eked out their expenses by doing housework in the college. In her address at Oberlin's semicentennial, Lucy said, "Future governors of the State, members of Congress, generals of armies, were part of the working brigade of Oberlin. General Cox, with paper cap on his head, with apron and sleeves rolled up, made the crackers which, on Sunday mornings, with coffee, made the breakfast."

Most of the students were poor, and the college furnished them board at a dollar a week; but she could not afford even this small sum, and during most of her first year she cooked her food in her own room, boarding herself for less than fifty cents a week. Yet she kept healthy and happy, stood well in her studies, and found time also for good works. She often mended the clothes of the poor students, both white and colored, and was always ready to lend a hand to any one in need of help.

There was a Ladies' Board, made up mostly of the professors' wives, with Miss Adams, the Lady Principal. They were supposed to look after the manners and morals of the girls. Lucy's independence soon brought her into collision with them. It gave her a severe sick headache to sit with her bonnet on through the long church service which the students had to attend every Sunday morning; so she took her bonnet off. The next day she was called before the Ladies' Board, and reminded of the Scriptural injunction that women should keep their heads covered in church. She said, "If I do, I am good for nothing all the rest of the day. What account shall I give to God of my wasted Sunday afternoons?" It was finally agreed that she should sit in a pew at the extreme rear, and that she might have her bonnet off part of the time.

Oberlin had a long vacation in the winter, to give the students a chance to earn money by teaching school. Lucy taught during the vacations, and in her second year, Bowman and Sarah lent her money.

Oberlin was a station on the Underground Railway, and many fugitive slaves settled there. A school was started for them, and the committee in charge asked Lucy to teach it. But the colored men, densely ignorant and fresh from slavery, still thought it beneath their dignity to be taught by a woman. The committee did not tell her this, but took her to the school and introduced her as the teacher, thinking that they would not like to express their objections in her presence. But a murmur ran around the room, and presently a tall man, very black, stood up and said that he had nothing against Miss Stone personally, but he must say he did not think it was the right thing for men to be taught by a woman. She persuaded them, however, that it would be for their advantage to learn from any one who could teach them to read; and her dusky pupils soon became much attached to her. When the Ladies' Boarding Hall took fire, during her temporary absence, she was told afterwards that a whole string of colored men had arrived on the scene one after another, to save her property, each demanding breathlessly, "Where is Miss Stone's trunk?"

In her third year, Father Stone's objections to a collegiate education for girls yielded to his respect for Lucy's courage, and to the affection which, under his rough exterior, he really felt for his children. He wrote to her on January 11, 1845:

"Lucy: The first thing you will want to know, after hearing that we are all well, will be about money. When you wrote that you had to get up at two o'clock to study your lesson, it made me think of the old tanyard where I had to get up at one and two o'clock. I little thought then that I should have children, or a child, that would have to do the same; not the same work, but perhaps as hard. I had to work late and early. I was hardly able to live; and you have been under the same inconvenience, as far as money is concerned. Let this suffice. There will be no trouble about money; you can have what you will need, without studying nights, or working for eight cents an hour.

"I pay the postage on all letters that are sent and received, so pay no more postage.

"Your Father Stone."

We do not know for which of her activities Lucy had been getting eight cents an hour. Perhaps it was for teaching in the colored school.

Lucy's third year was therefore easier financially, and she could devote more time to study. She wrote to her father and mother:

"I want to tell you how I spend my time, so that you can think of me, and know each hour of the day what I am doing. I rise at five o'clock, and am busy until six taking care of my room and my person. At six we go to breakfast, which, with family worship, lasts until seven. Then I go and recite Latin until eight; from eight to nine recite Greek; from nine till ten, study algebra; from ten till eleven, hear a class recite arithmetic; from eleven to twelve, recite algebra; from twelve to one, dinner, and an exercise in the sitting room which all the ladies are required to attend. From one to two, hear a class recite arithmetic; from two to five, I study; five to six we have prayers in the chapel, and then supper. We study in the evening. These are the duties of every day except Monday, which is washing day. In the afternoon of Monday, from three to four, I attend composition class. In addition to what is done during the other days, we have, every Tuesday, to go to the Music Hall and hear a lecture from some one of the Ladies' Board of Managers — this from three to four o'clock. Every Thursday there is a prayer meeting which we are all required to attend, from three to four, and, from four to five, a lecture from some of the Faculty, which we are also required to attend. So you see every moment is occupied. Yet I find time every day, and many times in a day, to think of Father and Mother, brothers and sister, and all in that hill-side home which I love better than ever. It will be a long, long time before I can see it. The home I have here is very pleasant, though it is not my New England home. In Wellington, where I taught last vacation, they say I may have a home, and if I am sick they will take care of me. They came out to pay me the other day, and brought me a great lump of maple sugar, and some apples. When I left, they gave me a good new broom, which I presume will last as long as I stay here. They were very kind. I sewed for them a little, and they gave me soap enough and candles enough to last a year. Cousin John Locke gave me some candles, and says I may have a home there.

"I room in the highest story, so that I have to run up two pairs of stairs with water, though we only carry wood up one stair. I earn a quarter of a dollar a week more than my board costs. I have to take Institution orders as pay. Mr. Fair-child, who keeps the boarding hall, will take only one half his pay in orders, because the Institution is so much in debt that its orders are not available without discount; so I have to pay half money, that is, $2 per month. The rest, which I can earn by teaching, will go to pay my tuition and room rent, which is upwards of $16 per year. I have money enough, if I should not earn anything, to pay all my expenses more than a year; so I feel very well provided for.

"They offered me another colored class to teach, but I had not time, for each recitation occupies an hour.

"I hope Sarah did not go to sewing straw because I had her money, so that she could not go to school. I should be sorry indeed if it was so. When she goes to school again, I wish she would study Mental and Moral Philosophy.

"I have been weighed to-day. Weigh 119 pounds — more than I ever did before. I have but very little headache."

In another letter she says: "I have bought me a fine big rocking chair, with one arm-shelf. Cost $4, but I shall get that amount of comfort out of it, and rest for my headaches."

On July 4, 1845, she wrote: "This forenoon Professors Cowles and Morgan, and Mr. Orvis, talked to us on peace. It was very good as far as it went, but they take the ground that war is sometimes right. You know that is not half strong enough for me."

She wrote to her brother Frank:

"I do wish you could be here to read with me; but, since you are not, I do as you said you used to do at Marietta College. I look at the moon, and think that perhaps the loved ones at home are looking at it too."

A colored student at Oberlin fell in love with one of the white students. When she refused to marry him, he declared that he would kill himself. It was feared that he might really do it. Lucy, who was looked upon as a friend by all the colored people, went to labor with him. She found him in the depths of despondency. He was deaf to argument, and insisted that he would drown himself in the college well. Finally she told him that it would be a great shame for him to spoil the water for the whole college, and strongly advised him, if he must kill himself, to cut his throat instead. His wrath at this hard-hearted suggestion brought him out of his fit of black melancholy, and he gave up the idea of suicide.

In 1845, a young woman entered Oberlin who was destined to become the world's first ordained woman minister — Antoinette L. Brown, a beautiful, intellectual, and very religious girl from Henrietta, New York. Born in a log cabin, she had joined the Orthodox Congregational Church at nine years of age, "on profession of faith", and at once began to take part in the prayer meetings in a way that made the older members marvel and quote the text, "Out of the mouths of babes and sucklings." Every one thought she was cut out for religious work of some kind, probably that of a minister's wife or a missionary. She herself cherished the wish to become a minister, but this would have been considered so wild an idea that she kept it strictly to herself.

On her way to Oberlin, she had for a fellow passenger in the stagecoach one of the trustees of the college, who was a friend of her family. He took occasion to warn her against Lucy Stone. He said, in substance: "She is a bright student, and there is nothing against her character; but she is a young woman of strange and dangerous opinions. She is a Garrisonian, and she is planning to become a public speaker, and she is always talking about woman's rights. You had better not have much to do with her." Antoinette says, in her reminiscences:

"Of course, she became the one person whose acquaintance I most desired to make. When we assembled in the Boarding Hall, I diffidently surveyed my new environment. There were long tables at which the men were seated along one side and the women along the other. The first question I addressed to my neighbor was, 'Which is Lucy Stone?' By leaning forward and looking down the line of tables, I could see a small, fresh, round-faced girl in a neat calico frock, her hair cut round at the neck and hanging just above the smoothest, whitest, turned-down collar — which, by the way, she always washed and ironed herself.

"Among the cheerful, quiet babel which rose about us, I could catch the sweet, clear-cut tones of Lucy's voice. A discussion was going on at that table. She talked a great deal, and I could feel sure, without hearing what she said, that she was speaking with much earnestness and with very positive convictions. As she was seated near the Superintendent of the hall, a college graduate and a clergyman, I promptly decided that she talked altogether too much, and with an unfitting absoluteness of conviction and of authority, for any young girl. She appeared to be about sixteen. Afterwards, when I learned that she was nearly twenty-seven, and had been a teacher for years, I recognized that her speech and manner were appropriate for the more mature age."

Owing to her uncommon health and vitality, Lucy always looked much younger than she was.

Antoinette was already so far advanced in her education that she was able to enter Oberlin as a third-year student, and so became Lucy's classmate. The two girls soon became great friends, and their friendship was cemented in later life by their marrying brothers. Antoinette says in her reminiscences: "Mine was the intense admiration of a much younger girl for one much more experienced and influential."

Close friends though they were, they differed widely in their opinions. Antoinette was an abolitionist, but not a Garrisonian. Lucy kept a picture of Mr. Garrison hanging in her room, and the other students declared that she said her prayers to it. Her face lighted up with enthusiasm whenever she looked at the picture or mentioned his name; and she defended the Garrisonian doctrines warmly on all occasions. Antoinette was a devout Trinitarian Congregationlist. Lucy had become a Unitarian through listening to Professor Finney's lectures on God — a result which the professor had certainly not meant to produce. The proslavery attitude of most of the clergy and churches had inspired her with a distrust, if not an actual antagonism, towards organized religion, which lasted with her for many years. Though her object in going to college had been to satisfy herself whether the texts quoted in defense of the subjection of women were correctly translated, in later life she attached little importance to the texts; but she always believed and maintained that the Bible, rightly interpreted, was on the side of equal rights for women. Lucy at this time used an almost Quaker plainness of dress; but she was held up by the authorities as an example to the other young women because of the spotless neatness of her simple calico gowns. Antoinette liked pretty things and wore artificial flowers on her hat. Lucy remonstrated with her earnestly, and said, "How can a sensible girl like you carry a flower-pot on her head?" But they agreed to differ, and loved each other none the less. They took long walks together, and once, as they stood looking at a wonderful sunset, Antoinette confided to Lucy her cherished wish to become a minister. Lucy, for all her optimism, could not believe that women would ever gain admission to the revered ranks of the clergy; but Antoinette said, "I shall do it!" and she did.

These two students made abundant trouble for the Ladies' Board. Antoinette, in her old age, said that they rather liked to be called before it, because it gave them an opportunity to air their views.

The young men had to hold debates as part of their work in rhetoric, and the young women were required to be present, for an hour and a half every week, in order to help form an audience for the boys, but were not allowed to take part. Lucy was intending to lecture and Antoinette to preach. Both wished for practice in public speaking. They asked Professor Thome, the head of that department, to let them debate. He was a man of liberal views — a Southerner who had freed his slaves — and he consented. Tradition says that the debate was exceptionally brilliant. More persons than usual came in to listen, attracted by curiosity. But the Ladies' Board immediately got busy, St. Paul was invoked, and the college authorities forbade any repetition of the experiment.

A few of the young women, led by Lucy, organized the first debating society ever formed among college girls. At first they held their meetings secretly in the woods, with sentinels on the watch to give warning of intruders. When the weather grew colder, Lucy asked an old colored woman who owned a small house, the mother of one of her colored pupils, to let them have the use of her parlor. At first she was doubtful, fearing that the meetings might be a cover for flirtation; but when she found that the debating society was made up of girls only, she decided that it must be an innocent affair, and gave her consent. Her house was on the outskirts of the town, and the girls came one or two at a time, so as not to attract attention. Lucy opened the first formal meeting with the following statement:

"We shall leave this college with the reputation of a thorough collegiate course, yet not one of us has received any rhetorical or elocutionary training. Not one of us could state a question or argue it in successful debate. For this reason I have proposed the formation of this association."

From this time on, the club continued to meet, and debated all sorts of high subjects.

It was at Oberlin that Lucy seems to have first conceived the idea that a married woman ought to keep her own name. Antoinette says, in her reminiscences:

"Some time during a recitation in the senior class, a quotation was made, I think from Montaigne, 'Women are more sunk by marriage than men.'

" 'Professor Morgan,' asked Lucy, 'why are women more sunk by marriage than men?'

"The professor fidgeted, physically and mentally, offering several minor reasons; then he said emphatically: 'Women lose their names, and become identified with the husband's family; the wife's family is not as readily traceable in history as her husband's; the law gives her property into her husband's keeping, and she is little known to the business world.'

"Then and there began Lucy Stone's first protest against the wife's surrendering her own name. The matter dropped. But again and again she spoke to me about it.

"The fact of a woman's losing her name, and in some sense her personality, in this way, still dwelt in her mind. This led to her determination never to take her husband's name, at whatever disadvantage to herself. I honored her for the bravery of her decision, although I felt sure it was paying dear at that day for the minor point of a name."

Lucy made her first public speech while at Oberlin. The colored people got up a celebration of the anniversary of West Indian emancipation, and invited her to be one of the speakers. President Mahan and several of the professors were also on the program. She made her speech with the rest and thought nothing of it. The next day she was called before the Ladies' Board. All the texts commonly invoked against public speaking by women were quoted. Finally the president's wife said, "Did you not feel yourself very much out of place up there on the platform among all those men? Were you not embarrassed and frightened?"

She answered, "Why, no, Mrs. Mahan! 'Those men' were President Mahan and my professors, whom I meet every day in the classroom. I was not afraid of them a bit." She was allowed to go, with an admonition.

Among the lecturers who came to Oberlin were Stephen and Abby Kelley Foster. Lucy wrote that she "had a grand time with them. They lectured three times. Set the people to thinking, and I hope great good will result. Some of the faculty were pleased with them; some were not."

Lucy's family were divided in regard to her intention to lecture. Her brother Frank wrote, in 1846: "If you think you have got brass enough, and can do more good by giving public lectures than any other way, I say go to it. But Mother does n't like the idea."

Frank's wife added an anxious postscript: "Lucy, if there should be any probability of your changing your mind, I hope you will let Mother Stone know it the first thing, for she feels dreadfully about it. Mother wants you to think carefully of it, and see if you cannot do more good teaching than by lecturing. And if you think you must lecture, she wants to know if you don't think you could do more good by going from house to house, as Harlan Page did."

Bowman wrote: "I believe Sarah said in her last letter that if you intend lecturing she hoped you would not come into this State. I wish you to do what you think is your duty. If you violate your sense of duty to please your friends, you will lose more than you will gain."

Sarah urged Lucy to devote herself to educating women rather than to lecturing. She said, "I hardly know what you mean by 'laboring for the restoration and salvation of our sex.'" She declared that she knew of no respect in which women were oppressed, except in their unequal pay, and that that was their own fault, because most of them had not acquired an education. She wrote very affectionately, but assured Lucy that the course which she proposed to follow "by the grace of God" was wholly contrary to the divine teaching.

Her mother's distress grieved Lucy, but could not shake her resolution. She wrote:

"I know, Mother, you feel badly about the plan I have proposed to myself, and that you would prefer to have me take some other course, if I could in conscience. Yet, Mother, I know you too well to suppose that you would wish me to turn away from what I think is my duty, and go all my days in opposition to my convictions of right, lashed by a reproaching conscience.

"I surely would not be a public speaker if I sought a life of ease, for it will be a most laborious one; nor would I do it for the sake of honor, for I know that I shall be disesteemed, nay, even hated, by some who are now my friends, or who profess to be. Neither would I do it if I sought wealth, because I could secure it with far more ease and worldly honor by being a teacher. But, Mother, the gold that perishes in the using, the honor that comes from men, the ease or indolence which eats out the energy of the soul, are not the objects at which I aim. If I would be true to myself, true to my Heavenly Father, I must be actuated by high and holy principles, and pursue that course of conduct which, to me, appears best calculated to promote the highest good of the world. Because I know that I shall suffer, shall I, for this, like Lot's wife, turn back? No, Mother, if in this hour of the world's need I should refuse to lend my aid, however small it may be, I should have no right to think myself a Christian, and I should forever despise Lucy Stone. If, while I hear the wild shriek of the slave mother robbed of her little ones, or the muffled groan of the daughter spoiled of her virtue, I do not open my mouth for the dumb, am I not guilty? Or should I go, as you said, from house to house to do it, when I could tell so many more in less time, if they should be gathered in one place? You would not object, or think it wrong, for a man to plead the cause of the suffering and the outcast; and surely the moral character of the act is not changed because it is done by a woman.

"I received a letter the other day from a friend saying: 'I regret for the sake of others that your mother refuses her consent for you to become a public speaker. I regret it less on your own account. The position of a woman advocating the right is so painful that I feel as though I did not wish you to be subject to all the trials that will be heaped upon you.'

"But, Mother, there are no trials so great as they suffer who neglect or refuse to do what they believe is their duty. I expect to plead not for the slave only, but for suffering humanity everywhere. ESPECIALLY DO I MEAN TO LABOR FOR THE ELEVATION OF MY SEX. The little pamphlet that I sent you, written by S. J. May, gives a faint outline of what is to be done, and the changes that are to be wrought. But I will not speak further upon this subject at this time, only to ask that you will not withhold your consent from my doing anything that I think is my duty to do. You will not, will you, Mother?

"I am not boarding at the public hall this spring, because I could not room alone there, and I can improve so much faster alone that I choose to board in a private family, though I have to pay twelve and a half cents more a week. The family are perfect haters of Disunionism. They berate Garrison, Stephen and Abby Foster most unmercifully; but I have to bear it patiently, so it does me good, though it is not very pleasant.

"We are trying to get the faculty to let the ladies of our class read their own pieces when they graduate. They have never been allowed to do it, but we expect to read for ourselves, or not to write."

A little later Lucy wrote home:

"I must write you about my affairs here, and then I want you to tell me honestly just whether you think I have done right. This coming Commencement, you know, I graduate, and several members of the class are appointed to speak and write for that occasion. The class appoints its own speakers and writers, after the faculty have decided how many shall be appointed. This year they decided that half the class, that is, half the ladies and half the gentlemen, should take part in the Commencement exercises.

"It has been the custom for the ladies who were appointed to write for the Commencement to have their essays read by Professor Thome. Some of them thought ladies ought to have the privilege of reading for themselves. Accordingly, I prepared a petition to the faculty, and to the Ladies' Board, asking that we might do so; but the petition was rejected, on the ground that it was improper for women to participate in public exercises with men. I came at once to the conclusion that I would not write.

"The day for the appointment came. President Mahan and Mr. Whipple, principal of the Preparatory Department, met with the class to count votes. I received an appointment by a very large vote. I said to President Mahan that I could not accept without a sacrifice of principle that I had no right to make, and I wished to be excused. Several members of the class spoke at once; said they hoped I would not then resign, but would take time to consider. I told them I had already considered, and that it was not at all probable that any after consideration would change my mind. President Mahan said he thought that we ought to have the privilege of reading for ourselves; that he did all he could to get the consent of the faculty, but they were all against him. He thought I had better wait a little before I refused the appointment. I told President Mahan I thanked him for his efforts for us in the faculty, and the class for honoring me with the appointment, but I could not accept it. He said it must be referred to the faculty whether I should be excused. Mr. Whipple came home with me, and urged all the reasons he could think of to persuade me to write and let Professor Thome read for me. I told him that by so doing I would make a public acknowledgment of the rectitude of the principle which takes away from women their equal rights, and denies to them the privilege of being co-laborers with men in any sphere to which their ability makes them adequate; and that no word or deed of mine should ever look towards the support of such a principle, or even to its toleration. Miss Adams and some members of the class who were particularly anxious that I should read, called on President Mahan and asked him to request the faculty it might be granted to me as a special privilege, in view of my conscientious scruples. He said that he had just been speaking of the same thing to Mrs. Mahan; that he was very, very desirous that Miss Stone should read; that he thought she ought to; that she understood herself, and would represent the class well; that there had never been a student here who had gone through a course of study with whom he was better satisfied, etc., etc., etc.

"I would not have mentioned these last things to anyone but my own father's family, nor to them only that it does us good sometimes to know that our friends have the confidence of those with whom they are. The matter has been before the faculty and the Ladies' Board more than two weeks. I don't know what they will decide, but I certainly shall not write if I cannot read for myself. I have had long conversations with several members of the faculty on the subject, and the probability is that I shall not read, and that some one will be appointed in my place.

"Now, don't you think I did right? Is n't it better that I should be true to my principles than to have the honor (?) of writing for Commencement what another must read for me? Not because I could not just as well read it for myself, but because I am a woman, and women must not speak in the church when men are on the same platform.

"When you write, please tell me honestly just what you think of it.

"Now about another matter that will trouble Mother more still, perhaps. Abby Foster wrote me that she had mentioned to Mrs. Chapman and Mrs. Follen that I intended to lecture, and that they wish me to go directly to Massachusetts after I graduate and lecture there, both because they need lecturers of the right stamp, and because her circumstances are such that she cannot be in the public meetings at present. She said also that the Massachusetts Anti-Slavery Society would employ me as their agent. Since I received her letter, and before I answered it, the Western Anti-Slavery Association (formerly called the Ohio American Society) have requested me to lecture for them, as soon as I am ready to do so. They urge a multitude of reasons, and among others, not the least important, that there are fewer laborers at the west than at the east, and that here I could have a female lecturess with me, which I could not have in Massachusetts. Mercy Lloyd, whom I have mentioned to you, would probably go with me here. . . . It had been my plan to teach a year or two, and earn enough to pay my debts, and during the time lecture my scholars, and thus learn how to lecture publicly.

"I hoped when I came to Oberlin that the course of study would permit such practice, but I was never in a place where women are so rigidly taught that they must not speak in public.

"I have been accustomed for the last year to meet with four other ladies, sometimes at the house of an old colored woman, and sometimes in the woods, and practice declamation and discussion; but I need more general practice before I can do justice to myself or the cause as a public speaker."

A little later, she wrote:

"I am glad that you all approved of the course I took relative to writing for Commencement. I felt that I had done right, but it gave a kind of wholeness to the feeling to know that you agreed with me. I am going to write for the 'Public Library Item' on 'Religion without Philanthropy.' I intend to tell some plain truths about the prevailing religion of the country. I don't know but I shall speak it. I have not told the people here anything about it. I intend to get it all written during our class vacation, which comes next week."

She had sent to New York for a black bombazine dress in which to graduate. Bombazine was a silk and wool material, something like the "gloria silk" of to-day. Up to this time, during the whole four years, she had had but one new dress, a cheap print. Her graduation gown, including the lining, cost $4.66, and it was doubtless made by her own hands. It was without trimming and was worn with a small white collar. Thus modestly attired, she stepped forward to receive her diploma, the first ever achieved by a Massachusetts woman.

Many of the students evidently sympathized with Lucy's point of view, for "all the ladies, except one, who were appointed to write essays resigned, as did two of the gentlemen. Others were appointed to fill their places, and these too refused to accept the conditions."

It illustrates the curious vagaries of anti-woman prejudice that Antoinette, who had also been chosen to write an essay for Commencement, was allowed to read it, without the least objection. The reason was that she had been taking the "Ladies' Literary Course", instead of the regular classical course. The students of the two courses recited together in many subjects, and had their graduating exercises on successive days, in the same auditorium, and before practically the same audience. But when the graduates of the Ladies' Literary Course took their diplomas, the persons on the platform were all women, except the president; and when the students of the regular classical course received their degrees, the persons on the platform were almost all men. Hence on the one occasion it was thought permissible for a woman's voice to be heard, while on the other it would have been considered a direct defiance of a divine command.

William Lloyd Garrison wrote to his wife from Oberlin, on August 28, 1847:

"Among others with whom I have become acquainted is Miss Lucy Stone, who has just graduated, and yesterday left for her home in Brookfield, Mass. She is a very superior young woman, and has a soul as free as the air, and is preparing to go forth as a lecturer, particularly in vindication of the rights of women. Her course here has been very firm and independent, and she has caused no small uneasiness to the spirit of sectarianism in the institution."

But, in spite of the uneasiness caused by her progressive ideas, she was a favorite with both faculty and students. Long after, one of the professors, when he and she had been talking over the old disagreements, added, "But you know we always liked you, Lucy!" And both Lucy and Antoinette always kept a warm affection for their alma mater.

When Oberlin celebrated its semicentennial, thirty-six years later, Lucy was invited to be one of the speakers at that great gathering — the only woman on the program.

LUCY STONE
*Early Portrait*

LUCY STONE

REV. ANTOINETTE L. BROWN

*The first ordained woman minister*

HENRY B. BLACKWELL
*Early Portrait*

JULIA WARD HOWE

*The first President of the New England Woman Suffrage Association, writer, club woman, author of "The Battle Hymn of the Republic"*

MARY A. LIVERMORE

*Army nurse, leader in Sanitary Commission, lecturer, writer*

LUCY STONE
*Later Portrait*

HENRY B. BLACKWELL

*Later Portrait*

## *Chapter IV*

Lucy came back to the hillside home which she had never ceased to love, but to which she had not been able to afford even one visit during her four years in college. She rejoiced to see her old friends, and lent a strong and capable hand to help her mother.

In 1847, she gave her first lecture on woman's rights, from the pulpit of her brother Bowman's church at Gardner, Massachusetts. This was the year before the first local woman's rights convention was held, at Seneca Falls, New York. From that time on, she spoke upon the subject at every opportunity.

Mother Stone was still unreconciled; but when the neighbors blamed Lucy for lecturing, she stood up for her, and by dint of arguing with them, she finally converted herself.

The first time that Lucy spoke in West Brookfield, her father sat in the audience with his elbow on his knee and his chin in his hand, holding his head down with a sense of shame. But when he heard how well she spoke, his feeling changed. In after years he said to her, "You were right and I was wrong."

In 1848 she was engaged to lecture regularly for the Anti-Slavery Society. It took physical as well as moral courage. Abolitionists were mobbed and sometimes murdered.

Soon after Lucy began to speak for the society, a meeting held in a grove at Harwich was broken up by a furious mob, who assaulted the speakers and wrecked the platform, "with demoniac screams and yells which were heard at the distance of more than a mile", according to the report in the *Liberator*, signed by the two secretaries of the meeting, of whom Lucy was one.

She had great power as a speaker. A little, simple country girl, she had no tricks of oratory; but she spoke with a fervor of conviction, a complete forgetfulness of self, and an extraordinary natural eloquence that swayed great audiences as the wind sways a field of grain. Mobs would sometimes listen to her when they howled down every other speaker.

Even when there were no mobs, there were difficulties of every kind. Once she was sent to hold a Fourth of July celebration, and all the other speakers failed to arrive. She wrote to Samuel May, the agent of the Anti-Slavery Society:

"At Northampton the team(driven by a stranger to me, with a long segar in his mouth) was waiting. It was an open wagon, with only one seat, and a large barrel in front, filled with bottles of mead;

the back part of the wagon filled with tobacco and segars, with both of which the driver stopped to supply the grocers on the road. I comforted myself on the way by thinking that we were in a free country, and that it was a capital thing to be very independent. When within seven miles of Cummingtion, we were overtaken by a severe shower, which stood by us like a friend the remaining distance, and poured into the wagon such a quantity as to give us a delightful foot-bath. When we arrived, every article of my clothing was wet through, and my bonnet, which was almost new, hung round my face like paper."

The rain prevented a grove meeting, the town hall was engaged for a tea party, but in the little red schoolhouse she had a good meeting, helped by the Congregational minister, Reverend Mr. Chapman.

"He said he loved the antislavery cause, and would not knowingly do a thing to sustain slavery, though, when I inquired, he said he belonged to the Association (of Congregational Ministers), and hoped he could do good by staying in it. He, however, manifested a very friendly spirit. He has recently been preaching against slavery and the Fugitive (Slave) Law, and is raising a storm about himself. He said that several years ago, while he was preaching in Connecticut, his meeting-house was burned, his horse mutilated, and the carriage and harness literally cut to pieces, because they were going to hold an antislavery meeting in the church. The next day they went and held the meeting on the smouldering ruins."

She used to put up her own posters, with a little paper of tacks, and a stone picked up from the street. Sometimes the boys followed her, hooting, and preparing to tear the posters down as soon as her back was turned. Then she would call them about her and hold a preliminary meeting there in the street, telling them what a bad thing slavery was, and how boys like themselves were sold on the auction block, till she got them all on her side, and they let her posters alone.

One day of Lucy's experience was typical of many. When she went to Dalton and Hinsdale, she found that the Unitarian minister, who had been asked to give out the notice of the meeting, had not done so. He told her, with much insolence of manner, that he would have nothing to do with it. She said, "Well, there will be a meeting this evening, and I hope you will be there." She engaged the town hall, and then all day she went from house to house, giving notice of the meeting. She did not stop for dinner. Towards evening she toiled up the long hill to the tavern. She found the tavern-keeper's wife overworked and worried, with several small children clinging to her skirts. Lucy said, "Get me for supper whatever you can get most easily, and I will amuse the children meanwhile." She loved children, and they were always glad to come to her. She told them stories till supper was ready. The tavern-keeper's wife started to make hash, and wiped out the wooden chopping bowl with the dishcloth; but, in her haste, she forgot to take the dishcloth out, and it was chopped up with the meat. When Lucy took her first mouthful, she found a piece of the dishcloth in it and she could eat no more. She went to her meeting fasting.

She found the hall filled, but largely with hoodlums. She sat down at the desk, and as she arranged her tracts and antislavery papers, she was greeted with a sharp fire of spitballs. The hall looked very dreary, with dead ashes in the fireplace, and long rows of jeering faces before her; but the faces soon changed their expression. She had a thoroughly good meeting, and got some subscribers to the *Anti-Slavery Standard* who continued to take it as long as it was published. On her return to the hotel, she found that her chamber was separated only by folding doors from a room where five young men were drinking and carousing, and she lay awake, feeling herself hardly safe in their neighborhood. Next morning she asked for eggs, potatoes and dried beef, and made a hearty breakfast.

Pepper was burned, and all sorts of devices were

used to break up her meetings, but generally without success. Once at East Bridgewater, Connecticut, Parker Pillsbury was speaking, while she sat in a front pew of the church, awaiting her turn. Suddenly a man in the audience rose and hurled a hymn book at her head with such force that she was almost stunned. Mr. Pillsbury said that if the objector had had any better argument, he would not have used that one. In her own speech, she did not allude to the incident. Once, in the winter, a pane of glass was taken out of the window behind her, the nozzle of a hose was put through, and she was suddenly deluged with cold water in the midst of her speech. She put on a shawl and went on with her lecture.

At an antislavery meeting held in the open air in a grove on Cape Cod, a mob gathered, looking so black and ugly, and so evidently meaning mischief, that the speakers one by one got down from the platform and quietly slipped away through the crowd, till only Lucy Stone and Stephen Foster were left. Those two never feared the face of man. She said to him, "You had better run, Stephen; they are coming!" He answered, "But who will take care of you?" At that moment, the mob made a rush, and one of the ringleaders, a big man with a club in his hand, sprang up on the platform. Lucy turned to him and said, without hesitation, "This gentleman will take care of me." It touched his feelings, and he declared that he would. Taking her upon one arm, and holding his club in the other hand, he started to march her out through the mob, who were roughly handling Mr. Foster, and such of the other speakers as they had been able to catch. On the way, she talked to him; and presently he mounted her on a stump, and stood by her with his club while she addressed the mob. She made them so ashamed of themselves that they not only desisted from further violence, but took up a collection of twenty dollars on the spot, to pay Mr. Foster for his coat, which they had torn in two from top to bottom, half of them hauling him one way and half the other.

She went from State to State, and the reports of her great power as a speaker are unvarying. The *Rhode Island Freeman* (Providence) said:

"Amity Hall was crowded on Sunday to hear this gifted and eloquent woman plead the cause of the Southern bondman. Hundreds went away disappointed, for at an early hour every seat was filled and every standing-place occupied. Forenoon and afternoon, on the hottest Sabbath of the season, her matchless eloquence kept that compact assembly riveted in their places. Nothing moved but the hearts of the attentive listeners, — and these were stirred to their inmost depths. . . . The plaintive melody of her voice would enable her to throw a fascinating charm around the most commonplace subject. . . .

"At 6 P.M., Miss Stone lectured on Temperance in the grove on Smith's Hill. Full two thousand persons were in attendance. Many who never believed that a woman could or ought to speak to a promiscuous crowd, confessed they had found a solitary exception."

It added materially to her difficulties that she was a "Garrisonian." A Vermont correspondent wrote to the *Liberator:*

"We have a large number of people in this inland State who are strongly prejudiced against anything tinctured with 'Garrisonism.' When it was announced that Lucy Stone was coming into this county to lecture, they were thrown into such spasms that it was feared they would never fully recover. The cry was raised that she was a 'Garrisonian,' and was an advocate of doctrines absolutely dangerous to the 'peace and dignity of the State.' Some of the Free Soilers were almost made to believe that, if they countenanced such doctrines as she advocated, it would sink their party. . . . To prevent the people from hearing the gifted advocate of human rights was now their chief business, and every means which men or devils could invent was resorted to. They flew from one stratagem to another, in quick succession. The little country paper came out with all the self-confidence of a young bantam in its first attempts at crowing. But it was of no use. The people had made up their minds to go and hear her for themselves, and did so, in such numbers as to put to shame all who were engaged in the proceedings against her."

An interesting synopsis of one of Lucy's lectures is given by Henry C. Wright, in a letter to the *Liberator* from Brattleboro, Vermont:

"I arrived in this town to-day. . . . The first thing that attracted attention was a notice of a lecture on slavery, by Lucy Stone, in the Baptist church. I am just returned from that lecture. The church was filled, though twelve and a half cents admission was charged. Her power over an audience it is easy to feel, but not possible to describe.

"Her subject was the causes of the existence and perpetuity of slavery in this land, while it is being abolished, and slaveholders are being branded with infamy, amid the hardest despotisms of Europe. These causes were: first, the government; then the religion of the country. She drew a true, a terribly true picture of the Whig, Democratic and Free Soil parties, showing most conclusively that, while they remain in political fellowship with slaveholders, they are powerless for good to the cause of freedom; that all their political remonstrances and votes against slavery are utterly futile, while they consent to sit down with slaveholders as legislators, judges, executives, on terms of perfect political equality. As well remonstrate and vote against piracy, and then hold fellowship with pirates as worthy co-partners in a political confederation. She demonstrated to the head and heart of the audience that the only ground from which slavery can be assailed successfully, and overthrown, is outside the government.

"Then she took up the Church, and showed how her altars stand in a sea of blood and tears — drawn by deep and unmitigated cruelty and injustice from three millions of slaves; showing that at the tribunal where the testimony of the imbruted slave will be received, it will be more tolerable for the State than for the Church.

"By the power and pathos of her thoughts and her tones, combined with her earnestness, simplicity and directness, she held the audience in breathless silence."

In a long editorial on this lecture, the *Brattleboro Democrat*, though the editor differed with Lucy's views, censured those who denounced her as an infidel. It said:

"What member of the Christian church did not feel his cheek burn with shame, and conviction of the truth of her declaration that slaveholding would have been abandoned ere this, if professing Christian bodies had washed their hands of it —

that it could not stand a day if the nominal Christian church took the same ground toward the baby-stealer and his accomplices that it does toward the chicken-thief and his aiders and abettors?

"Christian apologists of things as they are, denounce Lucy Stone as an infidel; but, if she be what they call an infidel, the more is their shame that her self-devotion in enforcing the commands of Christ excels theirs."

She next went to Bradford, Vermont, and Jehiel Claflin wrote to the *Liberator* of "the great interest and unparalleled excitement in this section of Orange County on the subject of slavery, caused by the touching pathos and surpassing eloquence of that gifted and peerless advocate of human freedom, Miss Lucy Stone. She fully sustained her high reputation, even exceeding the most sanguine expectations. I heard her at four different times, and in four different places, and in every one the anxiety to hear increased at each succeeding lecture. The conservative priests and hunker politicians, as usual, opposed her, and raised the hue and cry that 'Garrison is an infidel.' But, thank God, the Vermonters are not to be intimidated in this way, and, despite all opposition, the good people of this county said they would go and hear, and then judge. . . .

"On two occasions, so great were the gatherings, it became necessary to take out a window and prepare a place for speaking, the meeting-house being sufficient to contain only the women. . . . Her heart and mind seem all luminous with love and truth; she holds her hearers in perfect captivity. . . . The high moral position which Miss Stone occupies gives her great power over all sects and parties. . . . Although the numbers are comparatively few that can come fully up to her radical standpoint, yet she seemed fully conscious of the truth that 'one with God is a majority anywhere.'"

Lucy went and came, the light and sunshine of the home on Coy's Hill. Bowman had resigned his pulpit and come back to help his father run the farm. It was always a gala day with her brother's children when Aunt Lucy got home from one of her long lecture tours. If it was winter, she took them out and played with them in the snow till they were all as rosy as apples. In summer, she could amuse them for hours with flowers, or with the simplest materials.

Old men at whose homes she had been entertained in their childhood recalled, long after, how she had played with them and told them stories, and how they had thought her the most delightful young lady they had ever met.

Meanwhile Lucy had been formally expelled from the West Brookfield church. It was announced to her in the following letter:

"West Brookfield, June 16, 1851.

"Miss Stone:

"It becomes my duty to inform you that the church, at a meeting holden June 13, passed the following Resolution, viz.: Whereas, Miss Lucy Stone has withdrawn from the communion of this church, and has engaged in a course of life evidently inconsistent with her covenant engagements to this church, voted that she be no longer a member with us.

"L. Sampson,
"Clerk."

She replied:

"West Brookfield, Mass.
"June 20, 1851.

"Deacon Sampson:

"Your communication as clerk of the church has been duly received, in which you say that the church has voted that I shall no longer be a member with them, as I have withdrawn from the communion, and engaged in a course of life evidently inconsistent with my covenant engagements.

"It is the first intimation that I have received from any source that either the church or any member of it was dissatisfied with my course. I should be glad of an opportunity to explain to the church the reasons of my withdrawal from its communion, and also to show that my course of life is not only not inconsistent with, but is demanded by, my covenant engagements.

"I regard myself still as a member of the church, inasmuch as the Gospel steps in the case of one towards whom the church feels grief have not been observed. But as, by the action of the church, I am, in its estimation, no longer a member of its body, it will feel under no obligation to grant me an opportunity for explanation. Indeed, I would not ask it on that ground, but simply as a matter of courtesy, which sinners even extend to sinners.

"My engagements will render my absence from town necessary most of the time until August 1, after which date I should be happy to meet the church at such time as they may give me due notice of, and explain my position.

"Faithfully yours,
Lucy Stone."

We have no record whether the opportunity for explanation was ever given.

## *Chapter V*

Soon after she began to speak for the Anti-Slavery Society, Lucy got into trouble because she mixed so much woman's rights with her antislavery lectures. In an account of it written many years later, she says:

"I began to lecture for the Anti-Slavery Society. But I was so possessed by the woman's rights idea that I scattered it in every speech. The wonderful statue of the 'Greek Slave', by Hiram Powers, was on exhibition in Boston. I went to see it one morning. No other person was present. There it stood in the silence, with fettered hands and half-averted face — so emblematic of woman. I remember how the hot tears came to my eyes at the thought of millions of women who must be freed. At the evening meeting I poured all my heart out about it. At the close, Reverend Samuel May, the General Agent of the Anti-Slavery Society, came to me, and, with kind words for what I had said, he admonished me that, however true, it was out of place in an antislavery meeting. Of course, he was right; but the 'Greek Slave' took hold of me like Samson upon the gates of Gaza. After thinking a little, I said, 'Well, Mr. May, I was a woman before I was an abolitionist. I must speak for the women. I will not lecture any more for the Anti-Slavery Society, but will work wholly for woman's rights.'"

The Anti-Slavery Society was very unwilling to give her up, however, as she had been one of their best speakers, and it was finally arranged that she should lecture for them on Saturday nights and Sundays — times which were looked upon as too sacred for any hall or church to be opened for a woman's rights meeting — and during the rest of the week she should lecture for woman's rights on her own responsibility.

Her adventures during the next few years would fill a volume. No Suffrage Association was formed till long after this time. She had no coöperation and no backing, and started out absolutely alone.

At first she would not charge a door fee, partly because she was anxious that everybody should hear and be converted, and she feared an admission fee might keep some one out; and partly from something of the Quaker feeling that it was wrong to take pay for preaching the gospel. She economized in every possible way. When she came to Boston, she used to put up at a lodging house on Hanover Street where they gave her meals for twelve and a half cents, and lodging for six and a quarter cents, on condition of her sleeping in the garret with the daughters of the house, three in a bed. She wrote:

"When I undertook my solitary battle for woman's rights, outside the little circle of abolitionists I knew nobody who sympathized with my ideas. I had some hand-bills printed, 12 × 10 inches. I bought a paper of tacks, and, as I could not pay for posting, I put up my bills myself, using a stone for a hammer. I did not take a fee at the door. But there was always the expense of hall and hotel. To cover this, at the close of my speech, I asked help for the great work, by a collection for expenses. Then I took a hat and went through the audience for the collection, for all were strangers to me. I always got enough to pay what was due, and sometimes more.

"I remember at one time in Salem I had engaged a hall when I had but fifty cents. The Hutchinsons [1] were to sing that night. They did not want to have their audience divided. John Hutchinson came and proposed that we should unite. They would sing and I should lecture, and we would divide receipts. This we did. I was sadly in need of a cloak, for mine was worn and very shabby. My proceeds of our joint entertainment sufficed to purchase the needed garment; and thereafter I always charged a fee, many times but

[1] A famous family of antislavery singers.

twelve and a half cents. It kept out the stampers and hoodlums, and in no wise prevented those who were interested from attending.

"I had large audiences, drawn partly by curiosity to hear a woman, and partly by the subject of the lecture. In three years I cleared about $7000. This I put by for old age. It represented my individual efforts."

Her work in getting up the National Woman's Rights Conventions and her later work in carrying on the Suffrage Association were all done gratuitously. But she gave the service gladly. She said:

"The cause has been like a daughter to me. The service I have rendered it has always been its own exceeding great reward. I have rejoiced in every helpful thing done for it, and I have felt the pain of any disadvantage.

"I went from city to city and from State to State, everywhere carrying the good gospel of equal rights for women, seeking to create that wholesome discontent among women which would make them resent their unequal condition, and wish to escape from it. But the good sought to be done was hindered by the falsehoods and misrepresentations of the press. After one of my lectures in Indiana, the morning paper reported that I was found in the bar-room, smoking a cigar and swearing like a trooper. Another paper said, 'You she-hyena, don't you come here!'[1] Another expressed its surprise at finding a modest woman, and said it had always thought of me as the lion-tamer in Van Ambergh's menagerie."

In many of the towns where she lectured, no woman had ever spoken in public before, and curiosity drew large crowds. The speaker was a great surprise to them. They expected a woman's rights advocate to be a tall, aggressive, disagreeable woman, with masculine manners and a strident voice. Instead they found a small, quiet woman, with gentle, unaffected manners, and the sweetest voice ever possessed by a public speaker. This voice became famous. It was so musical and delicious that those who had once listened to her, if they heard her speak a few words years afterwards, on a railroad train or in a stagecoach where it was too dark to see faces, would say unhesitatingly, "That is Lucy Stone!"

She generally gave a series of three lectures, the first on "The Social and Industrial Disabilities of Woman", the second on her "Legal and Political Disabilities", and the third on her "Moral and Religious Disabilities." At every place where she spoke, women came to her after the lecture and poured out the story of the wrongs they had suffered under the unequal laws, thus

[1] This was the *Springfield Republican,* afterwards for so many years one of the stanchest supporters of woman's rights.

giving her fresh illustrations to use at the next place.

Long before Lucy's time, an occasional voice had been lifted in America in behalf of larger rights for women — by Margaret Brent of Maryland in 1647, by Abigail Adams of Massachusetts in 1776, and by the sister of Richard Henry Lee of Virginia in 1778. Frances Wright of Scotland, who lectured in this country, the Grimké sisters, Mrs. Ernestine L. Rose, a beautiful Polish Jewess who settled in the United States, and Margaret Fuller, had all spoken for woman's rights. But they had pleaded this cause only incidentally to other subjects, which were their chief themes. Lucy Stone was the first and for years the only woman who made it her main topic, and went up and down the country lecturing upon it. It is for this that she has been called "the morning star of the woman's rights movement." In those early years, it was she who stood to the public as the representative of that cause, and bore the chief brunt of the obloquy connected with it. Elizabeth Cady Stanton said, "Lucy Stone was the first person by whom the heart of the American public was deeply stirred on the woman question."

## *Chapter VI*

Interest in woman's rights was growing, stimulated largely by Lucy's lectures; but no attempt had yet been made to focus nation-wide attention upon the question by a National Convention.

At the close of the Anti-Slavery Convention in Boston in the spring of 1850, it was announced that those interested in having a National Woman's Rights Convention would meet in the anteroom. Nine women responded. Among them were Lucy Stone, Abby Kelley Foster, Paulina Wright Davis, Eliza J. Kenney, secretary of the Anti-Slavery Society, Mrs. Eliza Taft of Dedham, Mrs. Dora Taft, a daughter of Father Taylor of the Seamen's Bethel, and Doctor Harriot K. Hunt, a practising physician on Green Street, Boston, who had been paying her taxes under protest for years.

It was nearly night. The room was dark and dingy. There the nine women sat and made their plans. A committee of seven was appointed to correspond, and, if enough coöperation could be found, to issue a Call for a National Convention. In her address at the celebration of the fortieth anniversary of this convention, Lucy said:

"We talked the matter all over, and decided that it was time something was done for the women as well as for the Negroes, and that the best way to do it was to hold a convention. We did not know then how much coöperation we should have. The antislavery people were full of their own work, but Mr. Garrison, Wendell Phillips, Gerrit Smith, Henry C. Wright, and most of the abolitionists who were on the side of Mr. Garrison, were in favor of equal rights for women. We had not any money or any organization, and the question arose, How are we ever to make this woman's rights convention known? We agreed that we would divide the correspondence. Some should write to one State and some to another, to see whom we could get to unite in calling the convention.

"I went to Mr. Garrison, and I shall never forget the tender sympathy with which he spoke to me about it. I said, 'We have n't any money or any friends, and we don't know what to do, only that we are bound to have a convention.' And he said to me, 'There never was a movement that began so small and so poor as the antislavery movement; but it was rich in truth, and, because it was, it has succeeded so far, and it will succeed. Yours is just as true, and it will succeed. Never be discouraged.' Mr. Garrison and Mr. Phillips were constantly suggesting methods of work, and names of persons to whom to write. At length a list of names was secured. A wealth of character and nobility joined in the Call for that first convention."

It was headed by Lucy Stone, and signed by eighty-nine men and women, from six States. It included many illustrious names, among them that of Ralph Waldo Emerson. Massachusetts contributed thirty-six signers, Pennsylvania eighteen, New York seventeen, Rhode Island eleven, Ohio six and Maryland one. The Call, a very fine one, was written by Doctor William Elder of Philadelphia, with suggestions from various women and men.

Lucy, who had done so much for this convention, came near being unable to attend it. Her brother Luther was taken very ill in Indiana. She went out to nurse him, but was unable to save his life. Then she herself fell ill with typhoid fever and very nearly died.

On her way home, she met her future husband for the first time. Passing through Cincinnati, while barely convalescent, she called at Henry B. Blackwell's hardware store to cash a small check from the treasurer of the Anti-Slavery Society. Mr. Blackwell wrote, long after: "She was thin and pale, but with something beautiful in her expression and wonderfully eloquent in her voice and manner." He was so much taken with her that he advised his elder brother Samuel, who was looking for a wife, to make her acquaintance; and he put off paying the check until the next day, in order to send Samuel to her with the money. Samuel, though he found her pleasing, was not moved to pay court to her; but the younger brother never forgot her.

On her return, she wrote to Samuel May:

"I am at home again, and no child was ever gladder to find shelter under a father's roof. . . . I think I shall be at the Women's Rights Convention at Worcester next week, though only as a looker on, for I have not sufficient command of mind or nerve to be able to do anything. . . .

"I hope to be able some time to aid you again in the lecture field, but my teeth almost chatter when I remember the cold beds and the cold rides (like the one from Harwich to Hyannis) last winter. I must be much hardier than at present, before I shall be able to endure it again. But it does seem a pity for even the weakest of us to lie on our oars now, when so many are ready to hear."

Lucy's strength returned rapidly, however, and she was able not only to attend the Convention, but to speak and take an active part.

The First National Woman's Rights Convention met in Brinley Hall, Worcester, Massachusetts, October 23, 1850. It was called to order by the beloved Sarah H. Earle, wife of the editor of the *Worcester Spy*. Paulina Wright Davis, who had done much of the preliminary correspondence, was chosen president. Among the speakers were Lucretia Mott, William Lloyd Garrison, Wendell Phillips, Ernestine L. Rose, Lucy Stone, Antoinette L. Brown, Charles C. Burleigh, Stephen and Abby Kelley Foster, Sojourner Truth, Frederick Douglass, Sarah Tyndall and Doctor Martha H. Mowry. The *New York Tribune* said: "Above a thousand persons were present, and, if a larger place could have been had, many more thousands would have attended."

The Seneca Falls Convention of 1848, while of great historic interest as the first, was a small local meeting, held in response to an unsigned Call, and it attracted chiefly local notice. This first National Convention, with its long list of illustrious signers from many States, attracted the attention of the whole country, and really launched the woman's rights cause as a national movement.

Susan B. Anthony said it was reading the report of Lucy's speech in the *New York Weekly Tribune* that converted her to woman suffrage. The *Tribune's* report of the convention was read in England by Harriet Taylor, who afterwards became the wife of John Stuart Mill, and called out an article by her in the *Westminster Review*, which was the beginning of the modern movement for women's rights in England. She wrote:

"In the quality of speaking, the proceedings bear an advantageous comparison with those of any popular movement with which we are acquainted, either in this country or in America. Very rarely in the oratory of public meetings is the part of verbiage and declamation so small, that of calm good sense and reason so considerable."

After this a National Convention was held every year. Until her marriage, Lucy generally did the main work of getting it up, and afterwards published the report of the proceedings in pamphlet form, at her own expense, and sold great numbers of the pamphlets at her meetings as she went up and down the country. They were called Woman's Rights Tracts.

She was very popular, a favorite both with the public and among the reformers. Mary A. Livermore recalled how she first saw her at an Anti-Slavery Bazaar, and was one of those who followed her about with admiration: "She could not have weighed more than a hundred pounds at that time — a tiny creature, with the prettiest pink color; and her girl look was just as sweet as her look of later years. I thought her the sweetest thing I had ever seen."

The second National Convention was held at Worcester in 1851. Here Wendell Phillips made the great speech which was used by the women as a tract until suffrage was won. The third National Convention was at Syracuse, New York, in 1852.

Here Miss Anthony made her début on the woman's rights platform; and from that time on, the banner of woman suffrage, which Lucy had been carrying for five years, had another courageous and indefatigable defender.

Several of the women who spoke at Syracuse were elaborately gowned in the height of the fashion, but, judging by the press reports, Lucy, in a simple Bloomer dress, carried off the honors. On her return to Boston, Theodore Parker, who had been at the convention, met her on the stairs leading to the *Liberator* office, and greeted her with the words, "Whether we like it or not, little woman, God made you an orator!" This was a quotation from the *Syracuse Standard*, which had given her great praise.

Her lectures brought practical results. A letter written from Rockland, Maine, by Eliza Spaulding, is typical:

"I doubt not the [woman's rights] tracts will do good. I frequently hear the remark that a great change has been effected in public opinion by your lectures; and the change goes beyond mere public opinion, it is taking a serviceable form. Two young women have but recently gone into the printing office in this city, and are even now earning their two dollars per week. They could not have been persuaded to accept of this employment before you came among us. Every one feels in duty bound to give them a word of encouragement. One year ago they would never have thought of expressing approbation, and most likely would have thought it highly derogatory to the female character."

## *Chapter VII*

Lucy wore the so-called Bloomer costume for three or four years, beginning about 1850. It was worn also by Mrs. Stanton, Miss Anthony, Sarah Grimké and several others.

It was invented by Mrs. Elizabeth Smith Miller, the daughter of Gerrit Smith, a prominent abolitionist, a great landowner in western New York. He gave away a thousand farms to poor men, largely to colored men. Mrs. Miller wanted a dress in which she could easily take long walks about her country home. It consisted of a small jacket, a full skirt descending a little below the knee, and trousers down to the ankle. It was not beautiful, but was very comfortable and convenient, and entirely modest. Mrs. Amelia Bloomer, editor of the *Lily*, the first woman's paper, was much pleased with it, and advocated it warmly in her paper, and thus it became associated with her name.

The young girls of to-day, with their emancipated legs, can hardly realize the bondage of the long, cumbrous skirts that custom imposed upon women, their weight increased by that of a multiplicity of petticoats. The conventional dress was not only a grievous inconvenience, but a constant drain upon women's vitality. In the eyes of the public, however, the "freedom dress" looked grotesque, and it was an endless source of ridicule.

Lucy's first Bloomer was made for home use. After she had worn it for about a year, she declared that all her future dresses should be of that type. She was small and slight, and was one of the few women who looked well in it. But it was not half so ugly, upon any woman, as many of the hideous conventional styles of those days, which still amaze us as we look over the old-time fashion plates.

Soon after Lucy put on Bloomers, there was some question whether she should be invited to speak at an antislavery convention, because of her unconventional costume. Wendell Phillips said, "Well, if Lucy Stone cannot speak at that meeting, in any decent dress that she chooses, I will not speak either." That settled it, for they could not do without him.

Some men were strong advocates of the hygienic dress. Mr. E. D. Draper of Hopedale, Massachusetts, offered to give enough silk for a Bloomer dress to any woman among his friends who would promise to wear it. Henry B. Blackwell said of the new costume, "When I first heard about it, it commended itself to my reason; but when I first saw it,

I acknowledge my taste recoiled from the novelty. I felt a shock, in spite of myself, as a figure which seemed neither man nor woman approached me. But I feel so no longer."

It was soon found that the dress made no difference in Lucy's success as a speaker. Wearing the Bloomer, she campaigned for Gerrit Smith and helped elect him to Congress. Yet she met with her share of discomforts. She told the following stories, among others:

"At one time Susan B. Anthony and I were in New York. We started to go to the post office. Unfortunately, it was the noon hour, when all classes of people were on their way to dinner. Gradually we noticed that we were being encircled. A wall of men and boys at last shut us in so that it was impossible to go on or to go back. There we stood. The crowd was a good-natured one. They laughed at us; they made faces at us; they said impertinent things, and they would not let us out. Every moment brought added numbers, who peered over to see what attracted the crowd. Among them was an acquaintance of ours, who, when he saw us, took in the situation at once. He went for a policeman and a carriage, and we escaped, with only a little rough treatment at the last.

"At another time, when a clergyman who was to speak for the Nantucket Lyceum failed, I was invited to take his place. When Mrs. Nathaniel Barney escorted me to the platform, the audience, who expected to see a dignified clergyman, but saw instead a young woman in a Bloomer costume, burst into roars of laughter. But Mrs. Barney was a member of the Society of Friends, a woman well known and highly esteemed, with a fine social position and much wealth. In the quietest manner she gave me a seat, and at the proper time introduced me. To the credit of the audience be it said that they listened quietly, and evidently soon became forgetful of the dress. When I was in Louisville, Kentucky, a Negro woman at the public pump put her hands on her hips, awaiting my approach, and asked, 'Be you one of them theatre women?' In all directions, and all the time, those who wore the Bloomer costume were the observed of all observers, and were looked upon with unfriendly eyes. Was it any wonder that, after three years of petty crucifixion, they left it off, with the feeling that the large freedom they gained for their feet bore no comparison to the bondage that beset their spirits?"

The "freedom dress" was not given up without much hesitation and discussion. Mrs. Stanton was the first to abandon it. Miss Anthony wrote to Lucy:

"She has a new style of dress, short, and no

pants. She even gave me a new dress, if I would have it made and come out with her; but I cannot feel that it would be best for me to make any such change. She has an idea of getting rid of the name (to her and many of us odious), 'Bloomer dress.' She cannot do so. It will only be said the Bloomers have doffed their pants the better to display their legs. She had on a dress when I was there. It was shorter, somewhat, than young girls wear; looks very well; but she had stepped on it and torn it twice. It will not be as warm in winter as our present style."

Later she wrote: "I am happy to say Mrs. Stanton is coming to Albany, and will read her own address to the Legislature. Her petticoats have assumed their former length, and her wardrobe is cleared of every short skirt. I am sorry, but still feel a great deal of sympathy for her."

Miss Anthony added that she herself had been so implored to give up the dress "for the sake of the cause", and so jeered at by rude men and boys that, but for a very strong sense of duty on the subject, she would have been utterly disheartened. Lucy wrote:

"Dear Susan — About the dress, it is all fudge for anybody to pretend that any cause that deserves to live is impeded by the length of your skirt. I know, from having tried through half the Union, that audiences listen, and assent, just as well to one who speaks truth in a short as in a long dress. Did you see any want of willingness on the part of the people to hear us at Syracuse, New York or Cleveland? No, no, Susan, it is all a pretense that the cause will suffer. I wish that the dress gave me no other troubles; but I am annoyed to death by people who recognize me by my clothes, and when I get a seat in the cars, they will get a seat by me and bore me for a whole day with the stupidest stuff in the world. Much of that I should escape if I dressed like others. Then again, when I go to a new city, where are many places of interest to see, and from which I could learn much, if I go out a horde of boys pursue me and destroy all comfort. Then, too, the blowing up by the wind, which is so provoking, when people stare and laugh. I have bought me a nice new dress. I have had it a month, and it is not made because I can't decide whether to make it long or short. Not that I think any cause will suffer by a short dress, but simply to save myself from a great deal of annoyance, and so as not to feel, when I am a guest at any house, that they are mortified by my dress, if other persons happen to come in.

"I was at Lucretia Mott's a few weeks ago, and her daughters took up a regular labor with me to make me abandon the dress. They said they would not go in the street with me, and when Grace Greenwood called, and others like her, I think it would have been a real relief to them if I had not been there. It gave me a most uncomfortable feeling. James and Lucretia defended me most bravely, and none of them knew that I did not feel perfectly at ease. In Kentucky and Missouri I was not the least annoyed.

"I think I shall have some long and some short dresses made, and then wear (as circumstances vary) the one that will give me the most comfort. . . . I am sure you are tired and all worn out, or you would not feel so intensely about the dress. I never shed a tear about it in my life, nor came within a thousand ages of martyrdom on account of it. And to be compelled to travel in rain or snow, in mud and dirt, in a long dress, would cost me more in every respect than the short dress ever did. I don't think that I can abandon the short skirts; but I will have two suits.

"I have not made any long dresses yet, and I do not know whether I shall this spring. I go to Cincinnati early in April, and may not get time. Then, too, I have this feeling: Women are in bondage. Their clothes are a great hindrance to their engaging in any business which will make them pecuniarily independent; and since the soul of womanhood can never be queenly and noble so long as it must beg bread for its body, is it not better, even at the expense of a great deal of annoyance, that they whose life deserves respect and is greater than their garments, should give an example by which woman may more easily work out her own emancipation?

> " 'I read the lesson of the Past,
> That firm endurance wins at last
> More than the sword.'

"With this feeling, added to my own greater comfort in the short dress, I have a strong aversion to change, and do not think I shall, except for some special occasions. . . .

"What a grand convention you had! And to get it [the bill for woman's rights] referred to a select committee was magnificent.

"Here in the Maine Legislature last week, a bill passed the Senate (not the House) securing to married women the right to their own earnings, protesting at the same time that the measure had nothing to do with the Woman's Rights humbug. 'A rose by any other name is just as sweet.' But, Susan dear, how beautifully everything is helping the woman's rights movement to its true place, as the central reformatory movement of this age! And what infinite blessings it will bring to the race! We shall not have them, for they will not come till we are gone. We enjoy the privilege of giving which is not less good than that of receiving."

The remark about women whose life is "greater than their dress" recalls a curious incident. A man who had never met Lucy blamed her severely for wearing a Bloomer. He went with his wife to hear her lecture. Afterwards his wife asked him what he thought of the Bloomer dress. He insisted that Lucy had not worn a Bloomer and could with difficulty be convinced that she had. The impression made upon him by her personality had been so overwhelming that it blotted out all remembrance of what she wore.

We do not know how long Mrs. Bloomer wore the dress. She was small, slight, young and very pretty, and looked well in it. She had other troubles besides those connected with the hygienic costume. In April, 1854, the printers on the *Lily* declared they would not work in an office with a woman typesetter. Mrs. Bloomer let them all go and called upon Lucy, who was then lecturing in Ohio, to come and help her. This Lucy promptly did. A meeting was held, and some progress made towards an adjustment.

When Lucy finally decided to have a long dress made, Miss Anthony wrote to her in February, 1854:

"Dearest Lucy — Your letter caused a bursting of the floods long pent up, and I went straight to Mrs. Stanton and read her the outgushings of your innermost. . . . She says she now feels a mental freedom among her friends that she has not known for the two years past. But, Lucy, if you waver, and talk, yea, and resolve to make a long dress, why, then, who may not? If Lucy Stone, with all her reputation, her powers of eloquence, her loveliness of character that wins all who once hear the sound of her voice, cannot bear the martyrdom of the dress, who, I ask, can?"

Mrs. Stanton adds a postscript: "I have but a moment to say, for your own sake, lay aside the shorts. I know what you suffer among fashionable people. Not for the sake of the cause, nor for any sake but your own, take it off. We put the dress on for greater freedom, but what is physical freedom compared with mental bondage? By all means have the new dress made long."

Antoinette L. Brown, who had never adopted the Bloomer dress, wrote to her: "Don't suffer martyrdom over a short dress, or anything else that can be prevented. Sorrow enough will come. . . . So let every avoidable thing go, and good riddance to it."

Even Miss Anthony finally gave it up. Lucy wrote, long after:

"Those who wore the Bloomer costume put it on in the hope that a dress at once comfortable and useful, in which you could walk up stairs and not step on your clothes, and down stairs and not be stepped on, a dress which was still clean after the longest walk in mud and slush, with no endless yards of cloth to brush, would commend itself.

But one by one those who had adopted it abandoned it. Mrs. Smith Miller wore it much longer than any of the others. Her father, Gerrit Smith, thought that a principle was involved; that the health of women was being ruined by their dress, and that, to make the new costume acceptable, it must be seen. Mrs. Miller, who had a fine figure, wore it to better advantage than any of the others. For her father's sake she kept it on. But, little by little, her skirts lengthened until they were no longer noticeably different from those of other women."

Now, nearly eighty years later, a shift of fashion has given women the freedom that the pioneers strove so hard to win for them without success. It is to be hoped that they will never go back to the old bondage.

## *Chapter VIII*

Benjamin S. Jones wrote to Lucy from Salem, Ohio, January 21, 1853, asking her, in behalf of the Woman's Rights Convention, to come out and work in Ohio. He added:

"A Women's State Temperance Convention was held in Columbus on the 13th inst., and it was a great one. Lizzie (Mrs. J. Elizabeth Jones) and Josephine Griffing addressed an audience of one thousand in Representatives' Hall. And who does thee suppose presided at that meeting of one thousand men and women? Mrs. Professor Cowles, of Oberlin! Six years ago Catherine Beecher delivered an address in Columbus, through her brother, she sitting silent in the pulpit by his side. Now the women call meetings, appoint officers, present resolutions, and speak upon them and vote upon them. Church members do these things, and the clergy ask divine blessings upon their proceedings, and there seems to be no thought of their having stepped out of their appropriate sphere."

The world had moved, indeed. Only six years before, the Ladies' Board of Oberlin, made up of the professors' wives, had rebuked Lucy for addressing a mixed audience, and the professors had unanimously refused to let her read her own essay.

But there was plenty of prejudice left. A meeting was held in New York City in May, 1853, to plan for a World's Temperance Convention, to come off during the World's Fair. All temperance societies had been invited to send delegates, and some of the women's societies did so. The chairman, Mayor Barstow of Providence, Rhode Island, asked the "gentlemen" to hand in their credentials. It was suggested that the ladies also be allowed to hand in theirs. Their credentials were accepted. The Reverend Thomas Wentworth Higginson said that in a World's Convention women should be represented, otherwise it would be only a Semi-World's Convention. But when a motion was made to put Miss Anthony on the Committee on Credentials, "a scene ensued which beggars description", wrote Lucy, in her report to the *Liberator*. When it was proposed to appoint Lucy on the same committee, "The Hon. Mr. Barstow angrily exclaimed that he would not put the motion; that, if such motions were made, he would leave the chair. T. W. Higginson and Abby Kelley Foster attempted in vain to get a hearing, as everybody was ruled out of order who did not speak against us. When it became absolutely certain that regularly-elected delegates were to be excluded because they were women, Mr. Higginson entered his protest, and invited those who were in favor of a Whole World's Convention to meet that afternoon at the home of Dr. Trall."

A large minority withdrew. At Doctor Trall's Water Cure, they made Miss Anthony secretary, and put Lucy on a committee to issue a Call for a Whole World's Temperance Convention.

As the time approached, however, there were grave doubts as to whether such a convention could be made a success, and many counselled delay. Lucy strongly urged the issuing of a Call, and she prevailed. Miss Anthony wrote to her: "My eyes have feasted on the Call for the Whole World's Temperance Convention. Who but you, Lucy, could have braved and conquered the objections of such an array of men? I feel so thankful to you for your perseverance!"

The Whole World's Temperance Convention passed off peacefully and triumphantly. At the Half World's Convention, Antoinette L. Brown unexpectedly became a storm center.

Her troubles at Oberlin had begun when Lucy's ended, with their graduation from the collegiate department. There was consternation among the authorities when it was learned that she meant to enter the theological school. Faculty meeting after faculty meeting was held on the subject;

but the founders of Oberlin had put it into the charter that all its opportunities were to be open to women. Finally Professor Morgan said, "Antoinette, I think you are all wrong. If I could keep you out, I would; but, since I cannot, I will do my very best to teach you." Her father and brother ceased to send the money they had been contributing toward her expenses, not wishing to aid what they considered so wild a project as her plan to enter the ministry. She had been teaching drawing in the preparatory department and had expected to continue to do so; but the Ladies' Board made a special rule to bar her out. Then Miss Atkins, the Assistant Lady Principal, got up a drawing class for her, of which Professor (afterwards President) Fairchild and several of the theological students were members, besides many younger pupils; and she thus paid her expenses with ease.

She had one colleague, Lettice Smith, who wished to study theology, but was not intending to preach. They were allowed to study with the rest, but had no part in the Commencement exercises, except as listeners, and for many years their names did not appear in the Alumni Catalogue as graduates of the theological class of 1850. Long afterwards, Oberlin became very proud of them, restored their names to the list of graduates, and gave Antoinette the degree of D.D.

She could have been ordained at Oberlin when she left the theological school. Father Shipherd and several other ministers were willing to take part in the ceremony. But it would have embarrassed the university authorities, most of whom were opposed to women's preaching. Also, she preferred to wait till she could be ordained in her own denomination. For several years she lectured with success, and preached as she had opportunity. Horace Greeley and Charles A. Dana of the *New York Sun* were so impressed by her ability that they invited her to preach regularly in New York City, promising to provide a hall and pay her board, and to give her one thousand dollars a year — in those days a large salary for a woman. But she thought herself too inexperienced for a metropolitan pulpit, and accepted instead a call to the struggling little Congregational Church of South Butler, New York, at a salary of three hundred dollars a year. She was about to be ordained at the time when the Whole World's and Half World's Temperance Conventions were held.

The Fourth National Woman's Rights Convention — arranged by Lucy, as usual — was going on at the same time, in the Broadway Tabernacle, with a brilliant array of speakers. Antoinette attended it. She had also credentials to the Half World's Temperance Convention, both from the church at South Butler and from a temperance society.

Leaders of the anti-woman party, wishing to discourage the holding of the Whole World's Convention, had declared that it was needless, as they were going to allow women to take part. At the suggestion of Wendell Phillips, Antoinette decided to test this. She went over to the Half World's Convention, accompanied by Mr. Phillips and Mrs. Caroline M. Severance. She meant to offer her credentials, and, if they were accepted, simply to thank the Convention for removing the ban upon women, and then to return to the Woman's Rights meeting. Her credentials were accepted, and she came to the platform to express her thanks. Her speech would not have taken three minutes; but the anti-woman element among the delegates kept up a running fire of interruptions and used up three days in preventing her from being heard. Most of the delegates were ministers, and many of them disapproved of her not only as a woman who spoke in public, but as a woman who had the audacity to wish to be ordained. Despite the efforts of Wendell Phillips and of General Neal Dow, who was presiding, she was not allowed to speak.[1]

Horace Greeley was indignant. In the *Tribune*

[1] A full account of this extraordinary affair, written by Antoinette L. Brown, is given in the "History of Woman Suffrage", Vol. 1, pp. 152–160.

of September 7 he said of the Half World's Convention:

"This convention has completed three of its four business sessions, and the results may be summed up as follows:

"First day — Crowding a woman off the platform.

"Second day — Gagging her.

"Third day — Voting that she shall stay gagged.

"Having thus disposed of the main question, we presume the incidentals will be finished this morning."

The immediate result was to get Antoinette a very wide hearing. At the National Woman's Rights Convention, Lucy said:

"It is said that women could not be ministers of religion. Last Sunday, at Metropolitan Hall, Antoinette L. Brown conducted divine service and was joined in it by the largest congregation assembled within the walls of any building in this city (hisses). Some men hiss who had no mother to teach them better. But I tell you that some men in New York, knowing that they can hear the word of God from a woman as well as from a man, have called her to be their pastor, and she is to be ordained this month."

At one session of this National Woman's Rights Convention, the mob made such a clamor that no speaker could be heard. One after another tried it, only to have his or her voice drowned forthwith by hoots and howls. William Henry Channing advised Lucretia Mott, who was presiding, to adjourn the meeting. Mrs. Mott answered, "When the hour fixed for adjournment comes, I will adjourn the meeting, not before." At last Lucy was introduced. The mob became as quiet as a congregation of churchgoers; but as soon as the next speaker began, the howling recommenced, and it continued to the end. After the meeting, when the speakers went into the dressing room to get their hats and coats, the mob surged in and surrounded them, and Lucy, who was brimming over with indignation, began to reproach them for their behavior. "Oh, come!" they answered, "You need n't say anything; we kept still for you!"

Wendell Phillips wrote to her of the National Woman's Rights Convention and the Whole World's Temperance Convention:

"Dear Lucy: Let me congratulate you on the pre-eminent success of *your meetings* in New York, that eventful week, for they were all most emphatically yours — planned by you, persevered in by you in spite of so much remonstrance, and arranged by you with so little aid, not to say sustained by you at last so largely by your own efforts. They did noble work. Sorry I was away from the Tabernacle so much, but it could not be helped."

He had been away fighting Antoinette's battle at the Half World's Temperance Convention.

Antoinette Brown was ordained a few days later.[1] The affair made a great commotion. Press and pulpit thundered denunciations. Doctor Cheever declared that any woman who would seek ordination was an infidel, and any church that would ordain her was an infidel church. But Harriet Beecher Stowe wrote: "If it is right for Jenny Lind to sing to two thousand people, 'I know that my Redeemer liveth', why is it wrong for Antoinette L. Brown to say the same thing?"

She wanted Lucy to come and address her congregation. Lucy refused, for fear her heterodoxy and her Bloomers might make trouble for her friend. Antoinette replied:

"You are the greatest little goose and granny-fuss that I ever did see! What nonsense to think of your injuring in any way my success as a minister by lecturing to them! They are all expecting you, and they know besides that you wear Bloomers and are an 'infidel.' Any congregation I may preach to will not be scared overmuch by anything you will say. They believe in free speech. Everybody knows you and your reputation as well, almost, now as they will after seeing you, for your fame is abroad in the land. They think you, of course, worse than you are."

[1] See Appendix, Note 2.

Later Antoinette passed through a period of religious doubt which led her to resign her pastorate. For a time she did social work with Mrs. Abby Hopper Gibbons in the prisons and slums of New York. It was a sorrowful and depressing experience. Samuel C. Blackwell was courting her; and, after reading Thackeray's "Vanity Fair", she made up her mind that, if there was only one good man in the world, she had better take him when she had the chance. Samuel really was a man of the highest and sweetest character, and the marriage proved extremely happy. She emerged from her period of religious doubt a Unitarian, and continued to preach as often as opportunity offered and family cares permitted. She had six children, wrote nine books, and lived to be ninety-six years old. When she died, the census showed that there were more than three thousand women ministers and preachers in the United States.

## *Chapter IX*

The time was now drawing near when Lucy was to reconsider her determination not to marry.

Massachusetts held a Constitutional Convention in 1853, and a hearing was given on a woman suffrage petition headed by Louisa Alcott's mother. The speakers were Lucy Stone, Wendell Phillips, Theodore Parker and T. W. Higginson. Mr. Blackwell had come east that year to attend the antislavery meetings. He had also brought with him a volume of manuscript poems for which he hoped to find a publisher. He heard Lucy speak in New York and was filled with enthusiasm. He came on to Boston, and while listening to her speech at the State House, he made up his mind to marry her if he could.

He was a man of great ability and much personal charm, an eloquent speaker, a good writer, a fine singer, and an active and capable man of business. He was full of energy and vivacity, and constantly overflowed with wit and fun. He kept everybody laughing, and, as everybody likes to laugh, he was a great social favorite. He had a kind heart and a most chivalrous disposition.

He had blue eyes, remarkably bright and sparkling, curly black hair, and such beautiful teeth that his friends nicknamed him Carker, after the villain with glittering teeth in "Dombey and Son."

He confided his wishes to Mr. Garrison and asked him for a letter of introduction. Mr. Garrison warned him that Lucy had made up her mind not to marry and had declined many offers; but he gave Mr. Blackwell a letter to her, and also one to Deacon Henshaw, West Brookfield's leading abolitionist. Deacon Henshaw's eyes twinkled when he read the letter and divined the young man's purpose.

When he arrived at the farm on Coy's Hill, he found Lucy standing on the table, whitewashing the kitchen ceiling. She introduced him to her family, and later went with him for a long walk, and showed him the wonderful view from the summit of the hill. They discussed abolition and woman's rights. She admired Doctor Elizabeth Blackwell, the pioneer woman physician, and the fact that he was Elizabeth's brother was a recommendation to her friendship; but she gave him no encouragement as a suitor. He persisted, however, and would not give up hope.

His first love gift was offered with the following letter:

"You told me you were going to remain at

home and study this summer. Please oblige me by accepting the enclosed translation of Plato. Do not refuse my little gift. It will be such a luxury to me this summer, amid the hot and fetid air of Illinois, to imagine you amongst the cool, green, granite hills of Massachusetts, comfortably chatting with Socrates and his old Greeks, that I shall find the idea a better tonic than quinine. . . .

"I told Elizabeth that you had not yet seen her book, and she desires me to present you with a copy from her. I think you will like her lectures very much. If my partiality for her does not mislead me, they are full of sound good sense, and animated by a very noble idea. As for Plato, I am desirous to know how you will like him. . . .

"The evening I left you, I came straight to New York to wind up my Eastern visit. Yesterday [Sunday] I spent very pleasantly with Mr. and Mrs. Weld [Angelina Grimké] and Miss Sarah Grimké. They live at Belleville, N. J., some three and a half miles north of Newark, on the Passaic River. A beautiful place, shaded by trees and overlooking the water. On going up to the house with my friend Dr. Dorrance, we first met the two ladies, dressed in the Bloomer costume, which I have learned to like of late. They were surrounded by a dozen children, three of their own, comfortably seated on the piazza, reading and enjoying themselves as though Sunday was actually made to be happy in. Mrs. Weld is a sensible, earnest and very intelligent woman; wide awake and well up to the times. She has evidently been living, not vegetating, during her married life. We found Mr. Weld working in the garden — a middle-aged man, with a noble forehead, a little bald, clear complexion, a mouth compressed with an expression of firmness and energy, and brilliant, piercing eyes, full of intellect and fire.

"He welcomed me very warmly, touching me on a weak point by recognizing my father's face in mine, though twenty years had passed since he had known him.

"After dinner we adjourned to a sort of parlor built in the branches of a pine tree, and I tried to draw Mr. Weld out on the reasons why he withdrew from the active advocacy of reforms. He says the immediate cause was a narrow escape from drowning, which destroyed his voice entirely, stopping his public speaking short. This, he says, for the first time in years, gave him time to reflect. He found he himself needed reforming. He was all wrong. He had been laboring to destroy evil in the same spirit as his antagonists. He suddenly felt that fighting was not the best way to annihilate error, and that he could no longer act as he had been doing. All his old opinions and principles began to loosen and scale off. He threw aside books, newspapers, everything, and for ten years found there was nothing on earth for him to do but to dig ditches and work upon his farm. And so he did so.

"I tried to attack his position, but he says it was all right. That for him it was no longer possible nor proper to continue combating. He had done so manfully, and when his work in that way was ended, he was obliged to resign it to others, while he himself entered into a higher sphere of experience. So, since then, he has thought, and worked, and taught his children, and occasionally lectured, and helped all whom he has met who needed help, and, in short, endeavored to live a true, manly life. This all seemed very strange to me. I tried to argue the duty of fighting error so long as it existed, but both he and his wife simply say, 'There is a fighting era in everyone's life. While you feel it so, fight on; it is your duty, and the best thing you can possibly do. But when your work in that line is done, you will reach another and a higher view.' But, though I can't understand the position of the Welds, I see plainly that in their case they have acted rightly. I don't think it was marriage which is to blame for their withdrawal from public life, as so many suppose, but that it arose from a combination of physical, intellectual and moral causes quite independent of it. I wish I had more time to comprehend it. Certainly I dare not criticize too harshly two people so noble and earnest.

"If there ever was a true marriage, it is theirs. Both preserve their separate individuality perfectly, and on many points differ heartily, with the utmost good will. I do hope that some day you will meet them, Miss Lucy.

"For myself, my battle has yet to be fought, and, God helping me, I will fight it as I can. Yet it may be that the Welds are right. These twenty or thirty brave, strong, earnest children whom they have educated to work in the future, may make a deeper mark than we can imagine. Theodore's 'Thousand Witnesses' produced 'Uncle Tom', so says Mrs. Stowe. Perhaps his ten years' conscientious ditch-digging may eventuate in still more. And I believe that another active era will yet dawn for Mr. and Mrs. Weld. I hope the great problem of problems, 'the associative life', will meet their assistance in its solution. Feeling the necessity of a more perfect education for their children, they are about to join the 'Raritan Bay Union', and endeavor to realize a life which will be of itself an education to all.

"What a great thing it is to live! If, as I believe, your views on certain subjects change, prove your consistency to Truth by changing with them. If not, stay where you are. In any case, I shall esteem it a good fortune to have known and still to know you. If I know myself, my object is not happiness in itself, but to live a manly life, and to aid everyone else to do so.

"Meantime, try actual marriages, not by your own standard, but by that of those who are parties to them. You will greatly modify your estimate of it. I believe it is as imperfect as the people themselves, no more so. I believe, some day, you ought to and will marry somebody; perhaps not me, — if not, a better person. Believe me, the mass of men are not intentionally unjust to women, nor the mass of women consciously oppressed."

"The associative life" was always an idea of interest to him. His elder sister Anna spent some time at Brook Farm, and the thought of a co-operative colony of congenial friends appealed to him strongly, though he was never able to carry it out.

In September of this year, he wrote to Lucy, asking leave to call upon her at Niagara Falls, where she was to speak. She replied:

"I expect to be at Niagara at the time specified, and am very willing you should be there too, though I fear you will not find me very companionable. My soul is always silent before that great Presence: and, while I have a world of feeling, words always fail me. But we are friends, and can understand silence or speech.

"I think you know me well enough to put the right construction upon my consent to meet you at Niagara. I am glad of the friendship of the good, whether they be men or women. But believe me when I say that, in the circumstances, I have not the remotest desire of assuming any other relations. I should incur my own heavy censure if, by fault of mine, you did not understand this. But, since you do, I shall be very glad of the opportunity to have one good, long, frank talk with you."

He had urged her to come West and lecture, offering to make all the business arrangements for her. This he afterwards did, very efficiently. Her lectures on her Western tour took the public by storm. No halls would hold the audiences. She spoke in Cincinnati, Pittsburgh, Wheeling, Columbus, Sandusky, Toledo, St. Louis, Louisville, Madison, Indianapolis, Terre Haute, Lafayette and elsewhere, giving her series of three lectures in each place.

Some amusing incidents happened on this trip. At St. Louis, after giving her three lectures on woman's rights to great audiences, she was asked to give a fourth on temperance. Meanwhile she was taken for a drive around the city. She saw signs up that said, "Hot Tom and Jerry", "Irish Punch", etc., and others that said, "Negroes Bought and Sold." Her mind was full of the two ideas. The crowd on the fourth night was as large as ever and greeted her warmly. She had meant to end a sentence with the words "rum and rum-sellers", but, by a slip of the tongue, she said "rum and slaveholders" instead. She saw a flash go over all the faces. She stopped, and for a moment you might have heard a pin drop. Then she said: "I meant to say 'rum and rum-sellers'; but, while I was thinking of the ruin that comes to you by your rum-selling, I could not forget the deeper ruin that comes to you by your slaveholding; and in spite of myself, the word came out of my mouth." Generally it was almost as much as a Northerner's life was worth to say anything in the South against slavery; but the audience broke into applause. They thought she had done it on purpose, and they admired her courage.

At the close of the lecture, Doctor McDowell, dean of the Medical College, made his way to her side, for fear she might be attacked; but the people pressed around her with broad smiles, saying, "You thought you would n't go away without giving us a slap, did n't you?"

"No," she answered, "it was not meant for a slap; it happened just as I told you." And they believed her.

At Louisville, Kentucky, she had a like series of three great meetings. George D. Prentice, editor of the *Courier Journal*, and Doctor Bell, a prominent citizen, came to interview her at the hotel. Among other questions, they asked her if she believed in the inspiration of the Bible. She answered, "Why, not altogether; probably about as much as you do. You do not believe the whole of it, do you?" This seemed to amuse them greatly. The *Courier* gave her high praise, and the editor urged her to extend her tour to New Orleans, assuring her she would find that what the *Courier* had said had opened the door for her everywhere.

At Louisville, in the night, she heard a donkey bray, for the first time in her life, and lay awake in anguish, thinking it was the cry of a slave under the lash.

A correspondent of the *Cincinnati Columbian* describes a laughable incident of her journey on the Maysville packet:

"Soon after the boat left the wharf, the ladies' cabin became a scene of considerable excitement, which increased in intensity. It soon became fully known that Miss Lucy was on board. Curiosity was on tip-toe."

But many were Kentuckians and were opposed to her views. She had been on deck watching the scenery. When she came in, one and another engaged her in argument: "The crowd was dense and suffocating in and about the ladies' cabin, and a profound silence reigned except when at times the fair orator's sallies of wit and sarcasm 'brought down the house.' A portion of the controversy I must repeat; but words of hers that glow and burn, wrapped in the halo of her own soft voice and pleasant style, must lose their characteristic features when transcribed. The old minister, her adversary, was sorely troubled about women standing with uncovered heads in the presence of men. After adducing scriptural proof that the covering was not meant in a literal sense, Miss Lucy asked:

" 'Does your wife pray before you, her earthly lord and master, with covered head?'

" 'No,' he replied; 'I would give her money if she would pray before me at all. I believe in prayer, and always pray as often as I break bread with my family, that they may not forget their dependence upon their Heavenly Father.'

" 'We surely should never forget the goodness of our Creator; but I am not impressed that any set forms are necessary,' said Lucy.

" 'Are you a Christian woman?' he asked.

" 'I certainly consider myself such,' she said.

" 'How can you possibly get over the scriptural text which says a woman should not speak in public? I advise you to look into these matters more; to study the scriptures more thoroughly.'

" 'I have studied them in their original. I have read them in Greek and can translate them for you.'

"Had a thunderbolt fallen at the reverend's feet, he could not have looked more astounded, when she went on to say that the Greek verb, which is falsely rendered 'speak', should be rendered 'gabble.' By the time we reached the depot, Miss Lucy had added an extra leaf to her laurels, for she was not content merely to show up the important divine as utterly ignorant of the Scriptures in their original, but proved that he actually knew but little of them as rendered in our own tongue."

## *Chapter X*

In Cincinnati Lucy first made the acquaintance of the Blackwell family, with whom she was to be so closely connected. They were a remarkable group.

Henry's father, Samuel Blackwell, was a sugar refiner of Bristol, England. He was a deeply religious man, an Independent, and in the intervals of business he used to go out and do field preaching. During the Chartist riots, when a number of the public buildings in Bristol were burned, the rioters set out to destroy the church of St. Mary Redcliffe. He took his stand on the church steps, and made a speech to the mob which turned them from their purpose. As a well-known Liberal and Dissenter, he got a hearing when a man of different opinions would probably have failed.

When he became engaged to the beautiful Hannah Lane, her uncle, a rich goldsmith and jeweler, offered to let her choose any tea-set in his shop as a wedding present. She picked out a very handsome one; but her lover refused to let her accept it, on the ground that so splendid a tea service was unsuitable for a Christian. She thought seriously of breaking off the engagement, fearing that if he claimed so much authority while only engaged, he would prove a tyrant when married. But she was a merry and sweet-tempered girl and finally forgave him, realizing that his insistence was not due to a domineering disposition, but to a genuine scruple of conscience.

His reputation for integrity stood very high. When his sugar house burned down and he decided to emigrate, the merchants of Bristol united to offer him the loan of as much money as he might need to reëstablish his business, at one and a half per cent, if he would remain among them. But he was in love with American institutions — such as he supposed them to be — and wished his children to grow up in the great republic of the West. In 1832 he sailed for New York, with his wife, their eight children, his four sisters, and a governess and nurse — a company of sixteen persons. His youngest child, born soon after they landed, he named George Washington. Henry (born May 4, 1825) was then seven years old.

Mr. Blackwell started sugar refining in New York and set up the first vacuum pans ever used in America. His business brought him in contact with slaveholders from the West Indies and elsewhere, and he was much shocked by their attitude and that of the public in regard to the slaves. He joined the Anti-Slavery Society, and composed and published a small volume of "Slavery Rhymes." The children worked for the Anti-Slavery Bazaars: the family named their carriage horses Garrison and Prudence Crandall;[1] and prominent abolitionists, when in danger of being mobbed in New York, took refuge at the Blackwell home on Long Island.

He kept an open mind towards new ideas. His daughter Emily remembered the horrified faces of her mother and aunts when he announced one morning at breakfast that he had been to hear Frances Wright the night before. He added, "Much of what she said was very good sense."

His sugar refining in New York did not prosper, and after six years he moved to Cincinnati, partly with the hope of introducing the cultivation of beet sugar and thus indirectly striking a heavy blow at the slave-grown cane sugar of the South. But he died soon after reaching Cincinnati.

The widow and the eldest three daughters, Anna, Marian and Elizabeth, opened a school for girls and supported the family until the boys, who were younger, were able to earn.

Elizabeth pioneered the way for women into the medical profession. She applied in vain to

[1] Prudence Crandall was a young Connecticut school-teacher who underwent almost incredible persecution because she persisted in teaching colored girls.

all the medical colleges in the large cities. Doctor Pankhurst, a distinguished surgeon of Philadelphia, offered to admit her to his classes, but only on condition that she would disguise herself as a man. This she refused to do. Finally she secured admission to the Medical College of Geneva, New York, now the medical department of Syracuse University. The late Doctor Stephen S. Smith, who was a member of that year's medical class, has told how it happened.

The class consisted of about one hundred and fifty young men. They were so riotous and noisy that the neighbors had repeatedly threatened to have the college indicted as a nuisance. One morning the dean appeared before them, and told them that the faculty had received a most extraordinary request. A young lady had applied for admission. They had decided to refer the question to the students; if they were all willing, she might enter; if even one objected, she would be refused. Doctor Smith said the faculty did not really wish to admit her, and they thought some one would be sure to object. But it struck the class as an enormous joke. A class meeting was held, at which a series of speeches was made, each more extravagant than the last, and all in favor of admitting the young lady. When the vote was taken, there was a great shout of "Aye" and a single faint "No." Then the other students fell upon the solitary objector and cuffed and mauled him till he changed his vote. Some days passed; they had forgotten all about the matter. One morning, while they were waiting for the professor, and making their usual uproar, the door opened and he came in, accompanied by a young lady, of small stature and plainly dressed, but of a very firm and determined expression of countenance. At once every student seized his notebook and scudded to his seat, and you might have heard a pin drop. Perfect order prevailed till the close of the lecture; and it continued till the end of the course. The presence of one self-respecting girl wrought the change. But the people of Geneva felt sure that she was either a bad character or a lunatic. A doctor's wife at her boarding place refused to speak to her. Women passing her on the street held their skirts aside and sometimes made insulting remarks. She graduated in 1849, at the head of her class, the first woman in modern times to take a medical degree.

Her younger sister Emily afterwards applied for admission to the Geneva Medical College, but was refused. Pressure had been brought to bear upon the faculty, and they had decided to admit no more women, although they had testified that Elizabeth's presence had "exercised a beneficial influence upon her fellow students in all respects." Emily was refused admission by ten medical colleges. She got permission to study in the free hospital at Bellevue, New York, and was later admitted to the Rush Medical School in Chicago. But again the State Medical Association brought pressure to bear, and at the end of her first year the school excluded women. She was at last admitted to the medical college in Cleveland, Ohio, and completed her course there.

After post-graduate studies in Europe, the Blackwell sisters, with Doctor Marie R. Zakrzewska, opened in 1857 the New York Infirmary for Women and Children, with the double object of helping a poor neighborhood and affording women medical students the opportunity for hospital practice which was denied them elsewhere. It was the first hospital conducted wholly by women; and for more than half a century it remained the only place in New York, except one small homeopathic hospital, where poor women could be attended by physicians of their own sex.

Later, Doctor Emily Blackwell was for many years Dean of the Women's Medical College of the New York Infirmary, and was an inspiration to generations of the younger women doctors. The college always stood for the most thorough medical preparation and for the highest standards of professional honor. When Cornell opened its medical school to women, it merged with Cornell.

In the early days, the women physicians in New York were almost ostracized. Hardly any one but the Quakers would employ them.[1] Doctor Elizabeth finally settled in England, and was the first woman physician to have her name inscribed on the British Medical Register, in 1859. She lived to be eighty-nine. When she died, the census showed that there were in the United States more than seven thousand women physicians and surgeons.

Anna, the eldest sister, composed music, was a remarkably fine translator, and wrote a volume of poems that called out praise from Edgar Allan Poe. She settled in Paris and supported herself for many years as newspaper correspondent for a widely separated group of papers, when such work was unusual for a woman. The youngest sister, Sarah Ellen, was an artist, and author of a life of Anna Ella Carroll. Marian, one of the most gifted of the family, was handicapped by lifelong ill health. She kept house for the others. None of the five sisters ever married; but, among them, they took five poor children to bring up. The four brothers, Samuel, Henry, Howard and George, all went into business, some of them with much success.

[1] Elizabeth Blackwell's experiences and those of the Infirmary are described in her autobiography, "Pioneer Work for Women." E. P. Dutton and Co., Inc.

Anna gave Henry a year at Kemper College, near St. Louis. Here he distinguished himself in his studies, but the family finances did not permit him to stay longer. At fourteen he began to be a bread-winner. At twenty, he was the manager of two mills. He bought a small brick house near Lane Seminary at Walnut Hills, placed it in his mother's name, and it was the family home for years. Harriet Beecher Stowe and her husband were among their neighbors and friends.

Henry later became partner in a hardware firm, and for seven years traveled on horseback through Indiana, Ohio, Illinois, Kentucky and Wisconsin, securing orders; journeying often over unfathomably muddy roads, or riding by compass through the unbroken forest, sleeping in log cabins, and meeting the plain people of the West in a way that he always said was worth more to him than a liberal education. He built up a large trade in the Wabash valley.

He worked in districts where it was popularly believed that the only way for people to escape fever and ague was to keep themselves soaked in whisky. He let liquor alone, however, and kept his health.

It was in his mother's home at Walnut Hills that Lucy was a guest in 1853. Samuel Blackwell's diary says:

"Oct. 9, 1853. Henry spent last Sunday and

Monday delightfully at Niagara, where Lucy Stone was staying; then, returning to Cleveland, encountered on the train several well-known advocates of woman's rights on their way to a convention there. Some of them he had met before. He spent two days in Cleveland attending the convention, at which he acted as secretary and spoke. He seems to have enjoyed it exceedingly."

This was Mr. Blackwell's first woman's rights speech.

The Convention was held under the presidency of Mrs. Frances D. Gage of Missouri, the beloved "Aunt Fanny." Henry's speech was published in full in the pamphlet report of the proceedings. It began:

"In one of the letters read this morning, it was suggested that woman's cause should be advocated by women only. Yet I feel that I owe you no apology for standing on this platform. But, if I do, this is sufficient, that I am the son of a woman, and the brother of women. I know that this is their cause, but I feel that it is mine also. Their happiness is my happiness, their misery, my misery. The interests of the sexes are inseparably connected, and in the elevation of the one lies the salvation of the other."

Samuel's diary continues:

"Oct. 16, 1853. During the last three days we have had quite an excitement on 'woman's rights.'

Mr. and Mrs. Mott, Mrs. Wright, Mrs. Jenkins and Lucy Stone are here. They spoke in Smith and Nixon's Hall to immense audiences.

"Oct. 23. Last night Lucy Stone spoke on woman's rights to a large crowd. She exceeded all her former efforts, and delivered one of the very best speeches I ever heard. Tuesday evening she spoke on slavery, and Thursday she made an address at the Anti-Slavery Bazaar.

"Oct. 30. After two days' visit and speaking in North Richmond, Miss Lucy returned last Monday, and has been with us almost constantly since. She is a most admirable woman. By her quiet decision, steady purpose and lofty principle, she reminds me strongly of Elizabeth; and by a certain precision and distinctness of utterance, and personal neatness and good judgment. We have quite adopted her. This morning Henry went down to Louisville to provide for Miss Lucy's lectures there."

Mr. Blackwell believed that his suit was promoted by the acquaintance that Lucy thus made with his family, and especially by the affection that grew up between her and his mother, a noble, genial old lady, who took to Lucy greatly, and already began to love her like a daughter.

The next year Samuel wrote in his diary again:

"April, 1854. During the past week the Cincinnati Anti-Slavery Convention was held in Greenwood Hall. Henry took an active part. Most of the resolutions were his, and were good. Fred Douglass, Lucy Stone, Charles C. Burleigh, from abroad; Livermore, Boynton, Elliott and others in town, spoke. Henry spoke at length on the Nebraska question. The audiences were enormous, many hundreds going away unable to get in."

## *Chapter XI*

Henry and Lucy corresponded, and discussed all the questions of the day. He continued to press his suit and she to refuse. Then an incident happened which greatly advanced him in her regard. He wrote to her in September, 1854:

"Having received an invitation from the Western Anti-Slavery Society to attend their annual convention at Salem, I went up last week, in company with Mrs. Ernst, Mrs. Coleman and Christian Donaldson. I spoke four times during the three days. . . .

"During an afternoon session, a dispatch from Allegheny City (opposite Pittsburg) was received, stating that at 6 P.M. the train going West through Salem would contain a colored girl, with her master and mistress, on the way to Tennessee, and requesting us to stop her. You know that, being voluntarily brought into the State, she was legally free. Accordingly, after the adjournment of the convention, a meeting of about 1200 persons assembled at the depot and were addressed by Charles Burleigh. A committee of four were appointed to see the conductor, and ask the girl if she wanted her freedom. The committee selected a respectable colored man to act as spokesman, and when the cars arrived, I found myself along with them. We found the little girl, only eight years old, with her mistress and baby, and the colored man asked her whose child she was. Getting no answer, he asked the lady, who promptly told him 'it was none of his business.' The committee then inquired of the lady, and found she and her husband were on their way to Tennessee, and that the child was their slave. The child was asked if she wished to be free, and replied 'Yes', whereupon I told the owners, the husband (Mr. Robinson) having meanwhile come in, that the child was now legally free under the law, and must go with us. I took the child's arm and commenced lifting her from the seat, seeing that the passengers seemed to sympathise with the owners, and that there was no time to be lost. At that moment a young Cincinnatian, of the name of Keyes, collared me and remonstrated with me. I let go of the child, who was instantly caught up by the other members of the committee and passed out, and carried swiftly off into the town in the arms of a colored man, while I shook off Keyes. As soon as I found the child safe, I returned and explained to the astonished Tennesseans the motives of our conduct, and, after a very animated and angry discussion of a few minutes, the bell rang, the cars started, and the assembled multitude gave nine hearty cheers.

"In the evening we had a spirited and crowded meeting at the Town Hall. Dr. Thomas, one of the committee, stated the facts. I then spoke. Charles Burleigh followed; we had songs, and, at the request of the audience, I named Miss Topsy, who had appeared on the platform, Abby Kelley Salem — the Christian name from the lady who has done so much in that section of the country, and the surname from the place which had the honor of saving her.

"A Whig lawyer spoke well in favor of a resolution endorsing our action, and the audience passed it unanimously.

"From the platform Keyes, and other conservative acquaintances, denounced me in unmeasured terms, as the one participant whom they recognized. So, when I reached Cincinnati next day, I found the city buzzing like a hornets' nest. I was at once indicted for 'kidnapping'; but the case, as it happened, was placed by the owners in the hands of the eminent law firm of Taft and Mallon (Taft was the father of President Taft). Judge Mallon was an intimate personal friend of mine, and a fellow member of the Cincinnati Literary Club. They sent for me soon after, and privately informed me that they were satisfied that slaves could not be held upon free soil, when brought with consent of owners, and that they had so advised their Memphis clients.

"I find the matter very much misrepresented in the papers, as was to be expected. The *Gazette* gave a tolerably fair account; the other papers, which I send you, are very abusive. I have, however, published my statement of the facts, and have sent to Salem for a corroboration of them. . . .

"I do not regret the part I took. I regret the odium and misunderstanding which attaches to anything of the kind. The worst attack upon me is to-day, in the *Commercial*, signed 'An Eye Witness.' It is written by a member of our club,[1] and asserts that I assaulted the lady, scratched her neck, and tumbled the baby on the floor. Christian Donaldson will reply in Monday's paper with an equally flat denial of all this. And, if I succeed in obtaining a contradiction, signed by the citizens of Salem, I hope eventually to set the matter right. Meanwhile, I have at least the comfort of success. We saved the child, and vindicated the State. The systematic publication of falsehood was threatened me beforehand,

[1] The Literary Club of Cincinnati. It brought Ralph Waldo Emerson, Theodore Parker and other prominent men to the city to speak. It had many members who later became famous, including Rutherford B. Hayes, afterwards President of the United States, and Ainsworth R. Spofford, for forty years librarian of Congress.

if I would not produce the child, and have the matter decided by its wishes, with the promise of free papers if the child wished to be free. I told the parties that she was free already, and wanted no papers, and that they might publish me as much as they pleased.

"So you see, Lucy, that, with all my love of approbation, I am not, at present, on the road to popularity, apparently. What you say in your letter about the importance of perfect sincerity and fixed antislavery principle, is very true. I am not willing to admit, however, that the Disunionists are necessarily more radical or consistently antislavery than myself. But why cavil about means? Our aim is the same, and we all work towards it in our own way. I agree with you in regarding the operations of the Emigrants' Aid Societies in settling Kansas as very hopeful. I begin to hope that she will come in as a free State."

Mr. Blackwell was never sued for his part in this affair, but it caused much indignation in the South. A reward of ten thousand dollars was offered for his head at a large public meeting in Memphis, and for months Kentuckians would come into his hardware store and look long and fixedly at him. When he asked, "What can I do for you, gentlemen?" they would answer, "Ah, damn you, we shall know you if we ever catch you on the other side of the river!" They meant to lynch him.

Lucy wrote:

"Dear Harry: I am very proud and glad of the part you took in that rescue. Your statement of the facts was well. But do not defend the deed; it is its own best defense, and needs no other. The newspaper bitterness will pass away and their falsehoods be forgotten, while deep down in the hearts of all who know of the rescue will live forever real esteem for those who made it. Many who are not capable of a noble action themselves, do yet respect all the more those who are.

"What an exciting scene it must have been! How much of intense thought, feeling and action were crowded in that little space of time! What a change in one human destiny! What material for pleasant memories was furnished to many! God bless you all, as He will, and as every worthy deed does ever. It is possible your enemies may try to make this matter interfere with your business. But, even then, you will be richer with your self-respect, even though you may have less in dollars. The only safe wealth, after all, is that which does not 'perish in the using.'"

His business did suffer. In March, 1855, he wrote to "Dearest Lucy":

"I do not intend to take any active part in the (Anti-Slavery) Convention this year, although I am doing all in my power to aid it. My partners [1] feel desirous of my not doing so, until we can make a change and dissolve the firm. Of course the odium which attaches to me from the Salem affair has been, to a certain extent, injurious to our business, and much more so to its reputation (for purposes of selling out) than to its actual condition. People are so cowardly that they overestimate the effects of a popular clamor; and we actually did just miss an opportunity of selling out, a few weeks since, by the purchaser's fear that the business had been greatly injured by the Salem Spree.

"I hope you do not misunderstand me, dear Lucy, as regretting that affair, or as willing to compromise one iota of independent thought and action from sordid motives. On the contrary, I will endeavor to assume a position where I shall have no partners to object to my course, as an injustice to themselves. Only three or four days ago, I was obliged very much to offend them by getting out a writ of habeas corpus for two slaves who were brought to this city on the Maysville steamboat, and thence transferred across our Landing to the Louisville mail-boat. These men were chained round the body and to each other, and were being transferred from Dover, Ky., to Missouri, by a man who had bought them

[1] The firm was Coombs, Ryland and Blackwell.

only two days before. . . . The writ was granted by Judge Storer. Joliffe and I went to the Landing, and saw the deputy sheriffs on board. The captain denied the presence of the slaves, but on search they were found, and taken to jail. I called on them in the afternoon with a young free colored man, and represented the advantages of freedom. I found them both desirous to be free and not to go to Missouri. But the claimants and their friends got the trial postponed two days successively, and meantime talked to them, and bribed the jailor, turnkeys, etc., till they got the poor fellows bewildered and intimidated, representing that there were hundreds of men in Cincinnati out of work; that they would be starved to death, or put into the chain gang, etc., etc. However, we sent friends to see them on our side, and yesterday the case was very ably argued on both sides.

"The question is an important one, which we have wanted for a long time to bring up. It is this: Does a slave become legally free if, while being carried from one State to another on the Ohio river, the steamboat incidentally lands on the Ohio shore? We contend that the jurisdiction of Ohio extends to low-water mark. . . . If, as we confidently anticipate, the decision is in our favor, an important principle will be established. . . . We shall try to get the poor fellows clear.

"Of course the *Enquirer* came out with an infamous half column of abuse against me as a 'public nuisance', a destroyer of the business of the city, a British renegade, a Negro-thief, etc., and invoked a mob and a coat of tar and feathers, etc., etc. — all of which I shall be well satisfied to endure, if we can get Ohio one step nearer a free State than before."

The case ended without the decision of the important point at issue:

"The poor men, perplexed and ignorant, intimidated and deceived, finally consented to go back with their master, and the court dismissed the case. So I have the satisfaction of paying $100 costs and of being blackguarded in the newspapers, and nothing to show for it but my good intentions and a fixed resolution to try it again the first opportunity."

The correspondence continued. His letters breathe fervor and devotion, hers reluctance and doubt. But her heart warmed to him more and more. He wrote:

"You do not know the pleasure I feel in the assurance of your affection for me, which you so frankly express. I should be either more or less than human if I did not feel ennobled by being the object of an affection so pure, so elevated. Believe me, I shall try hereafter to prove myself worthy of it. Still more happy do I feel at the possibility, which you admit, of your feelings becoming hereafter still more strongly enlisted in my favor.

"While I do not believe one word of the poetical fiction that any two human beings are constituted peculiarly and in all respects fitted for each other — perfect counterparts, capable of a mystical and absolute union — I do believe that certain temperaments, tastes and dispositions naturally attract or repel each other, and that we are so constituted that we need to form an alliance, the most pure and intimate possible, with one individual of the opposite sex. Although the ideal of marriage, as of everything else, can only exist in possibility. . . . I still believe that the majority of people may, and many do, realize on earth a union more beautiful and desirable than any other which the present stage of the world's development permits. To undertake that relation is equally a privilege and a duty. To conceive one's self precluded from assuming it, because the existing laws of society do not square with exact justice, is to subject one's self to a more abject slavery than ever actually existed. Will you permit the injustice of the world to enforce upon you a life of celibacy? The true mode of protest is to assume the natural relation and to reject the unnatural dependence. I say unnatural, because there is no degradation in dependence if it be mutual and natural. The infant is dependent on its mother, but it would be a foolish baby who would knock its brains out to escape that relation.

"Now you know that I fully admit the injustice of the present law of property as regards married people (and, indeed, all others, in a more or less degree). But as to the right of personal custody, however true in theory, consult any lawyer you can trust, in any State in the Union, as to whether a husband can control his wife's movements, or residence, and my life against a dime, every lawyer, everywhere, will tell you 'No.' Universal custom and experience prove otherwise. . . . No husband can prevent his wife leaving him, except by refusing to support her, or holding on to the children. As you refuse, in any case, to be supported, I suppose the first threat would have no terror. As regards the second, you are aware that the custom has now grown to be a law in many of our States that the children are awarded by the judge to the party considered not in fault. And we should remember that, in case of marital separation, give the children to whom you will, there is hardship somewhere.

"It is rather bad for a father to give up a child. I hope you do not think that the male sex have no parental affection! I think in most cases, where there is fault on both sides the children should be divided. Where very gross criminality exists, either in father or mother, or both, the children should be removed from the one, or both. . . . And it is really true, is it not, that the welfare of the children should be made the paramount consideration?

"You ask me, if the laws placed a man in the same position, on marrying, as they now do women, would I marry? I certainly would. I should indeed be cautious in entering into the relation, and should first satisfy myself that you would not be likely to lock me up, or rather attempt to do so (for the law would soon get me out with a writ of habeas corpus if you did). Second, I should require you to promise not to avail yourself of any unjust laws giving you control of more than half my future earnings. Third, I should place beyond your control all my present property. These things I should do, not against you, but from a sense of personal duty, and with your full concurrence. Certainly, Lucy, I should not act unwisely. If the marriage were harmonious, the laws would not exist so far as we were concerned, because the provisions only apply where appeal is made to them. If it proved discordant, and you should lock me up, I should let myself out by habeas corpus, and sue you for assault and battery. . . . I should steal at least half my children from you, and put you to the trouble and expense of a law suit to get them back. . . . In short, I should be my own master, in spite of much unjust annoyance.

"Why, then, are women so terribly oppressed, you may say? Because they have not, as a class, the education, the spirit, the energy, the disposition to be free. Give me a free man, he can never be made a slave. Give me a free woman, she can never be made one either. Surely you enormously exaggerate the scope and force of external laws at the expense of internal power, when you lay such frightful and hopeless stress upon a few paltry enactments. . . .

"I think when a woman has taken the first step, she need not greatly fear ever to suffer from dependence. The only danger she should guard against is to avoid trying herself to play the despot; most intelligent, energetic women (and men, too) do that thing. . . . You did n't make the external law, and are in no sense responsible for it. The law of marriage existed before Blackstone. . . .

"Lucy dear, if I could express to you, properly, my view of matters and things, you would see that, as to marrying, I am right and you are wrong, and you would marry me, and be all the freer for doing so. Your views on the subject are warped from the unfortunate impressions of your childhood. I hope that your soul will be large enough eventually to outgrow these impressions. Meanwhile, dearest, love me all you can, and believe me

"Yours ever,

"Harry."

She feared that she could not make him happy. She reminded him that she was seven years his senior. He answered that in some ways he was older than she. It was true. To the end of her life, there was always something childlike about her.

Even after her heart was won, she felt that she ought to stay single, in order to devote herself wholly to her work for woman's rights. But he promised to devote himself to the same work, and persuaded her that, together, they could do more for it than she could alone. No promise was ever more faithfully kept.

The opponents of equal rights had often expressed the wish that somebody would marry Lucy, which it was assumed would be the end of her public speaking. At some time in the late forties or early fifties, the *Boston Post* published a parody upon a song then popular, called "Lucy Long." It began:

I just come out before you
  To make a little moan;
I 'll put it in the Boston Post,
  And call it Lucy Stone.

The first time I heard Lucy,
  The "slave power" she did tackle;
The second time 't was temperance,
  In Broadway's Tabernacle.

The poem went on to describe feelingly how much the sons of men were suffering under Lucy's speeches on woman's rights, and said in conclusion:

A name like Curtius' shall be his,
  On fame's loud trumpet blown,
Who with a wedding kiss shuts up
  The mouth of Lucy Stone!

But in after years the enemies of equal rights felt anything but gratitude towards Mr. Blackwell. He added his own eloquent voice to hers, and together they made a great team.

At last, after two years of arduous courtship, they were married, on May 1, 1855.

The famous Protest which they published on this occasion was Mr. Blackwell's idea. A good while before the wedding, he had written to Lucy:

"I want to make a protest, distinct and emphatic, against the laws of marriage. I wish, as a husband, to renounce all the privileges which the law confers upon me, which are not strictly mutual, and I intend to do so. Help me to draw one up. When we marry, I will publicly state before our friends a brief enumeration of these usurpations, and distinctly pledge myself never to avail myself of them under any circumstances."

The Protest, as finally adopted, was written by him, with some suggestions from Lucy and from friends.

Lucy had wished to be married by the Reverend Antoinette L. Brown, but she found that, to be legally valid, the ceremony must be performed by a Massachusetts minister or magistrate. The choice therefore naturally fell on the Reverend Thomas Wentworth Higginson, better remembered as Colonel Higginson.

Like Wendell Phillips, he was a man of the bluest blood in New England, who devoted his high talents to the cause of the poor and oppressed. When the Civil War broke out, he became the commander of one of the first colored regiments. He was desperately wounded, recovered, and returned to the front. After the war he did not reënter the ministry, but devoted himself to literary and political work. At this time he was pastor of a Unitarian church in Worcester, which was derisively called by its pro-slavery neighbors, "The church of the Jerusalem wildcats", because the preacher and his congregation were interested in so many unpopular good causes. He was a personal friend of Lucy's and had for years been actively associated with her in reform work. Of course, he never used the word "obey" in the marriage service. In a letter to his mother, Mr. Higginson gives the following account of the wedding:

"May 1, 1855. We went yesterday afternoon at four by cars to West Brookfield, where we found rather a short, stout, pleasant-looking person, with very black hair and whiskers, blue eyes, and a good forehead, who turned out to be the Blackwell. There also got from the cars a rather peculiar-looking personage, but of beautiful soul — Charles Burleigh, the lecturer[1]; we were all the company, Antoinette Brown and Elizabeth Blackwell (Medicine and Divinity in female forms) not having appeared, though expected.

"We rode three miles over a road among rocky hills till we reached a high little farm house, round which the misty sky shut closely down, revealing only rocks and barns and cattle, small children at the back door, and little Lucy beaming at the front door. She ushered us in; the children turned out to belong to the married brother, and his wife appeared also. While I was uncloaking Mary (Mrs. Higginson), Lucy disappeared, and came in leading a fine, hale, sturdy, stout old lady, saying, with an air of love and pride, "Mr. Higginson, this is my mother, my *own* mother," and the old lady looked as happy as she did.

[1] A saintly but eccentric abolitionist, who held it a matter of conscience to let his hair and beard grow.

"We had provided a box of greenhouse flowers, but no orange blossoms, being unattainable; but we found that Anna Parsons had supplied that deficiency, and we had everything else, including cloth-of-gold roses. The children flocked round to see me arrange them in glasses, and Lucy was very sweet to them; her word seemed to be law and love together. A handful of fallen blossoms she distributed among them. . . .

"It was a large, low old room, with an open wood fire; the children sat in little arm-chairs before its glow; and Charles Burleigh's long hair looked like the locks of an ancient bard.

"We went in to tea at a great table; Lucy presided, and cared for everybody; Mr. Blackwell sat opposite, in quite a domestic manner, the gentlemen of the family not having appeared. After tea they came in from the farm or elsewhere; the elderly father as sturdy as the mother, with a keen face, but saying little; the brother looked like Lucy, a plain likeness; an ex-semi-Orthodox minister, now farmer; he has her low, sweet voice, and we liked him very much. Mr. Blackwell also we liked more and more; he is thoroughly true and manly, earnest, sensible and discriminating; not inspired, but valuable. They seemed perfectly happy together. So the evening passed happily away, and we went at last up the steep stairs, Lucy piloting us, and looking to see that fire and water and all were right. She took such care of everybody that I felt as if some one else in the family were to be married, and she was the Cinderella.

"In the morning there was to be rather a struggle or 'match against time,' literally, as the wedding was to be before breakfast, and we were to ride three miles before 8.20. We gradually assembled in the parlor. Mr. Burleigh and Mr. Stone talked over Mr. Blackwell. The latter said: 'When he used to come up to our place first, I never thought it would end in anything; there had been a good many after Lucy, first and last, but she had made short work of them.' 'Yes,' quoth Burleigh, 'and some of them were such as some ladies who have ridiculed Lucy would be very glad to receive attentions from.' 'Yes, indeed,' nodded the brother knowingly. Meanwhile the queer old father had his dry chuckle on the other side of the room: 'Our Lucy thought there was n't anybody in these parts good enough to marry her, so she had to fetch somebody from Worcester for it, hey?' The quiet old mother meanwhile sat silent, though she had something to say afterwards.

"Presently in came the small lady, and with her the bridegroom; he in the proper white waistcoat, she in a beautiful silk, ashes-of-roses color. They stood up together and read their Protest, which I enclose; and then my usual form of service proceeded. She had had some scruples about the form, but she seemed to think a great deal about what her mother would wish, and after all, our views agreed pretty well; and so she expressed her purpose to 'love and honor' (not obey) very clearly and sweetly, and he as bridegroom should; and I have to add with secret satisfaction that, after this, Lucy, the heroic Lucy, *cried*, like any village bride! And I could hardly help it when, after I had ended, Charles Burleigh came forward and addressed them so nobly and sweetly that I have felt, since, as if it were he and not I who united them. This over, there was some little kissing; . . . and then the speedy necessity of breakfast effected an easy transition. For it was now 7.30 A.M., and we must leave the house in fifteen minutes. So in we went. Lucy soon swallowed her tears and gave others tea to swallow, and we plunged into a hasty breakfast. And I record for posterity that Lucy was presently heard to say quietly, 'And is n't the bride to have any breakfast?' Whereupon we all discovered that, though we had not sentiment enough to fast ourselves, we had enough to neglect her; which was soon remedied, in moderation. But soon we all jumped up and prepared to go. . . . It was the most beautiful bridal I ever attended."

The Protest read:

"While we acknowledge our mutual affection

by publicly assuming the relationship of husband and wife, yet, in justice to ourselves and a great principle, we deem it a duty to declare that this act on our part implies no sanction of, nor promise of voluntary obedience to, such of the present laws of marriage as refuse to recognize the wife as an independent, rational being, while they confer upon the husband an injurious and unnatural superiority, investing him with legal powers which no honorable man would exercise, and which no man should possess. We protest especially against the laws which give to the husband:

"1. The custody of the wife's person.

"2. The exclusive control and guardianship of their children.

"3. The sole ownership of her personal and use of her real estate, unless previously settled upon her, or placed in the hands of trustees, as in the case of minors, lunatics, and idiots.

"4. The absolute right to the product of her industry.

"5. Also against laws which give to the widower so much larger and more permanent an interest in the property of his deceased wife than they give to the widow in that of the deceased husband.

"6. Finally, against the whole system by which 'the legal existence of the wife is suspended during marriage,' so that, in most States, she neither has a legal part in the choice of her residence, nor can she make a will, nor sue or be sued in her own name, nor inherit property.

"We believe that personal independence and equal human rights can never be forfeited, except for crime; that marriage should be an equal and permanent partnership, and so recognized by law; that until it is so recognized, married partners should provide against the radical injustice of present laws, by every means in their power.

"We believe that, where domestic difficulties arise, no appeal should be made to legal tribunals under existing laws, but that all difficulties should be submitted to the equitable adjustment of arbitrators mutually chosen.

"Thus, reverencing law, we enter our earnest protest against rules and customs which are unworthy of the name, since they violate justice, the essence of all law."

Mr. Higginson had the Protest published in the *Worcester Spy* with the following comment:

"It was my privilege to celebrate May Day by officiating at a wedding in a farmhouse among the hills of West Brookfield. The bridegroom was a man of tried worth, a leader in the Western Anti-Slavery Movement; and the bride was one whose fair name is known throughout the nation; one whose rare intellectual qualities are excelled by the private beauty of her heart and life.

"I never perform the marriage ceremony without a renewed sense of the iniquity of our present system of laws in respect to marriage; a system by which 'man and wife are one, and that one is the husband.' It was with my hearty concurrence, therefore, that the following Protest was read and signed, as a part of the nuptial ceremony; and I send it to you, that others may be induced to do likewise."

The Protest had wide publicity, and helped to get the unjust laws amended.

Some opponents of woman suffrage, of the baser sort, pretended that their marriage was not legal, and represented their protest against the inequalities in the marriage laws as a protest against any legal union. Francis J. Garrison, the youngest son of the Liberator, said at the memorial meeting held after Mr. Blackwell's death:

"Seldom have a husband and wife been subjected to more atrocious misrepresentation, calumny and abuse than were they, when they entered into that noble marriage covenant. But they lived to hear the taunts change to tributes, the abuse to praise."

Comments on the match were many and varied. Harriet Beecher Stowe, who had known Henry for years as a young fellow bubbling over with fun, frolic and audacity, was amazed at his marriage to the serious and earnest young reformer. She said, "Is it possible that that wild boy has married Lucy Stone!"

The *Washington Union* said:

"We understand that Mr. Blackwell, who last fall assaulted a Southern lady and stole her slave, has lately married Miss Lucy Stone. Justice, though sometimes tardy, never fails to overtake her victim."

Lucy sent this to Miss Anthony, with the comment, "They evidently think him well punished." What he himself thought of it was shown in an editorial written just after his wife's death:

"In behalf of the great principle of equality in marriage, I desire, in this hour of inexpressible bereavement, to say, with all the added emphasis of a life-time's experience, that the Protest read and signed by Lucy Stone and myself on the first day of May, 1855, as a part of our nuptial ceremony, has been the key-note of our married life. After the lapse of more than thirty-eight happy years (how happy, I to-day more keenly realize than ever before), in her behalf and on my own, I wish to reaffirm that declaration."

## *Chapter XII*

Lucy looked upon the loss of a woman's name at marriage as a symbol of the loss of her individuality. Not believing in the thing, she would not have the symbol. With her it was a matter of principle. Her name had for years been widely famous, but, if she had been the most obscure of women, she would have felt the same necessity to keep her own name.

She consulted several eminent lawyers, among them the Honorable Salmon P. Chase, who was afterwards Chief Justice of the United States. All of them assured her that there was no law requiring a wife to take her husband's name; it was only a custom. So, with her husband's full approval, she determined to remain Lucy Stone.

Among the first to congratulate Mrs. Stone, as she now wished to be called, was Elizabeth Cady Stanton. She wrote:

"Nothing has been done in the woman's rights movement for some time that so rejoiced my heart as the announcement by you of a woman's right to her name. . . . It may do for the slave to be

Cuffee Brooks or Cuffee Douglass, just whose Cuffee he may chance to be; but for us, who have grown up into the full stature of womanhood, demanding all our social, civil, and religious rights, and diligently fitting ourselves to maintain them, too, it does seem to me a proper self-respect demands that every woman may have some name by which she may be known from the cradle to the grave. . . .

"Again, under our new property rights, married women may make contracts — buy and sell, and give deeds and mortgages. It becomes very important, therefore, that a woman should not change her name two or three times in one short life.

"But, if the mother retain her name, what should the children be called? It matters but little what, so that the girls have a name; for heretofore a woman, like other mere chattels, has been known but by the name of her owner."

Miss Anthony wrote:

"I am more and more rejoiced that you have declared, by actual doing, that a woman has a name, and may retain it throughout her life."

Mr. Higginson wrote:

"As to your scruple about your name, dear Lucy, it would be strange indeed if I did not respect it, when I have always wondered that women did not feel as indignant about the merging of their own individuality as I felt for them. I have always reproached my wife with not caring about it, and I rejoice that you do. . . . I hope others will follow your example. My wife sends her love, though she does n't agree about the name."

Keeping her own name brought much criticism, of course, and some inconvenience. She received many remonstrances from friends who thought she was making a mistake. She wrote to one of these:

"I am sorry any of my friends should be made to suffer on my account. I counted all the cost beforehand, and am so sure I am right that nothing that can be said or done moves me in the least. A thousand times more opposition was made to woman's claim to speak in public. But then, and now, a quiet adherence to the right will win.

"'Never a storm but the tainted air needs it;
Never a storm but the sunshine succeeds it.'

"So don't mind what people say. It is not of much account."

She was able to make the innovation accepted and respected, in her own case, even by those who disapproved of the general principle. The only serious loss that it brought her was the inability to vote when Massachusetts gave school suffrage to women in 1879.

The right at first was rigidly hedged about. A woman wishing to vote for school committee had to pay a two-dollar poll tax and make a sworn statement of all her taxable property. But Mrs. Stone prepared to vote, as a matter of course. The *New York Tribune* of November 25, 1879, said:

"Although the assessors have little sympathy with the new movement, . . . no pains have been spared to give the women fair play. . . . No complaints have been made of the way in which the law has been interpreted and carried out.

"Exception must be made, however, in the case of Mrs. Lucy Stone Blackwell, who has proved a thorn of great magnitude in the sides of the unhappy officers of the election. The trouble all arises out of her name. When she married Mr. Blackwell, it was with the understanding that she should retain her maiden name. . . . There is no statute in this State which compels a woman, on marrying, to take her husband's name, but common law sanctions the custom. . . . The assessors and registrars refused to accept her taxes, or place her name on the voting list, except as Mrs. Blackwell, and this name she strenuously refused to acknowledge. By a curious train of circumstances which have not been made public, she appears on the assessors' books as Lucy Stone, to the great confusion of the officials.[1] When it became known that she was determined to vote

[1] She had been paying her taxes under that name for years.

as Lucy Stone or not at all, strict orders were given that under no circumstances was she to be allowed the privilege except as Mrs. Blackwell.

"Before this, however, a clerk in the assessor's office, who had never heard of her except as Lucy Stone, happened to be on duty when she presented herself to pay her taxes (*i.e.*, the two-dollar poll tax), and, as he happened to have heard nothing of the order, he made out her bill in her maiden name, received her dues and receipted for them. Armed with the receipted bill, she moved upon the Board of Registration, and, by a most extraordinary piece of good luck, found in the office the only clerk who would take her name — a young man who had just come into the office, and who had somehow also failed to hear the prohibition. As soon as the officials found out how easily she had evaded all their snares — and innocently too, for she had heard nothing of the safeguards taken against her — they were naturally much chagrined, and were compelled to resort to the unpleasant necessity of erasing her name from the list and sending her a notification that a mistake had been made, and that she must not attempt to take advantage of it."

The *Boston Post* of June 5, 1879, called the decision of the assessors the only one possible, and added:

"We yield to no one in our respect for the lady

who has labored with so much devotion, energy, intelligence and sincere conviction to break down the barriers which she has believed kept her sex from its full rights and privileges. She has done more perhaps than any other single person to bring into the cause of woman suffrage a host of powerful friends, and with their aid she has elevated it into the horizon of a hopeful future. More than that, she has led her forces up to the attack again and again, undismayed by repeated repulses, until the outworks have been brilliantly carried; and we congratulate her upon the result. But . . . we hope there will be no change in the present custom by which the wife takes the name of her husband. Were this convenient arrangement to cease, almost endless family complications would ensue."

Mrs. Stone wrote to Benjamin Cushing, secretary of the Board of Assessors, on June 2:

"Replying to yours of the 28th ult., I will say that my name is Lucy Stone, and nothing more. I have been called by it more than sixty years, and there is no doubt whatever about it. If the use of a foot or cart-path for twenty years gives the right of way, surely the use of a name for three times twenty years should secure the right to its use. There is no law that requires a wife to take her husband's name. I have signed many important legal papers, and the signature has not been questioned, and it has no reason to be in the case of my vote."

She offered to sign herself "Lucy Stone, wife of Henry B. Blackwell", the form which she used in signing legal documents; but the chairman of the Board of Registrars wrote her that the City Solicitor held that this would not do.

I have seldom seen my father so indignant as on this occasion. He proposed that he and I should go before the Board of Registrars and make oath that we had known this woman for many years, and that her name was Lucy Stone. Of course, it would have been useless. She was barred from voting because a small Boston official thought he knew more about law than the Chief Justice of the United States.

Mrs. Stone said that if she lived to see municipal suffrage granted to women in Massachusetts, she would make a test case in the courts to deter mine whether she could not vote in her own name. School suffrage seemed too small to be worth going to law about; also, she believed that the later she brought her action, the more likelihood there would be of a favorable decision, since public opinion in behalf of equal rights for women was constantly growing.

The Lucy Stone League, organized in 1921, with headquarters in New York, aims to promote the keeping of their own names by married women, and has done much able and energetic work to establish their right to do so. Its members generally retain the prefix "Miss", their practice in this respect differing from that of Lucy Stone.

In Massachusetts, a comparatively recent enactment now makes it impossible for a married woman to register under her maiden name. It is to be hoped that sooner or later all the States will adopt the more liberal policy of England. There every woman may do as she chooses about a name, and the foundations of society have not been visibly shaken in consequence.

## *Chapter XIII*

The newly wedded couple spent the first year of their married life at the home of Mr. Blackwell's mother near Cincinnati.

Ohio was a border State, and feeling on the slavery question ran high. The people of the State were about equally divided between the friends of freedom and the advocates of slavery; but the Free Soilers were split into two factions, the Liberty party and the American party. Unless they could get together, they had no chance of defeating the pro-slavery men. Mr. Blackwell was active in politics, and in the critical year of 1855, soon after his marriage, he was able to render a signal service to the cause of freedom. A speech made by him brought about a coalition between the factions in Cincinnati, and the vote of the Cincinnati delegation at the State Convention turned the scale in favor of the nomination of Salmon P. Chase for Governor. A few years later, the vote of the Chase delegation in the National Convention turned the scale in favor of the nomination of Lincoln for President.

How the coalition in Cincinnati was effected

is told in a correspondence between R. B. Pullan and Thomas Spooner, who were local leaders in 1855 of the Liberty party and the American party, respectively. In a letter called out by the Lincoln anniversary banquet, Pullan wrote to Spooner on February 13, 1899, recalling the facts, and Spooner testified to the correctness of his recollection. At that time Mr. Chase was apparently "down and out" for good, in Ohio politics.

Mr. Pullan says that before the mass convention to be held in Cincinnati on June 23, 1855, to nominate delegates to the State Convention, he and Mr. Blackwell and other stanch Liberty party men had been holding conferences every evening, planning how they could secure the election of some Chase men as delegates. On the evening before the Convention, Thomas Spooner joined them, and said that he would support any candidate who got a majority in the convention: "All he wanted was harmony, and if we could agree upon a chairman, all would go well." Various names were suggested, but there was some objection to each. Then Mr. Blackwell proposed Judge Walker, who was acceptable to all. Mr. Blackwell at once walked out to Walnut Hills, roused up Walker at midnight, and secured his consent to serve.

Mr. Pullan continues:

"Next morning Greenwood Hall was packed.

As they gathered, storm clouds gathered also. At ten sharp, Judge Walker appeared. Instantly a motion was made to elect him president. He walked straight to the rostrum. 'Liberty' men, not more than twenty or thirty, were seated to his left, in a compact group, Blackwell about the center.

"The storm began. Motions and counter motions; rash things said on both sides. Judge Walker vainly rapped for order. 'Know Nothing' spread-eagle speeches were made, one after another, about Americans ruling America, and denouncing attempts of abolitionists, etc., etc.

"The crisis came. Pullan told Blackwell to get up. He refused; did not know what to say in such a turmoil. Pullan insisted: 'Play the role of Pitt — France and England, ancient enemies, unite to beat back Russian bear; so we beat back slavery. After that we fight again, if we want to.'

"The spread-eagle stopped. Blackwell arose. The crowd yelled, 'Englishman!' 'Rescue Blackwell!' [1] 'Pitch him down stairs!' 'Throw him out of the window!' The din grew. Blackwell was lifted into a chair. The fury increased; Walker could n't be heard; put on his hat. Silence for a moment, then he shouted, 'I came to preside over a convention, not a mob. The young

[1] Probably a derisive allusion to his rescue of the little slave girl.

man who has the floor shall be heard, or I 'll leave the hall and declare the assembly dissolved.'

"This brought silence, and Blackwell, pale with excitement, began in a trembling voice, partly choked, slowly but firmly saying that he admired the exhibition of patriotism and love of country, and, if he was not born in England, he, too, would be an American, etc., etc. The hall rang with applause, and it increased as burning sentence after sentence came from his lips."

He compared the two factions to two knights, honorable enemies, riding in opposite directions through the forest, who found a lady assaulted by ruffians. At once they joined forces to rescue her. Then they rode on their way again, honorable enemies once more. The endangered lady was the country. Mr. Pullan continues:

"The motion to appoint a committee was put, and carried unanimously. Judge Walker congratulated all, and predicted triumph. The storm had swept away divisions. All were now Americans."

Most of the delegates elected were Chase men. Mr. Pullan adds:

"Judge Walker, in coming down Main Street from the convention, was met by a distinguished lawyer with the remark,

'Well, you let an unknown young man run away with your convention, and turn it over to the abolitionists!'

"The Judge replied, 'Unknown young man! Well, I 've heard Mr. Webster, Mr. Clay, and all the great orators of the country; but, if eloquence is measured by its effect, I have just heard the most eloquent speech that ever fell from human lips. — Unknown young man!'"

Cincinnati was now the headquarters from which Mrs. Stone went out on her lecturing trips. There was no lack of thrilling incidents to serve as texts. Her heart was deeply moved by the case of Margaret Garner. A young slave, with his old father and mother, his wife and four little children, escaped from Kentucky; but they had hardly reached Cincinnati when they were recaptured. Mrs. Stone tells the story:

"The young wife, not yet twenty-three, when she saw that escape was impossible, seized the little daughter, a child of great beauty, nearly three years old, and almost severed her head from the body. She attempted also the lives of her other children, but was prevented. They were all lodged in jail, and, after a form of trial, with no judge and no jury, they were all returned to slavery.

"I saw the young mother once in jail and twice in court. She was a beautiful woman, chestnut colored, with good features and wonderful eyes. It was no wild desperation that had impelled her, but a calm determination that, if she could not find freedom here, she would get it with the angels. History furnishes no parallel to this kind of heroism of hers; and we were all powerless to help. No hall could be had for a public meeting. Two hundred special marshals, chosen from the ruffians of Kentucky, supplied with arms, crowded the court, hall and stairs, and formed the escort when the victims were returned to bondage."

While visiting Margaret Garner in prison, Mrs. Stone asked her, in case she should be taken back into slavery, if she had a knife. In court, Mrs. Stone was asked if it were true that she had offered Margaret a knife. She answered, "I did ask her if she had a knife. If I were a slave, as she is a slave, with the law against me, and society against me, and the church against me, and with no death-dealing weapon at hand, I would with my own teeth tear open my veins, and send my soul back to God who gave it."

Margaret had tried to kill all her children, but she had made sure of the little girl. She said that her daughter should never suffer as she had. Her master was in court. The sweat of shame and anguish rolled down his face while Mrs. Stone was speaking; and at the close he promised her to set Margaret free. But he did not keep his word. She was bound and put on board the boat that carried her down the Ohio river. Her baby was on her lap. The boat gave a lurch, and she let the baby roll off her lap into the river, without an effort to save it. Later her husband wrote to Mrs. Stone that Margaret was dead. He thought she would be glad to know it. An accident happened to the steamboat. Margaret, refusing to be saved, allowed herself to drown, and thus attained freedom at last.

Soon after, the family decided to move East. Mr. Blackwell had acquired some wild land in Wisconsin. To make this available to Eastern buyers, it was requisite to have a certification of each forty-acre piece of land, with a description of the soil and location. He went to Wisconsin to get the necessary data, and Lucy went with him. The trip proved a wild and picturesque experience. They drove from Chicago to Viroqua, Wisconsin, with a horse and buggy. He wrote from La Crosse to his brother Samuel:

"June 20, 1856.

"We left Chicago on Sunday afternoon, and drove to Jefferson Center same evening. Monday evening we stopped at a farmer's house, where Lucy was horrified by having to sleep in dirty sheets, and two girls and a dog kept passing through our room. We had passed during the day a beautiful lake named Zurich, where a queer, half-crazy reformer keeps a school, a farm, a newspaper, and a union store all going. He has also fitted up a huge stable for a free habitation to the human race.

Says he has kept cattle long enough, and now dedicates the stable to Man, under the title 'Humanity's Barn.' The simple farmer's family, when we took dinner, were quite disposed to accept all the father's isms. Tuesday noon we got dinner at one of the most beautiful farmhouses in America, on Queen Anne's Prairie, and, after passing one or two more lakes, reached a very good farm again, on Turtle Prairie. Wednesday we ate dinner of bread and milk at a farmhouse where we skimmed a pan of milk some three feet in diameter, and liked the thick, yellow scum exceedingly. That night we were caught in a violent thunder storm; but, as God guided us, we reached a nice farmhouse belonging to a locofoco politician named Burdick, whom Lucy identified, as usual, from her New England experience, as a genealogical Seventh-Day Baptist from Rhode Island. Indeed, Lucy or I were in every case intimate with everybody's relatives and connections. I knew all the Westerners, Lucy all the Easterners. She was profound east of Pittsburg; I was deeply saturated with Ohio, Indiana and Illinois.

"Thursday we drove to Madison, through such a wind-storm as is seldom seen. The sand from the lake shores fairly put out our eyes, and Madison from across the lake looked, in its cloud of dust, like a city in a conflagration. We stopped at night with some natives of Prince Edward's

Island, fresh from Nova Scotia. Next day, after driving through various Norwegian wheat-fields, and pulling down fences, and opening gates, we reached the village of Black Earth, and stopped at Mr. Love's tavern, on the wide and desolate sand-prairies of the Wisconsin River Valley. Saturday, after climbing one of the immense bluffs, called Point Judas, and digging into some Indian mounds, abstracting some human bones therefrom, we turned into Pine River Valley, dined at Sextonville, and in the afternoon went on to Richland Center. Here we called on Ira Hazeltine, a shrewd, money-making reformer, with long hair and beard, who, having resigned phrenological lectures for town lots, is now a small local millionaire, with spiritualistic affinities and a general love of lucre and liberty. By him we were induced to hold over and lecture that evening on woman's rights, which we did to a large and attentive audience, occupying the schoolhouse, the Odd Fellows' Hall, and the adjacent grounds generally. Lucy spoke first and I followed, and we went at it with a right good will.

"Next morning . . . we plunged into the dense woods of Richland County. We emerged from that leafy and stumpy wilderness into Mr. Ambrose's clearing about nightfall, with no further damage than a general removal of our epidermis that came in contact with parts of the buggy.

After a lecture from the old man upon clearings of forest, and the tenets of the Dunkards, we got with some difficulty into bed (while our six roommates stepped out to give us the opportunity), and next day crossed the Kickapoo and emerged upon the high rolling prairies of Bad Axe County, just as Lucy was sinking into despair. We lost our umbrella and sunshade at this juncture, and, in trying to find them, I lost my overcoat; but our joy on finding the overcoat consoled us for the loss of our head-protectors. Reached Viroqua in the afternoon, which surpassed Lucy's expectations, there being at least thirty shanties visible to the naked eye. Next day we drove, with the friendly County Clerk, Mr. McMichael, to some timber lands in 16 × 13 × 5, where men had been stealing our timber. Hoped to capture some rails, but did not. However, we railed at the robbers, and had the pleasure of counting some hundreds of stumps which they had left behind them. . . . I am in hopes of getting Meadows's assistance in surveying our lands. Yesterday Lucy and I took a long walk with him over the new town of La Crescent, and the magnificent bluffs above it. Our horse and buggy are just the thing. The horse is lazy, but kind, faithful, conscientious, strong, tough and imperturbable. He eats voraciously, can be left standing without hitching, and in bad places behaves like a hero."

During the summer in Viroqua, conditions were very primitive, but Mrs. Stone found opportunities to lecture both against slavery and for woman's rights. A Fourth of July celebration was arranged, a platform built in a grove, and she was invited to give an address. During her speech the platform broke down, but no one was seriously hurt. She said, "So will this country fall unless slavery is abolished!" [1]

She wrote her mother a lively account of a surveying trip:

"We have just returned from a novel expedition, which I must try to describe to you; but no description can reach the reality. I own 640 acres about twenty-five miles from here. We started last Friday morning to go and see it, in company with Mr. Grace, who wanted to trade with us. It was a bright, clear day, and rather too warm. We went about twelve miles over decent roads, and then it became bad. Our horse fell down. Mr. Grace's broke the harness; but we picked up and pushed on till we came to a log house at the end of the road. There a woman told us that, if we would take down two fences and go across a corn field, we should find a blind road about two miles, and she did not know whether

[1] A tablet now marks the site of this address, calling it the first antislavery and woman's rights speech ever made by a woman in the great Northwest.

there was any beyond. We went the three miles and found it indeed a blind road, which gradually grew more so, until we were entirely lost in grass as high as my shoulders, and which was full of sloughs, frightfully deep. Harry walked and I drove. At last no track could be seen. The men searched in all directions for nearly an hour, while I stayed and took care of the horses; but not the slightest trace of a road could be found. It was 6 P.M. The last house behind us was five miles away, and we were three hours getting over that distance with daylight to help. It would be utterly impossible to go back at that time, and we could go no further with the buggy. So we took out the horses, fastened them to a tree, gave them oats, and we travelled on through the nettles, briars, tall grass, sloughs and brush, bitten by mosquitoes and black with wood-ticks that fastened on us. Harry tore his pantaloons (one leg) from the bottom to the waist-band, so nettles, briars and bugs had free access. I was wet to my knees, Mr. Grace ditto. The sun had gone down, and the stars were thick over us, and we still toiled on, in the right direction, but not knowing whether a human being was to be found.

"At last we came to the junction of the Kickapoo and Otter Creek rivers. Both were in a freshet, and rushed past wild and high. The first thing, we quenched our horrid thirst; then shouted again and again, and only the bluffs answered the sound, and we began to be seriously afraid that we must remain out, when shouting was answered to ours from two directions. You never saw gladder souls than we. A young man came and told us to cross the Otter by a log; but alas! the log was swept away. So he went far up the Kickapoo and swam down, whirled like a straw by the current, our men pulling him out. He took us up a quarter of a mile to a log over Otter Creek, then another quarter to a log house. We went another quarter to a boat about as large as your hand, that took us, one at a time, over to the home of the young hero who had helped us. A log house with two rooms. Here we got supper, washed and dried our feet, and at 10.30 were in bed. We were now within eight miles of my land, but Mr. Grace would go no farther. So Harry went on foot the eight miles, and found the land already in demand. So that what cost me, last spring, $800, will within a year give me $3000. And if Harry had not come home with the skin all off his ankles, so that he could not get his boots on, we should have been satisfied. But he borrowed some soft moccasins, and the night saw us safe here. We stopped at a log house so far in the woods that the sun has never seen it (for the woods here are woods), where there was a good spring; and while we watered the horse, a woman came down to ask me if my bonnet (a sunbonnet that I had just made) was in the fashion!"

In the autumn, having finished their business, they drove back. The Blackwell family had disposed of the homestead at Walnut Hills and moved to New Jersey and New York. Mr. Blackwell wrote, many years after: "I have never seen Vernon County (Bad Axe) again. The whole incident of that summer's laborious, sequestered life is associated with the memory of my wife, and seems to me like a lovely dream. The cares and privations are forgotten; the beautiful scenery and the sweet, pure air of those romantic highlands will forever linger in my memory."

## *Chapter XIV*

They looked for a suitable home near New York, but had difficulty in getting one, as Mr. Blackwell had little to offer in exchange but Western land. Finally a cottage was found on Cone Street, Orange, New Jersey, whose owner wanted to go West. Mrs. Stone rejoiced in having a home of her own; and her husband often recalled, in after years, how cheerfully and capably she adapted herself to all the necessities and duties of a poor man's wife. She was skilled in every kind of housework. She wrote to a friend:

"It [the new home] is a Gothic cottage, 75 feet from the road, with an acre of ground — young fruit and ornamental trees growing about it, guarded by one venerable old apple-tree. I wish I could let you see just how pleasant it is, in this dear little home of our own, which is simple and unpretending, and where our friends are welcome. I do so enjoy its quiet, and the dear love that blesses it! . . . As soon as we can, we mean to have a larger domain, in the free, open country. But for the present, it is so good to say 'our own' to this little spot!"

Mr. Blackwell took a position with Augustus Moore, a publisher of agricultural books, who sent him West to try to arrange for the establishment in the school districts of Farmers' Libraries, to consist in part of the Moore publications. He says in his reminiscences: "Lucy and I had hardly bought our scanty furniture and moved into our cottage, when I had to leave her and spend months in the West."

A few days before their child was born, he wrote to her:

"Lucy dear, however this great crisis may eventuate, whether it result, as I hope and believe, in our assumption of new duties and cares, or whether in leaving me alone in this strange, uncongenial world, I will try to meet my responsibilities worthily and well. Dearest, you have made me very happy, in spite of surface cares and excitements, in feeling for you a love and esteem such as you may well prize from your husband. You have ennobled my life. . . . I hope to be yours always and forever. If God give me the great privilege and honor and blessing of your personal society, I will try to show my gratitude by living nobly in act and thought. If otherwise, I will stay in the world, awaiting the reunion — longing to join you, and working for the great cause of human progress, which you have helped, with all the ability which I possess. . . .

"And if, from beyond the grave, it be indeed permitted to influence and inspire, dear Lucy, you shall always find an open heart and an expectant longing.

"My own love, what can I say to comfort you in your lonely sufferings? I know of nothing better than to promise to live bravely and honestly, and to subject mere material aims to loftier purposes."

While he was on a visit home, their daughter Alice was born, on September 14, 1857. The question of a surname for her came up soon after. He said to her mother: "It is you and not I who have suffered to bring this child into the world, and if you want her to be called by your name and not mine, I am willing." But she thought that a child should bear the names of both parents.

Mr. Blackwell went West again, and in his absence she let her household goods be sold for taxes, as a protest against taxation without representation. The cottage in Orange stood in her name.

Notice of the sale was posted at the railroad station, and on January 22, 1858, it took place. A newspaper account mentions, among the articles carried out of the house on to the piazza to be sold, a table and two steel-plate engravings, one a portrait of Salmon P. Chase, the other of William Lloyd Garrison. According to family tradition, little Alice's cradle was also taken. The articles were bought in by a friendly neighbor, Rowland Johnson, and returned to Mrs. Stone.

This tax protest had wide publicity. Mr. Higginson wrote:

"Dear Lucy: I congratulate you on doing what I have often wished to be a woman that I might do. The effect of a multiplication of such protests would be great. The selection of those portraits will be so melodramatic for your biography that I suspect you of having bribed the sheriff to seize them. Well, 'Take joyfully the spoiling of your goods!'"

Fifty-seven years later, in 1915, a thousand suffragists crowded into the yard of the little house in Orange to see the unveiling of the tablet in honor of Lucy Stone's tax protest. The locality had changed. The house is now shut in by ugly buildings, and the hot sun beat down on the shadeless yard, but the crowd stood attentively through the ceremony. Lucy Stone's daughter unveiled the tablet, which is of bronze, and bears an inscription composed by Oswald Garrison Villard:

"In 1858 Lucy Stone, a noble pioneer in the emancipation of women, here first protested against their taxation without representation in New Jersey."

Mr. Blackwell succeeded in introducing fifteen hundred Farmers' Libraries into the school districts of Illinois. While there, he met Abraham Lincoln for the first and only time. He wrote: "Mr. Powell (the State Superintendent of Public Instruction) and I being in Springfield, Mr. Powell wanted to consult him on some law point connected with our libraries. We found him as he was coming out of the court-house with his law-books under his arm — a tall, middle-aged man, with kind eyes, and a frank, quiet manner, who impressed one with sincerity, sense and benevolence."

Mrs. Stone and the baby afterwards joined him and made their headquarters at Evanston. Later Mr. Blackwell opened real estate offices in Orange and New York, and dealt in real estate for some years, trading off his Western lands as opportunity offered. In the morning, while he kept office hours in New York, Mrs. Stone took their little daughter with her and kept the Orange office.

Mrs. Stone always found it easier to speak than to write. With Miss Anthony, in the early years, the opposite was the case. Generally Mrs. Stanton, who was kept much at home by her young family, wrote the speeches, and Miss Anthony read them. Lucy encouraged her to compose her own speeches and to deliver them without manuscript. She wrote to her in 1857:

"You ought to cultivate your power of expression. The subject is clear to you, and you ought to be able to make it so to others. It is only a few years ago that Mr. Higginson told me he could not speak, he was so much accustomed to writing, and now he is second only to Phillips. 'Go thou and do likewise.' You will have to be the president, doubtless, and must have an opening speech."

Miss Anthony did not like to have the suffrage lecturers fall in love and marry. When Lucy got engaged, Miss Anthony called her "a little dunce", because she treasured a pile of her lover's letters; and when Antoinette Brown also became engaged, Miss Anthony wrote to Ellen Blackwell, "Antoinette has become another little dunce."

She wrote to Antoinette, April 22, 1858:

"I am provoked at Lucy. Just to think that she will attempt to speak in a course with such intellects as Brady, Curtis and Chapin, and then, as her special preparation, take upon herself, in addition to baby cares — quite too absorbing for careful, close and continued intellectual effort — the entire work of her house! A woman who is, and must of necessity continue, for the present at least, the representative woman, has no right to disqualify herself for such a representative occasion. I do feel that it is so foolish for her to put herself in the position of maid of all work and baby-tender! What man would dream of going before the public on such an occasion, night tired and worn by such a multitude of engrossing cares? It is not best to have too many irons in the fire at one time.

"I have just returned from Mrs. Stanton's. She is consoling herself that she is doing the work of rearing for the world six of Mr. Higginson's model saints, versus bodies. She is preparing a history of the rise and progress of the Woman's Rights Movement, which, if I am President, as Lucy says I must be, I am going to read to the Convention."

Neither mobs nor matrimony had been able to "shut up the mouth of Lucy Stone", but mother love did it, for a time. In her, the maternal instinct was very strong and deep. A mishap or two that befell the baby, in the hands of a little nursemaid, while she was away lecturing, led her to announce that she would do no more lecturing while Alice was small, but would take care of her child herself. She wrote to Antoinette:

"I wish I felt the old impulse and power to lecture, both for the sake of cherished principles and to help Harry with the heavy burden he has to bear; but I am afraid, and dare not trust Lucy Stone. I went to hear E. P. Whipple lecture on Joan of Arc. It was very inspiring, and for the hour I felt as though all things were possible to me. But when I came home and looked at Alice's sleeping face, and thought of the possible evil that might befall her if my guardian eye was turned away, I shrank like a snail into its shell, and saw that, for these years, I can be only a mother — no trivial thing, either."

For two or three years, she spoke at few meetings. Then came the Civil War and put a stop, for the time being, to the agitation for woman's rights. Between 1860 and 1866, no woman's rights conventions were held. When the war was over, her little girl was old enough to be left, and she resumed her public work with her old eloquence and zeal.

During the war, she scraped lint for the wounded and helped in other ways. She presided at the great meeting that launched the Loyal League, and coöperated with Miss Anthony in its work, while it rolled up huge petitions for emancipation. But she never forgot to work for the women, both collectively and individually.

During her early married life in New Jersey, an old colored woman had been bullied by her husband into mortgaging her land, which was her only property. The mortgage was foreclosed. Mrs. Stone expressed her intention of attending the auction and trying to buy in the land for the old woman. She was told that it would be useless, as the Jews would be there, and a Jew could not be induced to give up a good bargain. She answered that a Jew was human, like any one else, and that, at all events, she meant to try. A number of Jews attended the sale, and not Jews of the best sort. She asked leave to say a few words before the bidding began. She explained the circumstances and asked to be allowed to buy in the land for the poor woman. Not a Jew bid, and she was allowed to buy in the land for the exact amount of the mortgage, which was much below its value.

The war was a sad time for Mrs. Stone, as for thousands of others. Its whole atmosphere of bloodshed and political corruption was alien to her, and intensified her sense of the wrong of shutting women out from the franchise. She said the government could take any mother's son away to be shot, "and afterwards put its bloody hand in her pocket to help pay the bills."

At the close of the war, the question of reconstruction came to the fore.

The Fourteenth Amendment to the United States Constitution proposed to guarantee to all citizens, irrespective of color, the equal rights, privileges and immunities of citizens. It also provided that, whenever suffrage was denied by a State to any class of its male citizens, the disfranchised citizens should be no longer counted in the basis of representation. This Amendment for the first time introduced the word "male" into the Federal Constitution.

Mrs. Stone went to Washington with her husband and pleaded with Charles Sumner, who had charge of the Amendment, to leave that word out. He answered, "I sat up all one night, and rewrote that clause of the Amendment fourteen times, so unwilling was I to introduce the word 'male' into the Constitution; but I could in no other way embody my meaning."

When the Fifteenth Amendment was pending, they went again to Washington, in the hottest weather, and secured the signatures of a number of members of Congress to an appeal to widen the Amendment so as to include women; but in vain.

In early New Jersey, where the Quaker influence was strong, women and Negroes had voted on a property qualification; but both had been excluded by the constitution of 1807. Mrs. Stone petitioned the New Jersey Legislature that, in restoring suffrage to the Negro men, the women also might be reënfranchised. A hearing was given her, and her address made a deep impression, but her appeal was refused.

The Eleventh National Woman's Rights Convention, held in New York in May, 1866, voted to resolve itself into the American Equal Rights Association, to work for equal suffrage for both women and Negroes. Lucretia Mott was chosen president, Mr. Blackwell recording secretary, and Mrs. Stone was on the executive committee. Mr. Blackwell arranged a number of conventions in New Jersey in 1867, under the auspices of the American Equal Rights Association, where he and his wife and sometimes others spoke. One series of conventions was held in towns on the railroads, another in places that had to be reached by stage.

In Princeton their meeting was mobbed and broken up by the students, who were mostly "copperheads." In the same year the New Jersey Woman Suffrage Association was organized, with Mrs. Stone as president.

Mr. Blackwell engaged in several different lines of business, steadily improving his financial position. The family lived for a few years in West Bloomfield (now Montclair) and enjoyed the beautiful scenery of the Orange Mountains. Sometimes they drove over to see Mrs. Stanton. Sometimes Horace Greeley dropped in for a chat and gave them advice about their garden and orchard. They spent a winter or two in New York and lived for seven years in Roseville, New Jersey. Here Mrs. Stone and her mother-in-law went to the polls and offered their votes, which of course were not accepted.

Lucy had hoped for a large family, but this hope was disappointed. All her wealth of deep maternal tenderness was poured out upon her one little daughter. But it was not a blind and unreasoning love, such as makes some mothers side with their own offspring, right or wrong. She was even more anxious that I should do right by everybody than that everybody should do right by me. As a child, if I got into trouble with any one, there was strict and close inquiry, and if I had been in the wrong, I had to make apology and reparation. For two things I have always been thankful — that my mother nursed me at her own breast, and that she made me mind. She nourished me with her soul as well as with her milk.

My father was not a disciplinarian, but he was the merriest and most delightful of comrades. All children adored him. He could spin fairy tales fully equal to "Alice in Wonderland", making them up as he went along, with an unfailing flow of imagination. Some were serials and ran for months. He was a man of wide reading and large intelligence. To live with him was a liberal education.

In 1868, while still residents of New Jersey, they came on to Boston and took part in organizing the New England Woman Suffrage Association, with Julia Ward Howe as president. Her social and literary prestige brought a new impetus to the movement. Mrs. Stone recalled on her deathbed the happiness it gave her when Mrs. Howe accepted the presidency. The New England was the first to be formed of all the large Suffrage Associations. It was for many years a very strong and active society. At its great May Festivals in Anniversary Week, a thousand persons sometimes sat down to table, and the after-dinner speaking was exceptionally brilliant. It organized most of the State Suffrage Associations of New England. At one of its first executive meetings, it urged

Mrs. Stone and Mr. Blackwell to return to the work in Massachusetts. In 1869 they moved to Boston, and in 1870 took an active part in forming the Massachusetts Woman Suffrage Association.

## *Chapter XV*

Events were impending that led to a serious split among the suffragists. The facts hitherto have been largely suppressed. Now they can be told. Both the race question and the sex question entered into the causes of disagreement. Those who are not interested in the history of the woman suffrage movement should skip this chapter.

The Kansas Legislature submitted two amendments to the State constitution, one to strike out the word "white", the other to strike out the word "male." Ex-Governor Robinson of Kansas, whose sister had married Mrs. Stone's brother, and the Honorable Samuel N. Wood, a prominent Republican politician, wrote to the Eastern suffragists, asking them to make a campaign in Kansas for the amendments.

Mrs. Stone's interest in Kansas was of long standing. In 1855 Sam Wood had asked her for the draft of a married woman's property rights bill for the new State, and he secured the adoption of the form of law that she sent him, with hardly the change of a word. She had also furnished, by request, the draft of the equal guardianship law passed by Kansas in 1862, the first in the Union. Her friendly connection with the State was an asset in the campaign.

She and Mr. Blackwell went out to Kansas when the spring of 1867 opened, leaving their daughter in the care of the Doctors Blackwell. They took part in a convention in Topeka which formed the Kansas Impartial Suffrage Association, and afterwards held meetings in every organized county in the State, with overflowing audiences. Mrs. Helen Ekin Starret says in her reminiscences: "Hon. S. N. Wood gave his whole time to the canvass, speaking with Lucy Stone and Mr. Blackwell in nearly all the towns in the western and northern parts of the State. There were no railroads, and it was at an immense expense of bodily fatigue that they accomplished their journeys, often in the rudest conveyances, and exposed to the raw, blustering winds of a Kansas spring. Their meetings, however, were ovations." Sam Wood telegraphed to the annual meeting of the American Equal Rights Association in New York on May 10: "With the help of God and Lucy Stone, we shall carry Kansas."[1]

After two months' work, Mrs. Stone and Mr. Blackwell came home feeling much encouraged.

[1] A number of letters from Mrs. Stone and Mr. Blackwell, written during the Kansas campaign, are given in the History of Woman Suffrage, Vol. 2, pp. 232–239.

They had paid their own expenses during the campaign, except as Kansas friends furnished local transportation; and Mrs. Stone afterwards raised money to enable the Reverend Olympia Brown to go out to Kansas and continue the work. Prospects looked bright. But there were snags beneath the surface, of which the Eastern suffragists knew little or nothing. After the Civil War, the Democratic party in Kansas had been almost wiped out; but the Republicans were split into factions, and there was great jealousy between ex-Governor Robinson's faction and that of "Jem" Lane, whose recent death had given him a halo of martyrdom. In 1867 the Lane machine was in control of the State.

From the first, the two amendments had injured each other. Many persons wished to concentrate on the Negroes and drop the women. When Mrs. Stanton and Miss Anthony arrived in September, they found the Republicans much divided. Governor Robinson toured the State with Mrs. Stanton, and many other prominent Republicans stood by the women; but the dominant Republican machine aligned itself definitely against woman suffrage. Then Miss Anthony invited George Francis Train to come and try to win the Democratic vote, he promising to pay the expenses of the meetings. This action had not been authorized by the Executive Committee of the American

Equal Rights Association. While meant for the best, it was a very serious mistake.

Mr. Train was a man of wealth, but so erratic that he was for a time shut up in a lunatic asylum as actually insane. His egotism and eccentricities had led him into all sorts of extravagant absurdities, and made him an object of general ridicule. He had nominated himself for President of the United States and urged his claims to election on all occasions. The general public looked upon the idea of woman suffrage as ridiculous, and it was highly undesirable to associate it with anything really ridiculous, like Mr. Train and his presidential aspirations. In addition, he was a virulent "copperhead", and represented in his own person everything against which the progressive elements in Kansas had been waging war.

When the Eastern papers announced that this fantastic personage was speaking for woman suffrage in Kansas, Mrs. Stone thought the report was a monstrous hoax, invented by the enemy. When she found that his meetings were actually being advertised as held under the auspices of the American Equal Rights Association, she felt constrained to publish a card explaining that the Association was not responsible.

Mr. Train drew large crowds, and his buffoonery tickled the rabble, but disgusted persons of sense. In the opinion of the best friends of the cause in

Kansas, he did much more harm than good. Both amendments were heavily defeated. In a vote of about thirty thousand, Negro suffrage got 10,843 votes, and woman suffrage 9,070.

Afterwards Mrs. Stanton and Miss Anthony held a series of public meetings with Mr. Train through the principal cities of the country, they advocating woman suffrage and he advocating his own election as President.

Mr. Train and David M. Melis, the financial editor of the Democratic *New York World*, furnished the money to start the *Revolution* in January, 1868, with Mrs. Stanton and Parker Pillsbury as editors and Miss Anthony as owner and business manager. It was agreed that "Mr. Train and Mr. Melis were to use such space as they desired for expressing their financial and other opinions."

In the *Revolution*, the often excellent and brilliant editorials of Mrs. Stanton and Mr. Pillsbury on woman's rights came out side by side with the insane ravings of Mr. Train, his presentations of his claims to the presidency, etc. At this time, at the close of the Civil War, the Republican party was all powerful, the Democrats very few and intensely unpopular. The *Revolution* constantly and vehemently assailed the Republican party, to which the vast majority of the suffragists belonged, and which at that time really was the party of progress. The *Revolution* also advocated an inconvertible paper currency, the prohibition of foreign manufactures, "America against Europe", and other peculiar theories.

A woman suffrage paper was needed, but many of the suffragists thought it would have been better to wait than to start one so loaded down with extraneous issues. Wendell Phillips felt so strongly on the subject that he would not allow an advertisement of the *Revolution* to appear in his paper, the *Anti-Slavery Standard*, for love or money. Miss Anthony wrote in her diary on January 1, 1868, in regard to the alliance with Mr. Train: "All the old friends, with scarce an exception, are sure we are wrong. Only time can tell, but I believe we are right." The following letter from William Lloyd Garrison expressed the general sentiment:

"Jan. 4, 1868.

"Dear Miss Anthony:

"In all friendliness, and with the highest regard for the woman's rights movement, I cannot refrain from expressing my regret and astonishment that you and Mrs. Stanton should have taken such leave of good sense as to be travelling companions and associate lecturers with that crack-brained harlequin and semi-lunatic, George Francis Train. You may, if you choose, denounce Henry Ward Beecher and Wendell Phillips (the two ablest advocates of women's rights on this side of the

Atlantic), and swap them off for the nondescript Train; but in thus doing, you will only subject yourselves to merited ridicule and condemnation, and turn the movement which you aim to promote into unnecessary contempt. The nomination of this ranting egotist and low blackguard for the presidency, by your audiences, shows that he is regarded by those who listen to him as on a par with poor demented Mellen, and Daniel Pratt, 'the Great American Traveller.'

"The colored people and their advocates have not a more abusive assailant than this same Train, especially when he has an Irish audience before him, to whom he delights to ring the changes upon 'nigger, nigger, nigger', ad nauseam. He is as destitute of principle as he is of sense, and is fast gravitating toward a lunatic asylum. He may be of use in drawing an audience, but so would a kangaroo, a gorilla or a hippopotamus. . . .

"Your old, outspoken friend,

"William Lloyd Garrison."

This letter had not been written for publication; but it was printed in the *Revolution* of January 29, 1868, with an editorial ridiculing Mr. Garrison and praising Mr. Train.

The Fifteenth Amendment to the United States Constitution proposed to forbid disfranchisement on account of "race, color or previous condition of servitude." The suffragists were divided into three parties in regard to the Amendment: (1), those who thought it unwise to try to incorporate woman suffrage in it; (2), those who thought that every effort should be made to include the women, but that, if this proved impossible, the Amendment ought nevertheless to pass; and (3), those who thought that, if it could not be widened to include the women, it ought to be defeated. Charles Sumner and many of the old guard of the abolitionists belonged to the first group, Mrs. Stone and Mr. Blackwell to the second, and Mrs. Stanton and Miss Anthony to the third.

To those of us who believe that suffrage ought not to be conditioned upon race or color, it must be fairly evident, at this distance of time, that Sumner and the abolitionists were right. A combination of circumstances had brought about a situation in which it was possible to wipe out race discrimination in suffrage in the National Constitution. It was not yet possible to wipe out sex discrimination. To unite the two things in one amendment would simply have been to defeat both. Later, when the States, one after another, were enfranchising women by State constitutional amendments, we should have thought it an unpardonable mistake in tactics to incorporate in the same amendment with woman suffrage any other innovation, no matter how just, to which there was strong popular objection.

Mrs. Stone, Mrs. Stanton and Miss Anthony all did their utmost to get the women included, and were acutely grieved when they failed. There, however, they parted company. Mrs. Stone said that it was a dreadful condition of powerlessness and helplessness to be disfranchised, and that she would not lift a hand to keep the Negro from getting out of "that terrible pit." Mrs. Stanton and Miss Anthony could not bear the idea of "boosting the Negro over their own heads." They joined hands with the Democrats and worked with all their might to defeat the Amendment.

The annual meeting of the American Equal Rights Association held in New York in May, 1869, was stormy. There were various causes of disagreement, but the subject upon which feeling ran highest was the attitude of the editors of the *Revolution* in regard to George Francis Train and the Fifteenth Amendment. The party opposed to the course taken by the *Revolution* had a large majority in the convention, and a majority of the newly elected Executive Committee, as of the out-going one, was also opposed to its policies. Resolutions in accordance with the opinion of the majority were adopted, and the meeting adjourned.

On the evening of the following day, the leaders of the minority party, who had been defeated in the convention, organized the so-called National Woman Suffrage Association, at a reunion in the house where the *Revolution* had its office. No public notice had been given that a Suffrage Association was to be formed on this occasion, and no public call had been issued for the friends of woman suffrage to meet at that time and place to form one. Prominent suffragists even in the immediate neighborhood knew nothing about it until it was over.

The society thus formed proceeded to hold weekly meetings in New York City, which were advertised both in the *Revolution* and in the daily papers as meetings of the "National Woman Suffrage Association", although it was obvious that no association really national could meet every week in the same city. At these meetings, resolutions on the subjects about which difference of feeling ran highest among the suffragists were passed, expressing views directly contrary to those of the majority; and these resolutions were sent out broadcast through the press as resolutions adopted by the "National Woman Suffrage Association." There was much dissatisfaction, and the feeling grew that a really national association was needed.

The Executive Committee of the New England Woman Suffrage Association appointed Lucy Stone, T. W. Higginson, Caroline M. Severance,

Julia Ward Howe and George H. Vibbert a committee of correspondence to confer with suffragists throughout the country in regard to forming a representative association on a delegate basis. The response was wide and general. A Call for the formation of an American Woman Suffrage Association was issued, signed by one hundred and ten active suffragists living in twenty-two States and Territories. The names included a large proportion of the men and women who had been most distinguished in the work for equal rights. After ample public notice, a convention, open on equal terms to all suffragists, was held at Cleveland, Ohio, on November 24, 1869, and the American Woman Suffrage Association was organized, with Henry Ward Beecher as president, and a strong and influential list of officers. It was nonsectarian and nonpartisan.[1]

Meanwhile the divorce question had begun to arouse lively discussion. The suffragists were of all shades of opinion in regard to it, most of them conservative. As the divorce laws were the same for men and women, the American Woman Suffrage Association held that the question whether divorce should be made easier did not properly come within

[1] The *Woman's Journal* of April 9, 1870, contained a history of the causes that led to the original division, written by William Lloyd Garrison and signed by him, Julia Ward Howe, Mary A. Livermore and Mr. Blackwell.

the scope of a Suffrage Association. Mrs. Stanton, the president of the National, was a strong believer in easy divorce, and held that its advocacy should be a part of the Suffrage Association's program. She herself advocated it on all occasions, on the suffrage platform as well as elsewhere, and most of the group associated with her held similar views. In believing in easy divorce, Mrs. Stanton, in my opinion, was right; but she was wrong in trying to make it a part of the program of the Suffrage Association.

Theodore Tilton sought to bring the two associations together under himself as president. He was a brilliant man, but lacking in balance and principle. Soon after this, he became a great admirer of Victoria C. Woodhull and wrote an extravagantly eulogistic biography of her. He said he believed in making divorce so easy that people could contract a new marriage every day if they wished.

At Mr. Tilton's request, a conference was held between three delegates from the American, three from the National, and three from those who had called the conference. He recommended that the two societies unite under the name of the Union Woman Suffrage Association, and read a proposed constitution for it, by which the annual meeting was always to be held in New York City, and every one paying a dollar was to have a vote. The

American, on the other hand, believed strongly in a delegate basis and a movable annual meeting. Its representatives were unanimous that it was not best to go into a union on the proposed terms. After they had left, the six persons remaining organized themselves into a "Union Woman Suffrage Association", adopted the proposed constitution, and elected Mr. Tilton president. The National Woman Suffrage Association voted to merge itself into the Union Association, and appointed a committee to arrange with a similar committee of the American for a union, if such a committee should be appointed.

The old American Equal Rights Association was now practically disrupted, the majority of its members having gone into the American Woman Suffrage Association and the minority into the National Woman Suffrage Association. That part of its object which related to the enfranchisement of the Negroes had been attained by the adoption of the Fifteenth Amendment, and that part which related to the women was covered by the two Suffrage Associations.

The Executive Committee of the Equal Rights Association voted unanimously that it was best to dissolve it, and appointed a business meeting of the society to act on the proposal. It was expected to be merely a perfunctory meeting, to pass a formal vote of dissolution. Very little interest was felt in it, and few attended. Mrs. Stone and Mr. Blackwell happened to be the only members present from what had been the majority party. The enterprising Mr. Tilton, however, brought to the meeting a number of the members who believed in making easy divorce a part of the program of the Suffrage Association, with some other persons who had never been members, but whose fees he paid on this occasion to enable them to vote; and they voted to merge the American Equal Rights Association into the Union Woman Suffrage Association. The American Equal Rights Association had several hundred members. There were present at this meeting just twenty persons, including those who joined for the purpose of giving this vote.[1]

No member of the Committee on Conference appointed by the Union Woman Suffrage Association attended the second annual meeting of the American Woman Suffrage Association, held at Cleveland in November, 1870, but Miss Anthony did. She made a speech warmly defending Mrs. Stanton's views on divorce, and, in the excitement of the moment, she asserted that Mrs. Stone and

[1] The secretary of the old Equal Rights Association pointed out, in the *Woman's Journal* of May 28, 1870, that the action taken was entirely unconstitutional, as the constitution required thirty days' notice of any change, and notice had been given of a proposal to dissolve the Association, but none of a proposal to merge it. The point was not worth disputing, however, as the old Equal Rights Association was practically dead.

Mr. Blackwell were not legally married. Colonel Higginson, who was presiding, said that he could testify to the contrary from his own knowledge, since he had himself married them; and Miss Anthony immediately retracted and apologized. But the incident irritated the convention and lessened the already small chance of union. The proposal to appoint a committee to confer in regard to a union was voted down, one hundred and twelve to forty-seven. Colonel Higginson, in the *Woman's Journal* of December 3, 1870, said several factors combined to defeat it: the letters received from Lydia Maria Child, Julia Ward Howe, and others, advising against a union; the indiscretion committed by Miss Anthony; and, above all, the reading of an editorial from the *Revolution*, written by Mrs. Laura Curtis Bullard. It asserted that woman suffrage as a political movement was dead, and added:

"Women know their own wants, and they know that they do not want suffrage a thousandth part as keenly as they want a reform of the marriage and divorce laws, and a general readjustment of the family relations. . . . What a woman wants is freedom to marry, and to be mistress of herself after marriage; freedom to freely sunder a yoke she has freely bound."

As George William Curtis had said in *Harper's Weekly*, in advance of the convention, the radical difference of opinion between the two associations as to the proper scope of the woman suffrage movement made union impossible.

The Union Woman Suffrage Association languished for a time and finally went to pieces. Mrs. Stanton, Miss Anthony and the group of women associated with them worked for a while under the name of the National Woman Suffrage Committee and then resumed the name of the National Woman Suffrage Association.

Meantime the partnership with Mr. Train had ended disastrously. He became absorbed in other interests, went abroad without providing for the maintenance of the *Revolution*, took part in one of the Fenian disturbances in Ireland, and was imprisoned. Miss Anthony was obliged to part with the paper and was left with a debt of ten thousand dollars for its expenses. This she paid off honorably, by hard work in the lecture field.

A sharper cause of disagreement arose between the American and National wings of the movement soon after when the leaders of the National took up Victoria C. Woodhull with enthusiasm. They gave her great prominence at their meetings; and she became the chief bone of contention between the two societies.

Mrs. Woodhull and her sister, Miss Tennessee Claflin, had been clairvoyant physicians. At this time, they were conducting a brokers' office on

Wall Street, New York, under the patronage of Cornelius Vanderbilt. Mrs. Woodhull was a Spiritualist, an eloquent speaker, and claimed to be controlled by the spirit of Demosthenes. The sisters were women of licentious lives. They preached free love in their paper, *Woodhull and Claflin's Weekly*, and also practised it. Emanie Sachs, in her biography of Mrs. Woodhull, entitled "The Terrible Siren", goes into detail on this subject. Their paper advocated some good things, as well as others that were very bad; but the bad ones were those that chiefly impressed the public. One of their statements often quoted was, "A woman has a right to take a new lover every day if she chooses."

Stephen Pearl Andrews, their associate in the conduct of the paper, advocated in its columns the most fantastic theories of the relations between the sexes, — as, for instance, that the best way to improve the human race would be to select a few of the finest men to be the fathers of all women's children, as a few of the finest stallions become the sires of innumerable foals. He argued against monogamy on all occasions. He compared the lifelong union of one congenial man and woman to the continual striking of two accordant notes in music, harmonious but monotonous; and declared that the best results required "variation and compound harmony."

By announcing herself as a candidate for President of the United States, and by other skillful methods of advertising, Mrs. Woodhull kept herself very much before the public. For a time there was no woman in America who was so much talked about, and none who was regarded with so much abhorrence by almost all decent people. To the general public, from one end of the country to the other, her name became a synonym for lawless licentiousness.

Mrs. Stanton and Miss Anthony had a generous but wrong-headed tendency to take up the cudgels for any woman who happened to be under fire, right or wrong. They were delighted with the argument put forward by Mrs. Woodhull, claiming that women already had the right to vote under the Fourteenth Amendment — a claim which the American Woman Suffrage Association believed to be untenable, and which was afterwards ruled out by the United States Supreme Court. They were also charmed with her personally. Miss Anthony said, "Mrs. Woodhull has youth, beauty and money, and youth, beauty and money are what we want." She wrote to her: "Go on doing, bright, glorious, young and strong spirit, and believe in the best love and hope and faith of S. B. Anthony."

Mrs. Stanton, president of the National Woman Suffrage Association, in a letter to Theodore

Tilton's paper, the *Golden Age*, copied in full in *Woodhull and Claflin's Weekly* for December 16, 1871, said that she was receiving many letters asking her to explain the difference between the two Suffrage Associations, and that, as she had not time to answer them separately, she would do so through the *Golden Age*. After explaining that the National claimed that women already had the right to vote under the Fourteenth Amendment, while the American asked for a Sixteenth Amendment, she added:

"Some people carp at the National organization because it endorses Mrs. Woodhull. When our representatives at Washington granted to Victoria C. Woodhull a hearing before the Judiciary Committee of both houses — an honor conferred on no other woman in the nation before — they recognized Mrs. Woodhull as the leader of the suffrage movement in this country. And those of us who were convinced by her unanswerable arguments that her position was sound, had no choice but to follow. Mrs. Woodhull's speeches and writings on all the great questions of national life are beyond anything yet produced by man or woman on our platform."

Mrs. Stanton went on to give Mrs. Woodhull further glowing praise, and laid it down as a principle that no more questions ought to be asked as to the morals of women who were willing to make speeches for suffrage than would be asked in wartime about the morals of men who were willing to fight for the flag.

The opposition had always declared that woman suffrage meant free love. The most innocent utterances of its advocates were often twisted and misinterpreted in this sense. When Mrs. Woodhull, the standard bearer of the free-love movement, was enthusiastically taken up by a few prominent suffragists, the public looked upon the accusation that woman suffrage meant free love as conclusively proved and visibly demonstrated. This was in the Victorian era, and the effect upon the movement was devastating. The cause was overwhelmed with a weight of odium which took many years to wear away.

Miss Anthony had by far the strongest common sense among the small group of suffragists who had allied themselves with Mrs. Woodhull, and she was the first to see that Mrs. Woodhull must be dropped. In the spring of 1872, although Mrs. Stanton and Mrs. Isabella Beecher Hooker called her "narrow, bigoted and headstrong", she refused to let the National Woman Suffrage Association unite with Mrs. Woodhull in holding a convention to form a new political party; and when Mrs. Woodhull came to the suffrage convention and insisted upon speaking, and offered a motion looking toward the formation of a new party, Miss

Anthony declared the meeting adjourned, and ordered the janitor to turn out the lights. Other officers of the National continued to champion Mrs. Woodhull for a little while longer, but all finally became convinced that it was best to have no more to do with her. Long before that, however, the harm was done.

The great majority of the suffragists were always opposed to the alliance with Mrs. Woodhull, as they had been opposed to the alliance with Mr. Train. During the two years after the American and the National Woman Suffrage Associations were formed, thirteen State Suffrage Associations became auxiliary to the American, while only two became auxiliary to the National; and, of those two, one severed its connection within a year. The controversy was often spoken of as a disagreement between New England and New York; but it was really a disagreement between a part of New York and almost all the rest of the country.[1]

The authors of the early volumes of the "History of Woman Suffrage" (Mrs. Stanton, Miss Anthony and Mrs. Matilda Josslyn Gage) were all warm partisans of the National, and the "History" is, naturally, somewhat one-sided. It gives no explanation of the causes that led to the division, but merely says: "During the autumn of this year [1869] there was a secession from our ranks, and

[1] See Appendix, Note 3.

the preliminary steps were taken for another organization. Aside from the divisions growing out of a difference of opinion on the Amendments, there were some personal hostilities among the leaders of the movement that culminated in two Societies."[1] The account of the efforts for union, as given in the "History", is wholly *ex parte*.

Mrs. Stone was the last person to be influenced by any petty motives in connection with the woman's rights movement. With her, the cause not only stood first, but overshadowed everything else. When the National came to hold a convention in Boston, she said fervently, in the bosom of her family, "Oh, I do hope they will have a good meeting!" Her great wish was that converts to woman suffrage should be made, whoever made them. Her grief over the early indiscretions of the National was because they hindered the making of converts.

When the "History of Woman Suffrage" came out, with its one-sided account of the division, many persons thought that the *Woman's Journal* ought to state the facts. But to do so would have been to put weapons into the hands of the enemy. Mrs. Stone refused, because she did not wish to remind the public that any suffragists had ever done the unwise things of which the National had been guilty. During the many years in which the two

[1] "History of Woman Suffrage", Vol. 2, page 406.

nation-wide associations were competing for the support of the suffragists, she would neither do it nor allow it to be done. She wanted that whole unfortunate episode to be forgotten as soon as possible. Women who had been aggressive in their endorsement of Mrs. Woodhull denied afterwards that they ever had endorsed her, and represented it as a malicious calumny; and so many malicious calumnies had been heaped upon the suffragists that it was easy for the younger generation, who did not remember the facts, to believe that this was one of them.

For many years, the two associations went their separate way. The National worked chiefly for Congressional action, the American chiefly for the granting of equal suffrage by the States. Conventions in Washington and Congressional hearings were useful for agitation and education; but it was only after the movement had built up a considerable group of woman suffrage States, where the women could vote in national elections, that the subject got serious consideration in Congress, and that the submission of a nation-wide amendment became possible.

Twenty years after the division, the two societies united again as the National American Woman Suffrage Association. The methods of the National, as time passed on, had gradually lost the characteristics that had aroused so much objection in its early years. The question of easy divorce was no longer pressed at its meetings. At the root of all the differences in the Train and Woodhull days lay the conviction on the part of the American Association that persons of conspicuous absurdity or of notorious immorality ought not to be invited to speak at suffrage meetings. The leaders of the National Association had fully come around to that view. There was no longer any good reason for continuing two associations.

When I began to work for a union, the elders were not keen for it, on either side, but the younger women on both sides were. Nothing really stood in the way except the unpleasant feelings engendered during the long separation, and those could be overcome, and were overcome, for the good of the cause to which both sides were sincerely devoted.[1]

The American had all along stood for a delegate basis and a movable annual meeting. The National was ready to concede a delegate basis, and, when once that was adopted, an annual meeting made up of delegates from all parts of the country soon voted for the movable annual convention.

The union strengthened the movement, and such divisions of opinion as arose afterwards were mainly along new lines, not the old. One incident

[1] See Appendix, Note 4.

happened, however, which was like a revival, in a milder form, of an old controversy.

Mrs. Stanton was really more interested in attacking orthodox religion than in promoting equal rights for women. In the early woman's rights conventions, she had loved to introduce some ultra-radical resolution that she knew could not pass, and it amused her to watch the fluttering in the dove cotes that followed. The fact that such a resolution had been offered was always used as a cudgel afterwards by the enemy.

In 1896 she brought out the so-called "Woman's Bible", a commentary on the Scriptures prepared by herself and a committee of her friends, written, of course, from a highly unorthodox standpoint. It greatly scandalized the church people. At the National Convention the following resolution was offered:

"That this Association is non-sectarian, being composed of persons of all shades of religious opinion, and has no official connection with the so-called 'Woman's Bible' or any theological publication."

Women who had done organizing in different parts of the country stood up in the convention and told how much their work had been hindered by the belief that the "Woman's Bible" represented the Association; and, after a long and lively debate, the resolution was carried. Mrs. Stanton and Miss Anthony were so much displeased that they at first determined to resign from the Suffrage Association, but, upon reflection, thought better of it.

Six years after Mrs. Stone's death, the official biography of Miss Anthony[1] appeared. Like the "History of Woman Suffrage", it omitted to state the reasons that led to the formation of the American Woman Suffrage Association, and implied throughout that it was a causeless division, due chiefly to personal motives. Then Mr. Blackwell published the facts, substantially as they are given here, in the *Woman's Journal* of March 11, 1899. In a friendly letter, he offered Miss Anthony free access to the columns of the *Journal*, if she wished to take exception to anything that had been said; but no correction was sent. The main facts were beyond dispute.

[1] "The Life and Work of Susan B. Anthony", by Ida Husted Harper.

## *Chapter XVI*

With the removal to Massachusetts, their family life entered upon a new phase. Mr. Blackwell had now accumulated a competence and was able to devote himself fully to the progressive causes which he had always had at heart.

Chiefly for the sake of its magnificent view, he and his wife bought a house on Pope's Hill in Dorchester, overlooking Boston Harbor, and commanding, on the south and southwest, the Neponset River and the Blue Hills of Milton. This beautiful home, with its wide outlook, its spacious grounds, its flowers and fruit and shade trees, became a Mecca to suffragists from all parts of the world. Many distinguished men and women were entertained there; and at Christmas, Thanksgiving and other festivals, the party generally included some of the many young men and women who were studying in and near Boston, far away from home. Professor Ellen Hayes of Wellesley said that whenever she went there, she longed to take five hundred Wellesley College girls with her, in order to show them what an equal-rights home could be.

Mrs. Stone was fully competent to supervise the horse and cow and poultry, and the large vegetable garden. She once said, "There was a good farmer spoiled when I went into reform." There was always a certain country strength and simplicity about her. To a grandniece living on a farm she offered a present of a new gown if she would learn to milk a cow. She said, "I consider it an accomplishment."

She was an admirable housekeeper, of the old New England type. She dried all the herbs and put up all the fruits in their season. She made her own yeast, her own bread, her own dried beef, even her own soap. She always thought the home-made soap was better than any she could buy. She was an accomplished cook, and her family were never better fed than during the occasional intervals between servants.

She was the most motherly of women. She was attracted by all children, dirty or clean, pretty or ugly. Her face always beamed at the sight of a baby; and on countless occasions, on boat or train, during her lecture trips, she helped some worried and anxious young mother to care for and quiet a crying child.

If she started home from a meeting, carrying flowers that had been given her, they were almost always begged away from her by the children in the poor streets that then led to the South Station.

Often when she started for her office she carried a load of flowers from her own garden, on purpose to distribute them to the children on the way.

Several of my father's nieces lived with us while attending school or college in Boston. They recall how kind and comforting she was when they felt lonely, and what capital and abundant school lunches she put up for them. One writes:

"She had such a motherly way and sweet voice that every one unburdened himself to her. . . . She was very kind in helping any one who needed it. I remember once getting on the train with her when an Irishwoman with several bundles and three small children was trying to get all her belongings on. Aunt Lucy picked up bundles and children in the most motherly fashion, and settled them all in their seats."

Another niece writes:

"Aunt Lucy sat with me each week while we did our mending. She taught me to take care of my own clothes. We used to run races with the stockings, each taking one, and finishing at almost the same moment. Aunt Lucy so arranged it that she always came out just ahead, so that I always had something to strive for. I was then about ten years old. . . . She had a way of always making a child see something just ahead for which to strive."

Her motherliness overflowed far beyond her

own family. Mrs. Florence M. Adkinson, a neighbor, and for many years an associate editor of the *Woman's Journal*, wrote:

"No one who was privileged to partake of Mrs. Stone's hospitality could fail to note her kindly concern for every one beneath her roof, and for all the dumb creatures belonging to the household. But few knew how far-reaching was that spirit of kindliness, how many her motherliness brooded over. Flowers and fruits were sent from her garden, boxes of clothing went West, North and South, a host of women who came to her in distress were helped to work or tided over hard places. She gave freely, and every gift was accompanied by thoughtful care and heart-warmth. Her heart went out strongly to young children and young people, and she sought to encourage them to do their best. She was never too busy to gladden the hearts of children who came into her presence, by gift of flower or fruit or picture, or by the telling of a story. And there were children of larger growth who went from her presence strengthened, helped and encouraged, to whom she was like a mother."

All the while she worked untiringly for woman suffrage, and her husband labored side by side with her, an invaluable coadjutor, his business ability and practical resourcefulness reinforcing her idealism and apostolic zeal.

Soon after her return to Massachusetts, she rendered one of her most important services to the woman's rights movement. She secured most of the ten thousand dollars that was raised to start the *Woman's Journal*, the paper which was destined to be a tower of strength to the cause for almost half a century. Her husband gave her the first thousand dollars, and then she went to others.[1]

Mrs. Mary A. Livermore, who was editing the *Agitator*, in Chicago, was induced to come to Boston, merge her paper in the new publication, and become its editor-in-chief. The assistant editors the first year were Lucy Stone, T. W. Higginson, Julia Ward Howe and William Lloyd Garrison.

Mrs. Livermore had been an army nurse during the Civil War and later a leader in the great Sanitary Commission which raised supplies for the wounded. She was a woman of noble presence and of extraordinary power and eloquence as a speaker. For years she was called "the Queen of the Platform", and she deserved the title. One of her lectures, "What Shall We Do with Our Daughters?" she gave more than eight hundred times. She was a woman of a big, warm and generous heart, and did innumerable kindnesses in private life. Her husband, the Reverend D. P.

[1] See Appendix, Note 5.

Livermore, was a Universalist minister, a learned man, and the author of several books. She said it was he who first converted her to woman suffrage, and that he encouraged and urged her to undertake public speaking, when she was afraid to attempt it. He was a fiery suffragist. It enraged him that his gifted wife could not vote, while every male loafer could.

The first issue of the new paper came out on January 8, 1870. The Salutatory by Julia Ward Howe said, in part:

"We implore our sisters, of whatever kind or degree, to make common cause with us, to lay down all partisan warfare, and organize a peaceful Grand Army of the Republic of women. But we do not ask them to organize as against men, but as against all that is pernicious to men and to women."

Lucy Stone's first editorial was on "The Legal Right of Mothers to their Children."

The paper was able and brilliant from the start. New England had at that time a galaxy of distinguished writers. Most of them were suffragists, and many became contributors to the *Woman's Journal*, as did prominent men and women all over the country and abroad. Colonel Higginson for years wrote a weekly editorial. Extracts from these were later published in book form, under the title "Common Sense about Women." The old fortresses of prejudice were assailed not only with facts and logic, but with wit and fun. Charlotte Perkins Gilman published some of her first poems in the *Journal*, and many writers afterwards famous began their literary life in its columns.

At the end of two years, Mrs. Livermore, whose time was under increasing demand in the lecture field, resigned as editor-in-chief, but she always remained a warm friend of the paper. The *Woman's Journal's* finances were very low at this time, and it became necessary to have editors who would serve without pay. Mrs. Stone and Mr. Blackwell shouldered the burden of the editorship and carried it to the end of their lives, with such help as I was able to give them later.

Mr. Blackwell had said in the beginning that he would always help the paper financially, but that there was one thing he would never do, and that was to assume any part of the editorial work. When the time of need came, however, he did that too, and carried his share of it for nearly forty years.

It was hard and heavy labor. Mrs. Stone compared the paper to a big baby which never grew up, and always had to be fed. There was also the ever-present problem of raising the money for its expenses. She gives a glimpse of it in an intimate letter written in 1874 to Mrs. Margaret W. Campbell of Iowa, a devoted worker, who spoke and organized for the American Woman Suffrage Association in more than twenty States and Territories. She and her husband had been campaigning for the suffrage amendment in Colorado. Mrs. Stone praised the good work they had done there and spoke with pity of their hardships. She said:

"I think of you with the five-cent loaf and ten cents' worth of meat a day for you two brave people, and the tears are in my eyes. But it is by just such sacrifice that the world will be saved. Mrs. Garrison was buried yesterday, and Wendell Phillips told how bravely she held up Mr. Garrison's hands when they did not know where the next meal was to come from.

"I wish I could rest. I am so tired to-day, body and soul, it seems as though I should never feel fresh again. I have been trying to get advertisements for the *Woman's Journal* to eke out its expenses. Yesterday I walked miles; to picture stores, crockery stores, to "special sales", going up flight after flight of stairs only to find the men out, or not ready to advertise. And for all my day's toil I did not get a cent; and when I came home at night, it was to find the house cold, the fire nearly out in the furnace, and none on the hearth; and it seemed as if the tiredness of a whole life came into my essence. I don't often complain, or feel like complaining, but I do wish there was some way of carrying on the *Woman's Journal* without such a hard, constant tug. If only the housekeeping would go on without so much looking after!"

Her general frame of mind, however, was cheerful and courageous. Whatever hardships went with the editing of the *Woman's Journal*, there was the solid satisfaction of knowing that the paper was doing good work. Not only did the suffragists look to it for news, counsel and inspiration, but innumerable articles from it were reprinted as tracts and leaflets and circulated far and wide. It was the great source of ammunition and information to the friends of the cause. It represented the Massachusetts, the New England and the American Woman Suffrage Associations; but, as Mrs. Carrie Chapman Catt truly said, "It was much more than the organ of any society; it was the Voice of the woman's movement." Its subscribers had a warm affection for it and were almost like a great family, scattered from Maine to California, and from Canada to the Gulf.

The paper was able to lend a hand to many good causes, as well as to help many individual women. It aided the movement for women's higher education, for dress reform, for the women's clubs, which were ridiculed and denounced, and the efforts going on all over the United States to secure equal property rights, and to obtain full privileges for women in the learned professions, and in new occupations. It stood by Josephine E. Butler in her long and valiant crusade against the State regulation of vice in England and Europe, and resisted attempts to introduce the system here.

It could not be stampeded into yielding to religious intolerance. The school vote of women in Massachusetts was small until 1888, when a report that a certain history had been taken out of the schools at the instance of a Roman Catholic priest led about twenty thousand Boston women to register, and to vote in one of the worst blizzards of the season. All the Roman Catholic candidates for the school committee were defeated, both that year and the next. The editors of the *Woman's Journal* took the ground that, since a large minority of the children in the public schools were Catholics, their parents were entitled to representation on the school board; and, later, it advocated the candidacy of a Catholic woman to the board, who was elected.

The *Woman's Journal* generally kept good-natured. The political newspapers used to put out a picture of a rooster crowing, when their party won a victory. When woman suffrage triumphed anywhere, the *Woman's Journal* put out a dove with an olive branch; and great was the joy among its readers when the dove appeared. Sometimes a long while passed without her once getting an airing; then she came out oftener and oftener, and finally we had to provide a second dove, because there were sometimes two victories in one week.

The paper was helped out by various legacies and gifts. About 1883, Mrs. Stone and Miss Anthony each received twenty thousand dollars left to them by Mrs. Eliza F. Eddy. Miss Anthony devoted her share to publishing the "History of Woman Suffrage." Mrs. Stone used part of hers to send out to about a thousand papers, which had agreed to publish it, a weekly "Woman's Column" of news items about women, strongly spiced with equal suffrage; and she put most of the rest into the *Woman's Journal*, which drew upon it year after year to make up its annual deficit. The Woman's Column was sometimes called the *Woman's Journal's* little sister. To save postage, it was published as a small newspaper. It was made up each week from the type already set for the *Woman's Journal*, so that the cost was trifling. It was issued for a number of years, and attained a circulation of seventeen thousand.

The *Woman's Journal* was published for forty-seven and a half years — a length of life almost unprecedented for a reform paper. During that time, its weekly issue never failed to appear, not even when the printing office burned down; and while it was under the control of Mrs. Stone and her family, as it was during most of its long life, it never went in debt except to its editors.[1]

Mrs. Carrie Chapman Catt, in the *Woman Citizen* of June 2, 1917, paid tribute to the *Woman's Journal*, "the great work in propagandist journalism initiated by Henry B. Blackwell and Lucy Stone. Pioneers in the field, they built up an enterprise compact of ideals, faith and endless generosity. Suffrage journalism has never been, could never be, a business to this historic family of suffrage journalists. It has been a duty, a joy, a consecration and an expense."

She added: "There can be no overestimating the value to the suffrage cause of the *Woman's Journal* in its long and vivid career. It has gone before and it has followed after; it has pointed the way and closed the gaps; it has been history-maker and history-recorder for the suffrage cause. The suffrage success of to-day is not conceivable without the *Woman's Journal's* part in it."

[1] See Appendix, Note 6.

## *Chapter XVII*

Mrs. Stone did a vast amount of woman suffrage work, beside that connected with the *Woman's Journal*. She was the leading spirit in the Massachusetts, the New England and the American Woman Suffrage Associations. There was endless organizing, petitioning, arranging of legislative hearings, and getting up of conventions and meetings of all sorts, besides press work and an enormous correspondence. There were occasional campaigns to elect or defeat a political candidate; there were countless attacks to be answered; there were vast quantities of tracts and leaflets printed; there were great suffrage fairs and entertainments to raise money. The long battle was full of interest and excitement at the time, but the details of it would lack color and spice in the retrospect.

She helped the suffragists of many States to secure improved laws for women. She was called upon, from all directions, to come and speak at legislative hearings where such measures were pending. Doctor Cameron says the married women's property law of Canada was passed under the direct pressure of her eloquence. Colonel Higginson wrote: "After one of those high-minded, high-hearted, silver-voiced pleas by Lucy Stone, Judge Greene, chairman of the Rhode Island Judiciary Committee, said, 'I have known all about these laws for twenty years, yet I never saw these injustices in them until a woman came to tell me of them.'" From that time on, Judge Greene was on the women's side.

In Massachusetts, as elsewhere, the suffragists hammered away year after year at the different legal injustices and got them amended one by one; and these minor victories cheered the long struggle towards the final goal. It took us ten years to get married women the right to own their own clothes, and the fight for other improvements was equally stubborn. The antisuffragists all along insisted that the laws were already "more than just to women." They opposed every change, and then, when it was carried, after years of hard work, they said, "See how easy it is for women to get any legislation that they need, without the ballot!" The women "antis" even opposed the equal-guardianship law, in a leaflet declaring that if two persons ride on one horse, one must ride in front, the inference being that if two persons are the parents of one child, one must be given exclusive control of that child. The joint-guardianship bill was not passed until fifty-five years after Lucy

Stone began to plead for it; and even now the law is not quite equal.

A large part of the woman suffrage work done in the United States radiated from the office of the *Woman's Journal*. The annual meetings of the American Woman Suffrage Association were held in different parts of the country, wherever the need at the time seemed to be greatest. Every State that submitted a constitutional amendment appealed to the American Association for help in money and workers and received it. Mrs. Stone and Mr. Blackwell took part in the amendment campaigns in Vermont, Michigan, Nebraska, Colorado and Rhode Island. In the Western campaigns, they and the other speakers ate all kinds of food, slept in every sort of bed, were bitten by every variety of insect, faced all weathers, as well as storms of opposition, and were exposed to all the hardships of primitive conditions and pioneer life, as in Kansas in 1867.

But, if the work was hard, it had ample compensations. Julia Ward Howe once said that she was glad to have come into the woman suffrage movement, if only because it brought her into "such high company." The workers for equal rights included a large proportion of the best brains and hearts in the community, men and women with whom it was a privilege and a joy to labor. A score of times I have had to resist the temptation to turn aside from the narrative of my mother's life to pay tribute to one or another of her co-workers. The limitations of space have made this impossible, except in the case of a few outstanding figures. But there was a great army of devoted workers, old and young, rich and poor, women and men, to whose tireless and heroic labors the final victory was due.

A campaign through the political conventions was undertaken by the suffragists in different parts of the country. Mrs. Stone and Mrs. Livermore were accredited delegates to the Massachusetts Republican Convention held in September, 1870, to the great displeasure of the extreme opponents of equal rights. One of them said, "If a local Republican organization elected a trained monkey as a delegate, would you feel obliged to accept him?"

The Massachusetts Republican Convention of 1871 endorsed woman suffrage, and at the Republican National Convention of 1872 Mr. Blackwell worked hard for similar action, but could only get it recommended to "respectful consideration." This was far from satisfactory; but the suffragists who appealed to the National Democratic Convention got nothing at all. The Prohibition and Labor parties both put woman suffrage planks in their platforms.

A few months later, the following — drawn up,

of course, by Mr. Blackwell — was adopted by the Massachusetts Republican Convention:

"Resolved, That the Republican party of Massachusetts, as the representative of liberty and progress, is in favor of extending suffrage to all American citizens, irrespective of sex, and will hail the day when the educated intellect and enlightened conscience of woman will find direct expression at the ballot box."

Mr. Blackwell got Democrats who were friends of the cause to push the matter in their party, and in 1882 the Massachusetts Democratic Convention also adopted a woman suffrage plank. But party endorsements did not prove very effective. Though elected upon platforms favoring woman suffrage, most of the members of the Legislature, both Republican and Democratic, continued to vote against it. Mr. Blackwell, however, continued to follow up the party conventions with hopeful persistency; and for years he went regularly as a delegate to the National Convention of Republican Leagues, for the purpose of securing a woman's rights resolution, which he generally got. Though an old-line Republican, he always scratched his ticket if the Republican candidate was opposed to equal suffrage and the Democratic candidate in favor.

The Beecher-Tilton scandal, which shook the whole country, had its repercussion on the woman suffrage movement. All the persons concerned in it were suffragists. Only a few years before, Mr. Beecher had been President of the American Woman Suffrage Association, and Mr. Tilton of the Union Woman Suffrage Association, and Mrs. Woodhull had been conspicuously affiliated with the leaders of the National wing. *Woodhull and Claflin's Weekly* now asserted that Mr. Beecher had been living in illicit relations with Mrs. Tilton and many other women of his congregation, and that it was perfectly right for him to do so.

Mr. Beecher at this time was the most influential and beloved clergyman in America. He had been a champion of the slave at the risk of his life, a champion of the early women doctors and women ministers, a strong friend of the New York Infirmary for Women and Children in its early and unpopular days, when it was mobbed, and a tower of strength to a score of good but unpopular causes.

The uproar and excitement were tremendous. The whole community was divided. The Beecher family itself was divided; his half-sister Mrs. Hooker believed the accusation, while the rest of his relatives scouted it, including the sister nearest to him in age and intimacy, Harriet Beecher Stowe.

The leaders of the National Woman Suffrage Association believed in his guilt, the leaders of the American Woman Suffrage Association in his innocence. With Mrs. Stone, it was especially a belief in Mrs. Tilton's innocence. She had known Mrs. Tilton for many years, and had known her to be devotedly attached to her husband; and she did not believe that any woman who really loved her husband could be unfaithful to him. The thing seemed to her simply impossible. When Mrs. Tilton declared herself guilty, Mrs. Stone thought her heart and spirit had been so crushed and broken by her husband's cruelty and infidelities that she let herself be browbeaten into saying what was not true.

In an editorial in the *Woman's Journal* of August 29, 1874, Mrs. Stone said:

"Of all the persons in the sad scene which has been passing before our eyes, Mrs. Tilton seems to me to be more wronged and injured than any other, and at the same time to be the most innocent. . . . Smarting under blows which human eyes could see, and bearing others which, though not seen, give the most cruel hurt; cowering before an infamous woman, who was installed over her in the house; carrying to the graves of her children the dead hopes of all her life; driven to the wall; in utter despair, endured for five miserable years, Elizabeth Tilton said what her tormentors required her to say. . . . There are women who could be drawn and quartered, but whom no stress of circumstances could compel to falsehood. Mrs. Tilton is of gentler mould. She lived in her affections, and when they were crushed, she was crushed. . . . I still hold her a good, true woman, unspeakably sinned against, and I do most cordially give her my hand, with all a woman's sympathy."

At the trial, after hearing all the evidence, the jury stood nine to three for acquittal.[1] An editorial by Julia Ward Howe in the *Woman's Journal*, on the untrustworthy character of the accuser (Mr. Tilton), was quoted in part by the ecclesiastical tribunal which afterwards investigated Mr. Beecher's case and acquitted him.

The public continued to be divided, and is divided to this day; but the antisuffragists made great capital out of the case. A suffrage amendment to the State constitution was then pending in Michigan, and Michigan suffragists attributed its defeat in large measure to the Beecher-Tilton scandal.

Mrs. Stone spoke in different parts of the country at the meetings of the Association for the Advancement of Women. It was organized in 1873, in response to a Call issued by Mrs. Charlotte B. Wilbour, President of Sorosis. For twenty-six years it held an annual "Woman's Congress", in places ranging from Canada to New Orleans, with papers and addresses by prominent women on literary, educational and philanthropic subjects. Mrs. Livermore was its first president. After-

[1] See Appendix, Note 7.

wards Mrs. Howe held that office for many years. Wherever the Association for the Advancement of Women went, it left behind it a trail of women's clubs, women's educational and industrial unions and other organizations then regarded as novel and dangerous. With the growth of the woman's club movement, the meetings of the General Federation and other societies finally supplied its place.

Mrs. Stone had an enthusiastic veneration for the old heroes and heroines of the American Revolution, and always insisted that the equal suffrage movement was only the logical application of "the principles of the fathers" — "Governments derive their just powers from the consent of the governed", and "Taxation without representation is tyranny." She never saw Bunker Hill monument without emotion. "It is our monument," she said. She liked to tell how it was built:

"The corner-stone of Bunker Hill Monument was laid by Lafayette in 1825, and lay there, with the gathered debris, until 1848. It was difficult to collect money for it, . . . but in 1843 the women undertook it. They held a fair, and with the proceeds, added to the contribution of Fanny Ellsler from her dancing, the Monument was completed."

The Centennial Exposition in Philadelphia seemed a suitable occasion to preach the principle, "Taxation without representation is tyranny." Mrs. Stone appealed earnestly to the various committees of the Woman's Building for space for an exhibit, and a place for woman suffrage on the program. All that could be obtained was a small space to hang up an exhibit of printed matter. It contained the tax protests of Harriot K. Hunt, Lucy Stone, Abby Kelley Foster, Sarah E. Wall and Julia and Abby Smith, with William I. Bowditch's pamphlet, "The Taxation of Women in Massachusetts." But it was hung so high that few could see it.

Abby Kelley Foster, in her old age, had refused to pay her taxes, and her home in Worcester, worth thousands of dollars, had been sold for a song.

Mrs. Stone could not get used to the annual defeats which woman suffrage met with in the Legislature for a long series of years. The justice of the claim was so clear, the arguments for it so convincing, that it seemed to her as if the legislators must see it; and, when they failed to do so, the disappointment brought the tears into her eyes. At the hearing before the Committee on Constitutional Amendments in 1879, she said:

"In this very State House, how often have women looked down from the gallery while our law-makers voted down our rights, and heard them say, 'Half an hour is time enough to waste on it.' When the half hour was over, we have seen them turn eagerly to consider such a question as what shall be the size of a barrel of cranberries. They took plenty of time to consider that, and did not regard it as time wasted. They comprehended that question. But when a great principle confronted them, they were not equal to it. A different history waits to be written by our law-makers, and, sooner or later, it will be written."

She had been deeply grieved by the refusal of Congress to include women in the basis of reconstruction. She said at that time: "I have no country, and no hope of a country. On this wide continent there is no mountain so high and no valley so deep that there I can take my child by the hand and be protected in my God-given rights as a mother under the American flag."

Twenty years later, at a meeting of the New England Woman Suffrage Association where the hall was profusely decorated with flags, she said:

"I can never look on this flag without thinking that nowhere under its shadow can a woman claim her child as her own; and so I never hang it up as an object of veneration, I never bow down to it, and I never sing

"'My country, 't is of thee.'

"But I suppose these young people did it in anticipation of 'a good time coming.'"

Massachusetts was not only, in the early years, the headquarters, to a large extent, of the suffrage movement; it was also the headquarters of the antisuffragists, and the seat of their first organization. Although they gave us much trouble, we had a great deal of fun with them, their arguments were so extraordinary. Every change was denounced in advance as certain to destroy the home and overturn the foundations of society. One member of the Legislature said that when a man came home tired at night, he did not want to kiss a member of the school board, or an Overseer of the Poor. Another member declared that, if women were allowed to vote, (1) there would be no more children born in Massachusetts, and (2) all the children that were born would be girls.

For some time, the women remonstrants presented their own case at the hearings; but for many years they hired an attorney to speak for them.

## *Chapter XVIII*

Meanwhile our family life flowed along quietly and pleasantly. My parents were too busy to do much social visiting; but we sometimes drove over to call upon William Lloyd Garrison in Roxbury, or Theodore D. Weld and the Grimké sisters at their home in Hyde Park. These visits were always like pilgrimages to a shrine.

The days were fully occupied. In the evenings, my father read aloud, while my mother darned the stockings. He was the best reader I ever knew.

It is said that no man is a hero to his valet; but Mrs. Stone was both loved and admired by her servants — the good ones, and even some who were not so good. One very capable middle-aged woman, whom we finally had to part with because she would occasionally get drunk, came out to Dorchester one night too much intoxicated to find her way home, and sat upon a neighbor's doorstep at one o'clock in the morning, singing Mrs. Stone's praises in her cups.

A good German girl worked for her during her early married life in New Jersey. Many years after, this woman was dying, a widow and destitute, in the Consumptives' Home near Boston. She told the matron she wished she could find a woman for whom she had worked in her youth, as she would like to leave her two little daughters in her care — Mrs. Lucy Stone. The matron said, "Why, she lives quite near here!" Mrs. Stone got one of the two little girls adopted by a good woman who proved a mother to her, and brought up the other in her own family.

A fine young woman from Cape Breton was our maid of all work when my mother was taken with her last illness. She refused to leave her at such a time, although she had been about to be married, and her lover was so vexed at the delay that he broke off the engagement.

Now and then there was some amusing manifestation of the old prejudice. When a minister in Malden was asked to give notice of a lecture by Mrs. Stone, he held the notice up before his face and said, "I am requested by Mr. Mowry to say that a hen will undertake to crow like a cock at the town hall this afternoon at five o'clock. Anybody who wants to hear that kind of music will, of course, attend." Mrs. Stone said, in telling the incident: "Everybody came, and Mr. Mowry was asked what kind of a hen it was, and all about it, and altogether it was a very good advertisement of the meeting." On another occasion, when Mrs. Stone, Mrs. Livermore and Mrs. Howe were to speak, it was announced that the "three old crows" would be heard.

But more and more the old odium and abuse died away, and gave place to affection and esteem.

She was as different as possible from the imaginary picture of an equal rights advocate, as drawn by the caricaturists. A woman who had strayed into a suffrage meeting and seen her for the first time, said afterwards: "What business had she there, that fresh, round, rosy little woman, whose very aspect suggested a husband and a baby?" Somebody else said she looked like "the grandmother of all good children."

She once went for a week's lecturing trip in Western Massachusetts with a younger woman, Mrs. Anna Christy Fall (the wife of George H. Fall, who afterwards, as a member of the Legislature of 1902, was chiefly instrumental in putting through the bill making mothers joint guardians of their children with the fathers). When Mrs. Fall got home, her voice and manner had become so much gentler that her husband noticed it. She told him it was due to that week's association with Mrs. Stone.

With most people, the objection to woman suffrage was one of sentiment rather than of reason; and there was something so sweet, not only in her voice but in her personality, that a whole parlor-meeting of antisuffragists sometimes went over to woman suffrage in a body, after hearing her speak. Colonel Higginson describes a similar sudden conversion on the part of Helen (Hunt) Jackson (H.H.), who went to a suffrage meeting with the avowed intention of turning it into ridicule, and came away saying, "Do you think I could ever oppose anything that a woman with such a voice as that wanted?" He said: "Her mere presence refuted all the popular impressions as to the unwomanly and shrieking qualities of the reformers. She went through the storms of life like Spencer's Una with the milk-white lamb:

"'So pure and innocent, like that same lambe,
She was in life and everie vertuous lore.'"

Although her own voice was so sweet, she had no ear for music, and could not tell one tune from another. She had but little sense of humor; and she grieved for both lacks. She said she hoped that when she got to heaven she should understand "music and jokes."

All the purely womanly qualities were strong in her. To the end of her life, her ideas of love were what many persons would regard as romantic; and she was as fond of a love story as a girl of sixteen, provided it was a simple and innocent love story.

She was as resolute as she was gentle. Once, when she thought it her duty to take some unpopular new departure — the letters do not make clear what it was — a friend remonstrated and predicted that she would lose her influence. She wrote in reply:

"I know it will cost me personal suffering and the loss of friends. But it has been ever so in my life. My right and wrong differed from that of my friends. When I went to college, when I became an antislavery lecturer, and then an advocate of woman's rights, — at each step, old friends left, and never returned to me; and it will be so now. But ever the high consciousness of right has been to me more than friends; and only God knows how dear to me is human love. 'We were not sent here,' says Wendell Phillips, 'to get influence, but to do our duty.'"

She respected the same right of private judgment in others. Once when I felt obliged to do something of which she did not approve, she said, after a short argument, "Well, I had to do so many things which my mother disapproved of that I suppose I ought not to be hard upon you."

She could adapt her remarks to her audience. Once she visited the Sherborn Reformatory for Women with Mary Grew, a saintly Quakeress from Philadelphia. They were invited to address the inmates. Mary Grew spoke to them about the love of God. It was entirely over their heads. Mrs. Stone told them how she had had to wrestle with her temper in her childhood; and they all brightened up into attention and interest.

She loved poetry. In her lonely early lecturing, she found great comfort in Bryant's "Lines to a Waterfowl":

"Whither, 'midst falling dew,
While glow the heavens with the last steps of day,
Far through their rosy depths dost thou pursue
Thy solitary way?

"There is a power whose care
Teaches thy way along that pathless coast,
The desert and illimitable air, —
Lone wandering, but not lost.

"He who, from zone to zone,
Guides through the boundless sky thy certain flight,
In the long way that I must tread alone
Will guide my steps aright."

She often quoted James Russell Lowell's lines:

"Get but the truth once uttered, and 't is like
A star new orbed, which drops into its place,
And which, once circling in its placid round,
Not all the tumult of the earth can shake."

She was fond of Anne Whitney's poems, especially her lines about the aloe:

"The aloe, in the northern clime,
Waits an hundred years for its flower.

"If the aloe wait an hundred years,
And God's times are so long indeed
For simple things, as flower and weed,
That gather only the light and gloom,
For what great treasures of joy and dole,
Of life, and death, perchance, must the soul,
Ere it flower in heavenly peace, find room!"

She quoted this to her lover, when refusing to marry him. It was often on her lips in later years, and she repeated it to her daughter on her death-bed.

Mr. Blackwell also knew much fine poetry, and quoted it in his speeches with great effect.

As time passed on, they were called upon to pay the last tribute at the funerals of most of their old colleagues, Garrison, Abby Kelley Foster, the Grimkés, and many more. The only time that I ever heard my mother literally "lift up her voice and weep", sobbing and crying out loud, like a little girl, was when she read the news of the death of Wendell Phillips. He had shown her much kindness in the hard early days, and she had a deep admiration and affection for him. She looked upon him as almost the ideal man.

She was one of the most modest and unassuming of women. She had no thirst for fame, no longing to live in history. She never kept a diary, preserved no record of her early work, and did not even save her press clippings. Fortunately, she sent them to her mother, and some of them were recovered, long after, from Mother Stone's repositories. She so loathed the idea of blowing her own trumpet that she went to the other extreme. When asked, as she often was, to furnish particulars of her life for books of "Famous Women", she refused, almost with horror.

A Philadelphia paper once offered a small prize for the best example of a girl's perseverance. I wrote an account of how my mother obtained her education, but did not let her know it until notified that my article had won the prize. The paper containing it arrived in my absence. When I got home, I found that she had hidden it at the bottom of a large pile of newspapers, with a feeling of bashfulness and shame.

When she could no longer climb the many and steep stairs to the printing office, she did not always know in advance about everything that was to appear in the *Woman's Journal.* Once we published a sketch of her life, with her portrait. She had been under the impression that there was to be a portrait and sketch of my father, and she opened the paper with eagerness and satisfaction. Great was her disgust to find a sketch of herself instead. In this matter she had two standards of morals, or rather of taste, one for herself and another for her friends; for she was delighted when they wrote their reminiscences.

She had no ambition for office. In the Massachusetts, the New England and the American Woman Suffrage Associations, in all of which she was much beloved, and could have been elected to any post, she habitually tried to secure for president the most distinguished and popular person who could be induced to accept the office, while she took the laboring oar in some less conspicuous position, generally as chairman of the executive committee. She always craved not the post of prominence but the post of work.

She had no vanity, and was even unduly lacking in self-esteem. She was always more conscious of her deficiencies than of her strong points.

In crossing a flooded river, during one of the Western campaigns, she caught a severe cold, which left her much crippled with rheumatism, and took away the strength of her voice, though not its sweetness. It had been said of this voice, in her prime, that it was "never low to the farthest, and never loud to the nearest." Now it was no longer adequate to addressing great assemblies. After 1887, she ceased to go upon the long Western trips. But she went about addressing women's clubs, schools, Granges, parlor meetings, and all sorts of audiences within the scope of her voice, as cheerfully and contentedly as she had done the huge crowds of her earlier days. Mr. Blackwell continued to take the far Western trips, sometimes alone, oftener with a group of able speakers whom he and his wife had helped to recruit.

His resourcefulness shone in these campaigns. Once he and Mrs. Carrie Chapman Catt were lecturing in South Dakota, and they arrived in a town where prejudice against woman suffrage was so strong that no hall could be had. He secured a wagon and stationed it in front of the post-office at the hour when the evening mail came in. He and Mrs. Catt mounted the cart. After ringing a big dinner bell until a large crowd gathered, he introduced Mrs. Catt in his sonorous voice, and she made her speech. She then introduced him and he made his. They won over the whole crowd, and at the close took a unanimous vote for woman suffrage. This incident was typical of many.

When the Territories of Washington, Montana and North Dakota came into the Union as States in 1889, he attended the Constitutional Convention of each, at his own expense, and labored for the adoption of woman suffrage. He addressed the Conventions of North Dakota and Montana, and the Suffrage Committee of the Convention of Washington. The North Dakota Convention, under the influence of his eloquence, voted to give women full suffrage, but reconsidered and limited it to school suffrage. Montana gave tax-paying women a vote upon all questions submitted to the taxpayers.

At the meeting of the International Council of Women, held in Washington in 1888, Susan B. Anthony, Julia Ward Howe and Frances E. Willard, the beloved president of the National Woman's Christian Temperance Union, all told how they had been converted to woman suffrage by Lucy Stone; and the elderly women joked about their own juvenility.

Miss Anthony said: "I was not at the Worcester Convention nor at the Seneca Falls Convention. Do not make any mistake about my being a pioneer. I am quite a young person. But I did take the *New York Weekly Tribune*." She told how reading the report of Lucy's speech at Worcester had converted her. She added:

"One of the things Lucy said, if I remember rightly, was that all that was left of a married woman to be marked on her gravestone was that she was the relict of somebody who had owned her. I made up my mind then that no one would make a relict of me. Now I want to bring before you a woman who has a million women at her back, Frances E. Willard."

Miss Willard said: "I think Susan brought me out to make me own up that I got very much the same sort of training from Lucy Stone that she did. Like Susan, I am very juvenile. I am not a pioneer. I remember when I was dreadfully afraid of Susan, and of Lucy too. But now I love and honor these women, and I cannot put into words my sense of what it means to have such women as have made it possible for more timid ones like myself to come along and take our places in the world's work. If they had not blazed the trees and pioneered the way, we should never have dared to come."

Mrs. Howe said: "When you have derided Miss Anthony's youth, what will you say to my white hair? When you have approved Miss Anthony's celibacy, what will you say to my opposite record? Because it was at about the same time when she formed that valorous determination not to be anybody's relict that I took my place beside a hero, to try to keep pace with his noble walk. But, like the others who have spoken, I am the convert of Lucy Stone. I remember vividly the woman suffrage meeting held in Boston, to which I went with a very rebellious heart. I came out very meek and have so continued ever since."

The main interest of both my parents was in the equal rights movement; but my father had many other interests as well. He was active in politics. He and his friends, Charlie Codman and the

Reverend Frederic A. Hinckley, called themselves "the triangle." At the caucuses of the Republican party in Dorchester, one of them would make a motion, another second it, and the third make a speech for it. They broke the ring which had been for many years in control of Dorchester politics, smashed the "slate", and threw terror into the machine politicians again and again. Dorchester people had been trying in vain for thirty years to get part of Savin Hill made a public park. Through his efforts it was finally secured. When a selfish millionaire bought up nine miles of shore adjoining our summer home at Chilmark, Martha's Vineyard, and tried to shut up a road which had been in use by the public for more than a hundred years, he led a successful fight against it.

The little republic of Santo Domingo in 1870 asked to be annexed to the United States, because it was afraid that it might be forcibly annexed by Haiti. President Grant sent Andrew D. White, Doctor Samuel Gridley Howe and Benjamin F. Wade to the island as a Commission to investigate and report. Mr. Blackwell went with them as a newspaper correspondent. He fell in love with the West Indies, lectured upon them after his return, and warmly backed up the Commission's report in favor of annexation. He labored to overcome Charles Sumner's opposition; but Sumner, in reply to all argument, only quoted the parable of Naboth's Vineyard. The request of the Dominicans for annexation was refused.

Mr. Blackwell had always been interested in sugar refining, and had twice engaged in it, in his early life. He carried on for years experiments aiming to find a substitute for cane sugar. With Frederick Ames, George S. Hunt and others, he tried to introduce the making of beet sugar in Maine. The farmers were supplied with seed and directions. Mr. Blackwell went to Germany and imported the best machinery. A considerable quantity of sugar was made, and he telegraphed joyously from Portland in 1878 to his wife: "Beet-sugar manufacture a success. Slavery in Cuba is doomed!" But the undertaking finally had to be given up for lack of a sufficient supply of beets. The cultivation of sugar beets is very laborious, and the Maine farmers preferred to raise other crops.

During his absence in Portland, Mrs. Stone took the whole charge of the paper and the voluminous correspondence of the Suffrage Headquarters.

He was an active member of the Twentieth Century, the Massachusetts, the Chickatawbut and the Victorian Clubs. Governor Long said that in the Massachusetts Club, which included the most prominent men of the State, he was easily the best debater.

Both Mrs. Stone and Mr. Blackwell wrote much

for the newspapers. Up to a few months before her death, she did a great deal of public speaking, being in continual demand to present her special subject before gatherings of all sorts. Her little figure, and plain black silk bonnet, were a familiar sight in many different meetings. She belonged to the New England Women's Club, the New England Women's Press Association, and the Association of Collegiate Alumnae (now the Association of University Women). For many years, she and I were the only mother and daughter in the last-named society. Now it is full of mothers and daughters.

However busy, she found time to go over the morning and evening paper, and took a vivid interest in the news of the world. She was particularly interested in the great organized movements of her day, the Grange, the working girls' clubs, the college settlements, the labor societies, the Woman's Christian Temperance Union, and the Christian Endeavor. She might not agree with them in all respects, but she recognized the value of their work as parts of a great whole, and wished to keep in touch with them.

She had to forego many things for the sake of her one great aim. She had always longed to see the Swiss mountains. Towards the end of her life, I asked her why she did not take a trip to Switzerland. She answered, "Oh, why don't I do so many things! It is too late. I shall never do it now." She added contentedly, "But I have done what I wanted to do. I have helped the women."

Brought up by such parents, I naturally came to share their views. In my childhood, I heard so much about woman suffrage that I was bored by it and thought I hated it, until one day I came across a magazine article on the other side and found myself bristling up like a hen in defense of her chickens. This happened when I was about twelve years old. After that I never had any doubt as to whether I believed in it. About 1870, a series of conventions was held in Vermont, and I distributed suffrage literature at the doors. At Chauncy Hall School, Curtis Guild (afterwards governor and general) was my classmate. He took a roguish pleasure in dropping a disparaging word about woman suffrage now and then, in order to set me off like fireworks. Later some of my classmates at Boston University amused themselves in the same way. Before leaving school, I was allowed to select poetry and stories for the *Woman's Journal*. The first time that I was entrusted with the sole charge of the paper was in 1882, when both my parents were away in Nebraska, campaigning for the suffrage amendment. Once when my father was conducting a hearing at the Boston State House, with a terrible cold, his voice gave out, and I took charge of the hearing.

After a while it became my regular task to answer the antisuffragists, at both State and Congressional hearings, and also to prepare most of the controversial literature. As I gained experience, I was able to help my parents more and more, both with the paper and with the work of the Suffrage Association; and after they passed away, I was in training to go on with both.

It was a satisfaction to my mother to have me take part in the work for equal suffrage, but she did not want my life to be so completely absorbed in it as hers had been. Without my knowledge, she asked our friend, Mrs. Isabel C. Barrows, to try to draw me out into wider and more varied interests. Mrs. Barrows was secretary of the National Conference of Charities and Correction. She and her husband, the Reverend Samuel J. Barrows, were editing the *Christian Register*. They had traveled, and were cosmopolitan in their friendships. I became a regular guest at their summer camp in Canada and at the informal daily lunches in the winter at the *Christian Register* office, frequented by distinguished men and women from all parts of the world. This led to my acquaintance with the Armenian question, and to many other interests of my later life. I did not learn until long afterwards that I owed this widening of my horizon to my mother.

## *Chapter XIX*

For some time Mrs. Stone had been urged to sit for a portrait bust, to be exhibited at the World's Fair in Chicago in 1893. Her daughter wrote to a friend:

"For more than a year, Mrs. Holmes and Mrs. Callanan,[1] Frances Willard and others have been urging Mamma to let a subscription be started for a bust of her, and she has absolutely and peremptorily refused, saying, very sensibly, that it was much better to devote the money to suffrage work. But at the New England Women's Club the other day, when she was not there, the project was started, and a committee formed, and about $150 subscribed, and Anne Whitney was interviewed (all this without Mamma's knowledge), and she agreed to make it; and Mamma's particular friend, dear Mrs. Judith W. Smith of East Boston, was appointed a committee with Mrs. Dietrick to talk Mamma into it. They have represented to her that the money which will go for

[1] Mrs. Mary E. Holmes of Chicago, President of the Illinois Equal Suffrage Association, and Mrs. Martha C. Callanan of Des Moines.

the bust is not money that would have otherwise been given for suffrage, and along that line they have persuaded her."

The bust proved an excellent likeness. It was exhibited in the Woman's Building at the World's Fair, and later was presented to the Boston Public Library. It stands in the main reading room. Lucy Stone and Julia Ward Howe are the only women represented there, among many busts of famous men. The face of the first Massachusetts woman to take a college degree now looks calmly and benignantly down upon the many college girls from Boston University and elsewhere who frequent the great library, and for whom she pioneered the way. There are two plaster replicas of the bust, one in the Shurtleff Public School of Boston, the other at Oberlin College.

The World's Fair offered a great opportunity to make propaganda for woman suffrage. Mrs. Stone went to Chicago and interviewed the most influential of the men and women who were making the preliminary arrangements. She wrote to Miss Anthony:

"The outlook is certainly very good for our cause. It will be lifted on a whole age by this effort in a new situation. The women themselves will learn so much. Mrs. John A. Logan said to me, 'Before they know it, they will be there.'

"I happened to be in Chicago at the time of the five-days' business meeting of the Women's Department. So many distinguished women were there from all over the Union, and so many of them were fine-looking, noble women, and the best of them were suffragists. I stopped at the Palmer House, where the headquarters of the women were. They came to me from everywhere to say that they were suffragists, especially the Southern women, to whom the question is a fresh gospel. It did my heart good to meet them, and to see and feel their enthusiasm. And they are still young, and able to fight when we are gone. Mrs. Potter Palmer is herself a host on our side. . . . Everything seems to be helping now. How good it is, after these long years of endeavor!

"At our meeting in the Winnebago County Fair in Illinois, the great audience almost unanimously voted their approval of woman suffrage. It was a sight worth seeing when the great audience rose up on our side, and the President of the Fair wore the yellow ribbon, as did the Mayor of the city.

"Yours in good hope of the victory, not so far off as it was once,

"L. S."

Mr. Blackwell was appointed a member of the Advisory Council on Woman Suffrage, and spoke at the Exposition on "The Evolution of Woman Suffrage Historically in this Country", an appropriate subject, as he had worked for the cause for forty years.

Mrs. Stone spoke in the Suffrage Department Room meeting of the World's Congress of Representative Women, under the auspices of the National American Woman Suffrage Association. The journey to Chicago to keep these engagements proved to be her last lecture trip. She wrote to her husband, May 21, 1893:

"The Congresses are all over, but I have to speak for Mrs. Governor Eagle in the Woman's Building, and tomorrow Mrs. Potter Palmer gives a reception. . . . Today I spoke to Jenkin Lloyd Jones's Sunday School, and stayed and heard John W. Chadwick preach. . . . We have been conferring with Mrs. Carrie Lane Chapman about Colorado, and with a Colorado woman."

In August Mr. Blackwell and his daughter went to Chicago and filled their respective dates on the program. Mrs. Stone was unable to go. She had greatly overtired herself upon her Chicago trip in May, and she developed a tumor of the stomach which made it impossible for her to digest. Her strength failed rapidly; but Colorado dwelt upon her mind. The last letter but one that she ever wrote was to Mrs. John R. Hanna of Denver, warmly commending to her Mrs. Carrie Lane

Chapman, who had gone to Colorado to work for the pending amendment. The last letter of all was to her brother Frank. She said:

"This may be the last letter you will ever get from me. But you have always been a dearly-beloved brother, and I have always had profound respect for your integrity, your honesty, your love of truth. Everyone knew your word was as good as your bond. You would not cheat or take advantage. I have no fear or dread of the life beyond, and some time, somewhere, I hope to meet you there."

This brother, twelve years her senior, came to take leave of her. He said, with tears, "You have always been more like a mother than a sister to me."

She was perfectly calm and fearless, and made all her preparations to go as quietly as if she were only going into the next room. She said, "I know the Eternal Order, and I believe in it. I have not a fear, or a dread, or a doubt."

While she was strong enough, she sat all day on the piazza, often with a favorite black cat on her lap, looking at the beautiful autumn landscape. She said she had never realized before how much beauty there was in the two elm trees in front of the house. After she was confined to her room, she still enjoyed the view from the windows, the sunlight, the songs of the birds in the morning, and the flowers with which her friends filled her chamber to overflowing. Later still, she lay quiet in bed, watching the tossing boughs of the great maple tree outside her window, and enjoying, as she said, "the wild pageant of the wind, and its wealth of music." She said, "I have had a full, rich life. I am so glad to have lived, and to have lived at a time when I could work!"

To a friend who expressed the wish that she might have lived to see woman suffrage granted, she said, "Oh, I shall know it! I think I shall know it on the other side. And, if not, I shall be doing something better." When something was said about her possibly coming back to communicate with those she had left, she answered, "I expect to be too busy to come back." To another friend she said, "I look forward to the other side as the brighter side, and I expect to be busy for good things."

She said something to the doctor about her coming death, and he answered, "We must keep as serene as we can." She answered, in a tone of slight surprise, "There is nothing to be unserene about."

She studied to save everybody steps and to give as little trouble as possible. As long as she could, she went on with the twofold line of thought that she had followed all her life, planning for the carrying on of the suffrage work after she should be gone, and planning also for the comfort of her family and the carrying on of the household. She gave us advice tranquilly about domestic details, and even told us what food to prepare for the relatives who would come to the funeral.

She lay and thought of Coy's Hill, and her mind wandered over all the old places. She spoke of the many little brooks that took their rise on the old farm. She had always loved their music, and their remembered voices soothed her still. She spoke of the great pleasure she had had all her life from the beauty of the world, — the birds, the leaves in spring, the autumn colors, the old rocks, the clouds. She named them over with the accent of a lover, dwelling especially on the clouds. She said, "I have had a pile of good out of the clouds!" and she added, "I fully expect that the next world will be just as good as this — very likely better."

She suffered much weakness and weariness, but little severe pain. "I have so much to be thankful for!" she said repeatedly; and, again and again, "Everybody is very good to me."

Loving letters and messages poured in from every side. To the friends who came to see her, she said good-by with more courage than they could muster. One, to whom she waved farewell from the window, said, "It was like getting a wave from heaven!"

As long as she was able, she read the daily paper with unabated interest. The accounts of the World's Parliament of Religions gave her especial pleasure. She was struck by a description in the *Nation* of the Grand Canyon of the Colorado. She said to me, "After suffrage is carried, you will still be here, and you must go to see that canyon." To the suggestion that she would do well to go and see it herself, when she was freed from fleshly limitations, she answered, with a twinkle of her old cheerful resolution, "You may be sure I shall, if I can."

When a letter from the Women's Press Association was read to her, speaking warmly of her work, she seemed touched. She said slowly, "I think I have done what I could. With one hand I made my family comfortable; with the other —." Here her voice failed through weakness. What she meant was that with the other she had worked to get the women their rights.

A flash of joy passed over her face when she heard that the New York State Democratic Convention had adopted a woman suffrage plank, and she said, "That ought to make the Massachusetts Republicans ashamed." A few hours later she looked up and said, faintly, but with one of her old bright looks, "Doctor Holmes's One-Horse

Shay! Democratic resolution for woman suffrage in New York! Landslide for woman suffrage in Colorado!" This referred to a letter from Colorado, saying that there seemed to be a regular landslide there, as all the parties were passing resolutions in favor of the pending amendment. The thought in her mind evidently was that the opposition was giving way in all directions at once, like the One-Horse Shay.

She said to her husband, "Send a hundred dollars to Mrs. Carrie Lane Chapman. She has a level head."

The news of the granting of suffrage in New Zealand also brought her joy.

She was to have addressed the New England Agricultural Fair, and her husband took her place. When a friend told her how well he had spoken, she answered, "He always does. Dear Mr. Blackwell, how he has helped!" She thanked him and me fervently, not for what we had done for her, but for what we had done for the cause. When she was told that all the papers were saying pleasant things about her, she said, "Oh, if they would only all come out for woman suffrage!"

The last editorial that she dictated for the *Woman's Journal* was published only eleven days before her death. It said:

"The Boston Herald last Sunday commented upon the Woman's Building at the World's Fair, and said it was a wrong idea to have a separate exhibit of women's work. The Herald said men and women ought not to be separated, but ought to go everywhere together, hand in hand and side by side. Whatever our opinion may be in regard to the Woman's Building, the Herald is right as to the general principle. The Herald is an able paper. Will it use its great influence to help men and women go side by side to the ballot box?"

The end came on October 18, 1893. On the last afternoon, she was very weak. She seemed to wish to say something. I put my ear to her lips. She said distinctly, "Make the world better!" They were almost her last articulate words.

The following poem was one that had pleased her during her illness. She had cut it out of some newspaper:

"Up and away like the dew of the morning,
That soars from the earth to its home in the sun,
So let me steal away, gently and lovingly,
Only remembered by what I have done.

"My name and my place and my tomb all forgotten,
The brief race of time well and patiently run,
So let me pass away, peacefully, silently,
Only remembered by what I have done.

. . . . .

"Needs there the praise of the love-written record,
The name and the epitaph graved on the stone?
The things we have lived for, let them be our
story;
We ourselves but remembered by what we have
done.

. . . . .

"I need not be missed, if another succeed me,
To reap down those fields which in spring I have
sown;
He who plowed and who sowed is not missed by
the reaper,
He is only remembered by what he has done.

"Not myself, but the truth that in life I have spoken,
Not myself, but the seed that in life I have sown,
Shall pass on to ages, all about me forgotten,
Save the truth I have spoken, the things I have
done.

"So let my living be, so be my dying,
So let my name be, unblazoned, unknown;
Unpraised and unmissed, I shall still be remem-
bered,
Yes, but remembered by what I have done."

She had advised us not to have a public funeral. She said there would not be enough people who would care to come, to fill a church, but she left us free to do as we thought best.

The funeral was held in the Church of the Disciples. Hours before the time set for the services, the throng began to gather, and when the doors were opened, hundreds were standing in silence in the street. Eleven hundred persons filled the historic church to its utmost capacity. The *Christian Register* said:

"An immense audience was present. Never have we seen in Boston a more representative gathering of people interested in social, philanthropic and political reform. . . . The occasion was deeply impressive and fitting, as were the addresses. The great, silent audience, which packed the floor, gallery and aisles, spoke still more eloquently its tribute."

The speakers and pallbearers were among the noblest citizens of the community. She had asked that her funeral should be bright and cheerful, and that everything should be as simple and natural as possible. Beside the pulpit stood a plaster cast of Anne Whitney's bust of her, and a life-size portrait of Wendell Phillips. The coffin was almost buried in flowers. Her face, under its familiar white lace cap, looked peaceful and serene, as lovely as in life, and wonderfully young. A little bunch of lilies of the valley, a flower she loved, had been placed in her hand. By her request, two of Whittier's poems were read, containing the lines,

Not on a blind and aimless way
The spirit goeth,

and

I know not where His islands lift
Their fronded palms in air;
I only know I cannot drift
Beyond His love and care.

The Reverend Charles G. Ames conducted the services. He said afterwards that it seemed less like a funeral than like a coronation.

As we stood behind the coffin, waiting for the funeral procession to move forward out of the church, my father whispered to me, "She leads us still."

She had wished to have her body cremated, and it was done in the new crematory at Forest Hills. This was the first cremation to take place in New England. A pioneer in death as in life, she still helped to make the world better.

Under the heading, "She Leads Us Still", Mr. Blackwell wrote in the *Woman's Journal:*

"The gentlest and most heroic of women has passed away. The woman who in her whole character and life most fully embodied our highest conceptions as daughter, sister, wife, mother, friend and citizen, no longer lives to disarm prejudice and convert even opposition into advocacy. For seventy-five years Lucy Stone has spent her life for others. We who are left must henceforth carry on our work without her.

"Pure-minded and simple-hearted as a child, no guile or duplicity marred her perfect sincerity. She was faithful to every duty and responsive to every call.

"Dear friends of woman suffrage everywhere, let the loving, unselfish life of our departed friend and leader be to us faith, courage and inspiration. In no way can we so cherish her memory as by promoting the cause that was to her more dear and sacred than any other."

Many ministers made her life the subject of a sermon.

The newspapers, far and near, paid tribute to her worth. An old opponent said that up to that time the death of no woman in America had called out so widespread a tribute of affection and esteem.

## *Chapter XX*

When my father and I came down from the chamber in which Lucy Stone had just breathed her last, he said to me, "We must try to keep Mamma's flag flying."

We found our chief comfort in working to carry forward the cause to which she had devoted her life. For the sixteen years during which he outlived her, my father was always at its service. No distance was too great, no weather too bad, for him to go wherever he was called to speak; and he was always ready to do any piece of hard and thankless work that nobody else cared to undertake.

At first his heart was broken. He had written to her in 1857: "If, from beyond the grave, it be indeed permitted to influence and inspire, dear Lucy, you shall always find an open heart and an expectant longing." Now he sat night after night alone in her room in the dark, to see if her spirit might come to him; but there was no voice or token, and neither he nor I could put any faith in the mediums who professed to bring us messages from her. But we knew what she would have wished us to do, and we tried to do it. Friends rallied to the cause; within a few weeks came the news of the victory in Colorado; and year after year her soul went marching on.

Some years after Mrs. Stone's death, hundreds of suffragists celebrated her birthday by a Pilgrimage to the old home on Coy's Hill where she was born. It is still occupied by her grandnephew and his family. Speeches were made on the lawn, a memorial tree was planted, and a tablet was placed upon the house.

Both of my parents had been members of the first society of the American Friends of Russian Freedom. They might truly have said, with James Russell Lowell:

Wherever wrong is done
To the humblest and the weakest, 'neath the all-beholding sun,
That wrong is also done to us; and they are slaves most base
Whose love of right is for themselves, and not for all their race.

Later Mr. Blackwell was an officer in the Friends of Armenia, and spoke at innumerable protest meetings against the Armenian massacres.

Our Armenian man of all work was the only child of a widow. He saved money and paid her fare to this country, only to be notified that she could not land and must be deported. The time was short. Mr. Blackwell took the next train to Washington, saw the head of the Immigration Bureau, secured the intercession of United States Senator George F. Hoar and others, went himself to New York, and, just as they were leading the old woman up the gangplank to send her back to a country where she had no longer a single living relative, he appeared with the papers that enabled her to stay till her case could be further investigated. She was finally allowed to stay for good.

He was a frequent speaker at the meetings held to protest against the Jewish pogroms in Russia. His age, his eloquence, and his connection with the old struggles for freedom in the United States, made the new citizens look upon him as the ideal American. The great Jewish audiences stood up when he rose to speak, as audiences of all kinds did for Mrs. Julia Ward Howe in her old age. At the last of these gatherings that he addressed — the jubilee meeting held when President Roosevelt refused to surrender Jan Pouren to the Czar — he got a greater ovation than Jan Pouren himself.

He had more leisure than in former years. A group of very capable young women took hold of the suffrage work in Massachusetts, and carried it forward, with great ability, till the victory was won.

At the annual meetings of the National American Woman Suffrage Association, there were never more than a few male delegates present. Sometimes Mr. Blackwell was the only one. He was always there, and he thoroughly enjoyed himself in the congenial society of a crowd of strong-minded women. He was always appointed chairman of the Committee on Resolutions, a position where he was able to render excellent service, because of his facility in writing fine English, his good nature in dealing with the many persons who presented freak resolutions, and his clear, strong voice in reading the report of the Resolutions Committee to the convention.

He attended practically every annual meeting for forty years — during the first twenty years, those of the American Woman Suffrage Association, and during the last twenty, those of the National American. His curls, so black in his youth, were now brilliantly white. The Reverend Anna Garlin Spencer's little daughter took him for Santa Claus. Other children often noticed the likeness. His face, beaming with kindness and mirth, aided the illusion.

He and William Lloyd Garrison the second were great friends. They were congenial spirits, both of them overflowing with fun. They were interested in many of the same good causes and worked for them together. At the celebration of Mr.

Blackwell's eightieth birthday, Mr. Garrison said:

"The conduct of his special cause does not diminish his interest in every struggle for human freedom. He breaks a lance for all downtrodden and oppressed peoples. Wherever a protest against tyranny is called for, you may be sure that Mr. Blackwell will answer "Adsum." When he does his sleeping, who can tell? Tonight an Armenian meeting may claim his presence, tomorrow Russian exiles enlist his aid. If the Chinese are in the toils of persecution, he counts himself among their friends. When his fellow citizens rise against the coal monopoly, he is at Faneuil Hall to make the rousing speech of the occasion. When prejudice against the Negro and lynching horrors are to be denounced, his eloquent indignation is assured. He abhors Imperialism, advocates with enthusiasm reciprocity and freer trade, is numerous at the State House committee hearings, day or evening, to speak the humanitarian word on topics of wide diversity. Pervasive, patient, modest, direct, kind in his judgments, and possessed of saving humor, he moves among his antagonists without exciting rancor, or having the capacity to cherish it himself. . . . Having finished his four-score years with juvenile freshness, he celebrates the beginning of his eighty-first year by helping organize a movement for the Initiative and Referendum. How fortunate for us that he was early transplanted from English Bristol!"

On this occasion, the Annual Festival of the New England and Massachusetts Woman Suffrage Associations in Faneuil Hall, a pleasant surprise awaited him in the presentation of a silver pitcher and salver from the Massachusetts Woman Suffrage Association, "In gratitude", said the inscription, "for his unswerving support of his beloved wife, Lucy Stone, in her life work, and for his fifty years of unselfish and untiring labor for the enfranchisement of women."

Mr. Blackwell, in his response, spoke of the assurance he gave to Lucy Stone, during his courtship, that, together, they could do more for woman's rights than she could do alone. He said, "If she had not believed that it might be so, she never would have married. Therefore, am I not under an honorable obligation to devote every energy of mind and body to make that promise good, knowing, as I do, that all I can do in a lifetime will not do as much as she did in the first three years after I knew her?"

The last of the long series of National Suffrage Conventions that he attended was that held in Seattle in July, 1909. As usual, he enjoyed much fun and sociability with old friends on the train that carried the large crowd of delegates across the country. There was one colored woman among them, and, as she was not acceptable to all, he took especial pains to show her kindness and courtesy. He addressed several open-air meetings en route, and spoke at the Seattle Convention with his old vigor. He came home afterwards by the Northern Pacific, and greatly enjoyed the sail to Vancouver and the magnificent scenery of the Canadian Rockies.

In the course of this trip, some one said, in introducing him to a friend, "This gentleman is the husband of Lucy Stone — or was the husband of Lucy Stone." "Is the husband of Lucy Stone," he said, in a tone of tenderness and pride.

His last public appearance was at a great suffrage festival given by Mrs. O. H. P. Belmont at the Marble House in Newport, Rhode Island.

He was active to the end. Most men of his age lean upon their children. To the very last, I leaned upon him. He was so vigorous physically, so alert and youthful mentally, that he was more like a brother than a father. However late at night I got back from a lecture trip, he was always waiting at the station to meet me and to carry my suit case up the hill. At eighty-four, he was eager to go out and "stump" the three far-Western States where suffrage amendments were pending, and seriously discussed the possibility of doing so.

He had worked for woman suffrage in more than twenty States. In many of them he and his wife had helped to organize the State Suffrage Association. He had been Corresponding Secretary of the American Woman Suffrage Association for nearly twenty years, and that of the New England Woman Suffrage Association twice as long. He never took a dollar of compensation for all his work, either in the Suffrage Associations or on the *Woman's Journal*, but, on the contrary, put money largely into both.

One hot day, he was unexpectedly invited by ex-Governor Foss to go with him to his summer home at Cohasset, to talk over with a few friends a plan for tariff reform, in which Mr. Blackwell was much interested. He went just as he was, very lightly clad, and took a chill, which led to an illness resulting in his death about ten days later, on September 7, 1909.

His sense of fun was indomitable. He joked with the doctor on his deathbed. His kindness of heart was shown to the last by his solicitude to spare everybody trouble. "Poor child!" he said of the trained nurse, "she has a hard life"; and he added, "I pity everybody." He left a half-written review of "Misery and Its Causes", by Edward T. Devine. Attracted by its title, he had sent for the book. The misery of the world had impressed itself upon him more and more during his latter years, and he wanted to see what suggestions could be made for a remedy.

He left directions that his body should be cremated. He rather disliked the idea of cremation, but he wished to follow his wife's example, and to have their ashes mingled in one urn.

He strongly disapproved of show and expense at funerals, and had often said that he wished to have no coffin, only a simple pine box. His directions were carried out. A dark cloth spread over the box covered all singularities.

The service at the Forest Hills Crematory was conducted by Doctor Borden P. Bowne. He said, in part:

"I do not know whether Mr. Blackwell belonged to any church organization, and I am not much concerned to know; but of this I am sure, that he belonged to the Church of churches — the Church of the Good Samaritan. In this church, Mr. Blackwell was a most efficient member, in good and regular standing. He loved righteousness and hated iniquity. He had a passion for justice, and devoted his life to securing it. Those who spoke wickedly concerning oppression found in him a determined and strenuous opponent. He lived with protest on his lips and with resistance in his will against everything that harmed or hindered humanity. The oppressed Russian knew him; the outraged Armenian knew him;

the Southern slave knew him; and they all loved and honored him. His individual benefactions were numberless, and generally wise. His life has been a blessing to multitudes. It would be hard, indeed, to find another such record as this, or another man so widely beloved as he. Social conditions are more just, laws are more equal, public morality has a higher tone, and the public conscience is more keen and discerning because of his life and work.

"'Never rode to the wrong's redressing
A worthier Paladin.
Shall he not hear the blessing,
"Good and faithful, enter in"?'

"And those lines of Whittier's remind me of what a knightly soul Mr. Blackwell was. The bravery and the tenderness, together with something of the romance we associate with knighthood, were all his. One could always locate him, for

"'He stood four-square to every wind that blew.'"

The regret for his death was widespread, even among those who had known him but slightly. For every one he had had a smile, a pleasant word and a joke. Even the attorney of the Anti-Suffrage Association, who had assailed him with jibes and jeers at the legislative hearings for years, said after his death, "He was a splendid man."

Edward A. Filene said, "He was an inspiration to men like myself, in his unconquerable youth and enthusiasm and efficiency for the good." Mrs. Carrie Chapman Catt summed up the feeling of many hearts when she called Lucy Stone and Henry B. Blackwell "one of the noblest of the world's women and one of the most heroic of the world's men."

The homestead at Number 45 Boutwell Street, Dorchester, was deeded in 1919 to "The Lucy Stone Home", a small corporation formed to use it for benevolent purposes. Ever since, they have given the use of it to the Morgan Memorial, which houses some of its social workers there, has meetings of its boys' and girls' clubs there in winter, and every summer brings out hundreds of mothers and children from the poor districts of the city for a day's country outing, and a bath by the children in the salt water of the bay. The sight of the happy children at play and the tired mothers resting under the trees would bring joy to the hearts of its former owners.

The lesson of such lives as theirs is summed up in a few words spoken by Harriet Beecher Stowe at a celebration in Boston of her birthday, at which Lucy Stone and Henry B. Blackwell were among the guests. After many famous men and women had paid their tributes to her, in prose and verse, the sweet-faced, white-haired little old woman stood up to reply. She said nothing could have seemed more hopeless, in her youth, than the effort to abolish slavery, so strongly was it entrenched in all the seats of power; yet it had all been swept away. She told those who were seeking to do away with other wrongs never to be discouraged, no matter how great the odds against them might seem, and she added, "Remember, whatever ought to be done can be done!"

In the beginning, the movement for woman's rights seemed even more hopeless than the movement against slavery. To-day the flag that Lucy Stone raised and that her husband and daughter tried to keep flying, floats on every breeze. Women are voting throughout most of the civilized world. But the warfare between the kingdom of darkness and the kingdom of light goes on without ceasing. Other great wrongs still remain. They seem as impregnably intrenched as the injustices that confronted Lucy Stone and Henry B. Blackwell in their youth; yet they are destined to go down, and the lives of the old worthies are a bugle call to the new generation to take up the fight against them, and, in the new times and under changed conditions, still to do their part to "make the world better."

## *Appendix*

1. Shays' Rebellion: Lucy Stone always maintained that there was much reason for that revolt by the farmers. A graphic description of Shays' Rebellion and its causes is given by Edward Bellamy in "The Duke of Stockbridge."

2. Antoinette L. Brown was ordained in the Orthodox Congregational church of South Butler, New York, on September 15, 1853. The ordination sermon was preached by the Reverend Luther Lee (Methodist Protestant), of Syracuse. Prayer was offered by Elder McCoon of South Butler (Baptist), Reverend Mr. Hicks of Walworth gave the charge to the pastor, and there was an address by Gerrit Smith of Peterboro.

While a Congregational church was the first to call and ordain a woman minister, the Universalists were the first denomination to authorize the ordaining of women, as a denomination.

3. The Brooklyn Woman Suffrage Association and many individual suffragists in New York always stood with the American. On the other hand, most of the Connecticut suffragists sided with the National.

4. The officers elected at the time of the union were: President, Elizabeth Cady Stanton; Vice President, Susan B. Anthony; Chairman of the Executive Committee, Lucy Stone; Treasurer, Jane H. Spofford; Recording Secretary, Rachel Foster Avery; Corresponding Secretary, Alice Stone Blackwell; Auditors, Eliza T. Ward and Reverend Frederick A. Hinckley; National Lecturer, Doctor Anna Howard Shaw.

In the American Association, men and women had worked together. Under the constitution of the National, men had been debarred from office. In the National American, no constitutional disabilities were laid upon men; but the later work passed almost wholly into the hands of women.

5. The *Woman's Journal* was a joint stock company, and was incorporated in 1870 by Henry B. Blackwell, Samuel E. Sewall and Ebenezer D. Draper.

The New England Woman Suffrage Association had urged the establishment of the *Journal*. It took stock in the paper, and repeatedly helped it financially, sharing with it the proceeds of some of the great Suffrage Bazaars. It finally expressed its appreciation of Mrs. Stone's services by making over to her all its stock in the paper.

6. Some years after Mrs. Stone and Mr. Blackwell died, the *Woman's Journal* was adopted for a time by the National American Woman Suf-

frage Association as its official organ; but this did not prove permanent. In 1917, under an amicable arrangement planned chiefly by Mrs. Catt, the *Journal* was moved to New York, was consolidated with two other suffrage papers to form the *Woman Citizen*, and became the property of the Leslie Commission. The *Woman Citizen* has lately resumed the old name of the *Woman's Journal*.

7. Paxton Hibben does not mention this fact in his "debunking" biography of Mr. Beecher, as he should have done, to be fair. His book seems, on the surface, to be strongly documented; but the references, if looked up, often fail to bear out what they are supposed to prove. This is emphatically true of those relating to woman suffrage. Any one taking the trouble to look up the references purporting to show that he became lukewarm in his interest in that cause will find that they show just the opposite. Mr. Beecher's record in regard to woman suffrage, after he became a convert to it, was one hundred per cent good.

# INDEX

Adams, Abigail, 94
Adams, John Quincy, 37
Adams, Miss, 50, 69
Adkinson, Mrs. Florence M., 235
Advocate of Moral Reform, The, 16
Agitator, The, 236
Alcott, Louisa M., 124
Amendment campaigns in Vermont, Michigan, Nebraska, Colorado and Rhode Island, 246
Ames, Rev. Charles G., 285
Ames, Frederick, 269
American Equal Rights Association, 202, 207, 209, 214, 218, 219, 224, 239
American Flag, Views about, 254
American Friends of Russian Freedom, 285
American Party, 170, 180
American Society of University Women, 270
American Woman Suffrage Association, 216, 218, 221, 223 to 229, 240, 241, 244, 249, 264, 290, 294, Appendix 300
American Woman Suffrage Association, takes part in organizing, 215, 216
Ancestry, Lucy Stone's, 7, 8
Andrews, Stephen Pearl, 222
Anthony, Susan B., 99, 101, 103, 105, 106, 107, 111, 112, 115, 116, 170, 172, 197, 198, 200, 208, 210, 211, 213, 214, 219, 220, 221, 223, 225, 226, 231, 242, 266, 267, 274, Appendix 300
Antislavery lecture, synopsis of, 83
Antislavery lecturing, 76 to 86
Anti-Slavery Standard, The, 17, 79, 211
Antisuffragists, The, 245, 251, 255, 296
Armenia, Friends of, 288
Armenian question, 272
Armenian woman, rescue of, 288
Association for the Advancement of Women, 251, 252
Association of Collegiate Alumnae, 270
Atkins, Miss, 117
Avery, Rachel Foster, Appendix 300

Barney, Mrs. Nathaniel, 106
Baptists, unpopularity of, 17
Barrows, Mrs. Isabel C., 272
Barrows, Rev. Samuel J., 272
Barstow, Mayor, 115
Beecher, Catherine, 114
Beecher, Henry Ward, 211, 216, 249, 251, Appendix 301
Beecher, Dr. Lyman, 48
Beecher-Tilton scandal, 248, 249, 250, 251
Beet-sugar making, 269
Bell, Dr., 132
Bellamy, Edward, Appendix 299
Belmont, Mrs. O. H. P., 293
Blackwell, Alice Stone, 195, 199, 271, 273, 276, Appendix 300
Blackwell, Anna, 130, 138, 142, 143
Blackwell, Dr. Elizabeth, 125, 126, 138, 139, 140, 141, 142, 145, 163, 207
Blackwell, Dr. Emily, 138, 140, 141, 207
Blackwell family, The, 136 to 143

Blackwell, George W., 137, 142
Blackwell, Hannah (Lane), 136, 137, 138, 143, 145
Blackwell, Henry B., 4, 97, 104, 124, 125, 137, 142 to 155, 163 to 165, 177 to 182, 197, 202, 203, 204, 207, 213, 216, 219, 220, 231, 232, 238, 246, 247, 262, 265, 275, 276, 281, 285 to 297, Appendix 300
Blackwell, Howard, 142
Blackwell, Marian, 138, 140, 142
Blackwell, Rev. Dr. Antoinette Brown, 56 to 60, 62, 73, 74, 99, 112, 116 to 120, 122, 123, 162, 163, 198, 199, and Appendix 299
Blackwell, Samuel, 127, 136 to 138
Blackwell, Samuel C., 97, 98, 123, 136, 137, 138, 142, 143 to 145, 185
Blackwell, Sarah Ellen, 142, 198
Blagden, Dr., 25
Bloomer, Mrs. Amelia, 103, 111
Bloomer dress, 101 to 113
Boston Herald, 281
Boston Post, 163, 175
Boston Public Library, 274
Boston University, 271, 274
Brattleboro Democrat, 84
Brent, Margaret, 94
Brook Farm, 130
Brooklyn Woman Suffrage Association, Appendix 299
Brown, Antoinette L., see Blackwell, Rev. Dr. Antoinette Brown.
Brown, Rev. Olympia, 208
Bryant, William Cullen, 261
Bowditch, William I., 253
Bowne, Dr. Borden P., 295
Bullard, Laura Curtis, 220
Buller, Judge, 4
Bunker Hill Monument, 252
Burleigh, Charles C., 99, 146, 147, 149, 163 to 166
Bust, Portrait, 273, 274
Butler, Josephine E., 241
CALL FOR FIRST NATIONAL WOMAN'S RIGHTS CONVENTION, 97
Callanan, Mrs. Martha C., 273
Cameron, Dr., 244
Campbell, Mrs. Margaret W., 238
Canada, secures Married Women's Property Law for, 244
Cape Cod, subdues mob on, 80, 81
Carroll, Anna Ella, 142
Catt, Mrs. Carrie Chapman, 240, 243, 265, 276, 281, 297, Appendix 301
Centennial Exposition, 252, 253
Chadwick, John W., 276
Channing, William Henry, 121
Chapman, Carrie Lane, see Carrie Chapman Catt.
Chapman, Mrs., 71
Chapman, Rev. Mr., 77
Chase, Hon. Salmon P., 171, 179, 180, 195
Chase, Rev. Moses, 48
Chauncy Hall School, 271
Cheever, Dr., 122
Chicago Exposition, 273, 274, 276
Chickatawbut Club, 269
Child, Lydia Maria, 220
Childhood, Lucy Stone's, 9 to 16
Chilmark, Martha's Vineyard, 268
Chosen delegate to Massachusetts Republican Convention, 247
Christian Register, 272, 284
Church denounced by Garrisonians, 48
Church denounced by Lucy Stone, 84, 85
Cincinnati Columbian, 133
Cincinnati Commercial, 150
Cincinnati Enquirer, 155
Cincinnati Gazette, 150
Cincinnati Literary Club, 149, 150
Civil War, 200, 201, 208, 210, 236
Civil War work, 200
Claflin, Jehiel, 85
Claflin, Miss Tennessee, 221

Clashes with Ladies' Board, 50, 60, 61, 63, 68, 70, 114, 117
Codman, Charlie, 267
College, preparation for, 37
College, resolves to go to, 16
Collins, Mrs. Emily P., 4
Colorado, 239, 281, 289
Colored School, teaches, 51, 52
Come-Outers, 47, 48
Commencement essay, refuses to write, 67 to 70, 72, 73
Converts Susan B. Anthony, 99
Congregational Church, Antoinette L. Brown joins, 56
Congregational Church, Lucy Stone joins, 22
Congregational Church meeting, Lucy Stone refused vote in, 22, 23
Congregational Ministers, General Association of, issues Pastoral Letter, 24
Congregational Ministers withdraw, 37
Congregational Church of South Butler, N. Y., ordains Antoinette L. Brown, 122, Appendix 299
Congregational Church of West Brookfield expels Lucy Stone, 86 to 88
Congregational Church, power of, 25
Constitutional Convention of Montana, 265, 266
Constitutional Convention of North Dakota, 265
Constitutional Convention of Washington, 265
Coombs, Ryland and Blackwell, 153
Courage, Lucy Stone's, 14, 15
Courtship, 124 to 131, 145, 146, 155 to 160
Cowles, Mrs. Professor, 114
Cowles, Professor, 55
Coy's Hill, 7, 279, 288
Cox, General, 50
Crandall, Prudence, 138
Cremation, 285, 295
Cummington, meeting at, 77
Curtis, George William, 220
Cushing, Benjamin, 176

Dana, Charles A., 118
Davis, Paulina Wright, 95, 98
Death of Lucy Stone, 282
Debating club of college girls, organizes first, 60 to 62, 72
Denounced by press as "she-hyena", etc., 92, 93
Delegate to Massachusetts Republican Convention, 247
Determines to work for woman's rights, 15
Devine, Edward T., 294
Dietrick, Mrs., 273
Discontinues lecturing, temporarily, for baby's sake, 199
Disunionism, 67
Division between American and National Woman Suffrage Associations, history of, 206 to 231
Divorce question, 216, 217, 219, 220
Donaldson, Christian, 147, 150
Douglass, Frederick, 99, 146
Dow, General Neal, 119
Draper, Ebenezer D., 104, Appendix 300

Eagle, Mrs. Governor, 276
Earl, Sarah H., 98
East Bridgewater meeting, 80
Eddy, Mrs. Eliza F., 142
Elder, Dr. William, 97
Ellsler, Fanny, 252
Eloquence, Lucy Stone's, 76
Emerson, Ralph Waldo, 97, 150
Emigrants' Aid Societies, 151

Fall, Mrs. Anna Christy, 258
Fall, George H., 258
Fairchild, Mr., 54
Fairchild, Professor, 117

Family life, 232 to 235, 256
Farmers' Libraries, 194, 196, 197
Fifteenth Amendment, 202, 212, 213, 214, 218
Filene, Edward A., 299
Finney, Professor, 47, 48, 59
First National Woman's Rights Convention, heads call for, 97
First public speech, Lucy Stone's, 65
First woman's rights lecture, Lucy Stone's, 75
First women college graduates, 43
Fourteenth and Fifteenth Amendments, urges inclusion of women in, 201, 202
Follen, Mrs., 71
Foss, Ex-Governor, 294
Foster, Abby Kelley, 24, 26, 32 to 37, 39, 63, 67, 71, 95, 99, 115, 253, 262
Foster, Stephen S., 33, 63, 67, 80, 81, 99
Fourteenth Amendment, 201, 223, 224
Free love, 222, 224, 225
Free Soilers, 82, 83
Free Soil Party, 83
Friendship with Antoinette L. Brown, 56 to 60
Fuller, Margaret, 94
Funeral, Lucy Stone's, 283

Gage, Mrs. Frances D., 144
Gage, Mrs. Matilda Josslyn, 226
Garner, Margaret, 183 to 185
Garrison, Francis J., 169
Garrison, Mrs., 239
Garrison, William Lloyd, 26, 29, 38, 41, 59, 67, 73, 96, 99, 125, 138, 195, 211, 212, 216, 236, 256, 262
Garrison, William Lloyd, Second, 290, 291
Garrisonian Abolitionists, 48, 82
Gilman, Charlotte Perkins, 238
Golden Age, The, 224
Graduation, Lucy Stone's, 72
Greek Slave, 89
Greeley, Horace, 118, 119, 203
Greene, Judge, 245
Greenwood, Grace, 108
Grew, Mary, 260
Griffing, Josephine, 114
Grimké, Angelina, see Angelina Grimké Weld
Grimké, Sarah, 26 to 32, 34, 35, 37, 94, 103, 126, 262
Guild, Gen. Curtis, 271

Haiti, 268
Hanna, Mrs. John R., 276
Harper, Mrs. Ida Husted, 231
Harper's Weekly, 220
Has hymn-book hurled at her head and is drenched with water, 80
Hayes, Professor Ellen, 232
Hayes, Rutherford B., 150
Hazeltine, Ira, 187
Henshaw, Deacon, 22, 125
Hibben, Paxton, Appendix 301
Hicks, Rev. Mr., Appendix 299
Higginson, Col. Thomas Wentworth, 115, 116, 124, 162, 163, 168, 172, 196, 197, 199, 215, 220, 236, 237, 245, 259
Hinckley, Rev. Frederic A., 268, Appendix 300
Hinsdale and Dalton meeting, 78, 79
History of Woman's Rights Movement, 199
History of Woman Suffrage, 119, 207, 226, 227, 231, 242
Hoar, Senator George F., 289
Holmes, Mrs. Mary E., 273
Hooker, Isabella Beecher, 225, 249
Housework in Ladies' Boarding Hall at three cents an hour, 49
Howe, Julia Ward, 204, 216, 220, 236, 237, 246, 251, 252, 257, 266, 267, 274, 289
Howe, Dr. Samuel Gridley, 268
Hunt, George S., 269

Hunt, Dr. Harriot K., 95, 253
Hutchinson Family, 91
Hutchinson, John, 91

Illinois Equal Suffrage Association, 273
Immortality of animals, 39
Imperialism, 291
Infidel, is denounced as, 84
Initiative and Referendum, 291
Interested in the Grange, the college settlements, working girls' clubs, labor societies, Woman's Christian Temperance Union and Christian Endeavor, 270
International Council of Women, in addresses at, Susan B. Anthony, Julia Ward Howe and Frances E. Willard ascribe their conversion to woman suffrage to Lucy Stone, 266, 267

Jackson, Mrs. Helen (H. H.), 259
Jewish pogroms, 289
Jews, makes successful appeal to, 200, 201
Joan of Arc, 199
Johnson, Rowland, 196
Joint guardianship bill, 245, 258
Jones, Benjamin S., 114
Jones, Mrs. J. Elizabeth, 114
Jones, Jenkin Lloyd, 276

Kansas Amendment Campaign, 206 to 210
Kansas, drafts two laws for, 206, 207
Kansas Impartial Suffrage Association, 207
Kelley, Abby, see Abby Kelley Foster
Kemper College, 143
Kenney, Eliza J., 95

Labor Party Endorses Woman Suffrage, 247
Ladies' Board of Oberlin College, 50, 53, 60, 61, 63, 68, 70, 114, 117
Lamb, Charles, 7
Lane, Hannah, see Hannah (Lane) Blackwell, 136
Lane, "Jem," 208
Lane Seminary, 48, 143
Lee, Rev. Luther, Appendix 299
Lee, Richard Henry, 94
Leslie Commission, Appendix 301
Letter to brother on the woman question, 37 to 40
Liberator, The, 17, 22, 49, 82, 83, 85, 101, 115
Liberty Party, 179, 180
Lily, The, 103
Lincoln, Abraham, 179, 196, 197
Livermore, Rev. D. P., 236, 237
Livermore, Mrs. Mary A., 100, 216, 236, 238, 247, 251, 257
Locke, John, 54
Logan, Mrs. John A., 274
Lloyd, Mercy, 71
Long, Governor, 269
Long, Lucy, 160
Louisville Courier Journal, 132, 133
Lowell, James Russell, 261, 288
Loyal League, 200
Lucy Stone Home, 297
Lucy Stone League, 177, 178
Ludlow, H. G., 38
Lyon, Mary, 20, 40

Mahan, President, 63, 68, 69
Mallon, Judge, 149
Margaret Garner case, 183 to 185
Marietta College, 56
Marriage, Lucy Stone's, 161 to 170
Marriage Protest, 161, 162, 165 to 170
Marriage Protest, calumnies arising from, 169
Massachusetts Anti-Slavery Society, 37, 71, 89, 90, 95
Massachusetts Club, 269

Massachusetts Constitutional Convention, 124
Massachusetts Democratic Convention, 248
Massachusetts, removal to, 205
Massachusetts Republican Convention, 247, 248
Massachusetts Spy, 16
Massachusetts Woman Suffrage Association, 205, 240, 244, 264, 292
May, Samuel, 76, 89, 98
McCoon, Elder, Appendix 299
McDowell, Dr., 132
Medical College of Geneva, N. Y., 139, 140
Melis, David M., 210
Memorial tablets, in Orange, N. J., 196, in Viroqua, Wis., 189, and in West Brookfield, Mass., 288
Michigan Amendment Campaign, 251
Middle West, lectures in; amusing incidents, 131 to 135
Mill, John Stuart, 99
Miller, Mrs. Elizabeth Smith, 113
Moore, Augustus, 194
Morgan Memorial, 297
Morgan, Professor, 55, 62, 117
"Morning star" of the woman's rights movement, 94
Mother love, 199, 203, 204
Mott, James, 109, 145
Mott, Lucretia, 30, 41, 99, 108, 109, 121, 145, 202
Mount Holyoke Seminary, 20, 40
Mowry, Dr. Martha H., 99
Mowry, Mr., 257

NAME, first conceives idea that married woman should keep her own, 62
Name for daughter discussed, 195
Name, keeps her own, 171 to 177
Nantucket Lyceum, 105
Nation, The, 286
National American Woman Suffrage Association, 228, 276, 290, Appendix 300
National Convention of Republican Leagues, 248
National Democratic Convention, 247
National Republican Convention, 247
National Woman's Rights Conventions: First, 95, 98, 99; Second, 100; Third, 100, 101; Fourth, 120, 121; Fifth, 144; Eleventh, 202; Fortieth, 292, 293
National Woman Suffrage Association, 215, 217, 218, 221, 224 to 229, 249
National Woman Suffrage Committee, 221
National Woman Suffrage Conventions, 290, 292
Nature, love of, 7, 11, 277 to 279
New England and Massachusetts Woman Suffrage Associations, takes part in organizing, 204, 205
New England Woman Suffrage Association, 204, 215, 240, 244, 254, 264, 292, 294, Appendix 300
New England Women's Club, 270, 273
New England Women's Press Association, 270, 280
New Jersey Legislature, appeals to, 202
New Jersey, removal to, 193
New Jersey, suffrage in early, 202
New Jersey, suffrage work in, 202, 203
New Jersey Woman Suffrage Association, 203
New York Infirmary for Women and Children, 141, 249
New York State Democratic Convention, 280

New York Sun, 118
New York Tribune, 99, 119, 174, 266
New York World, 210
New Zealand grants equal suffrage, 281

Oberlin College, 34, 42 to 46, 116 to 118, 274
Oberlin, day's work at, 53, 54
Oberlin Evangelist, 17
Oberlin, John Frederic, 43
Oberlin's semicentennial, 49, 74
Opens new occupations to women, 101
Orange, N. J., life in, 193
Orvis, Professor, 55
Overworks to save her mother, 19

Palmer, Mrs. Potter, 275, 276
Pankhurst, Dr., 139
Parker, Theodore, 101, 124, 150
Parsons, Anna, 164
Pastoral Letter, 24, 25, 27
Paxton, Mass., school teaching in, 23
Peace, strong views on, 55
Pennsylvania Hall, 31
Personal appearance, 21
Personal characteristics, 233 to 235, 258 to 264
Phillips, Wendell, 28, 29, 41, 96, 99, 100, 104, 119, 121, 124, 162, 198, 211, 239, 260, 262, 284
Pilgrimage to Lucy Stone's birthplace, 288
Pillsbury, Parker, 80, 210
Poe, Edgar Allan, 142
Poetry, love of, 261
Political Conventions, 247, 248
Political resolutions, 280
Pope's Hill, Dorchester, home at, 232
Porter, Zeruiah, 43
Portrait Bust by Anne Whitney, 273, 274
Pouren, Jan, 289
Powers, Hiram, 89
Prall, Elizabeth Smith, 43
Prentice, George D., 132
Preparation for college, 37
Princeton, mob at, 203
Prohibition Party endorses woman suffrage, 247
Pullan, R. B., 180 to 182

Quaboag Seminary, 37

Raritan Bay Union, 129
Refuses to rake up early misdeeds of National Association in Woman's Journal, 237
Religious intolerance, resists, 241
Removal to Massachusetts, 205
Rescue of little slave girl, 147 to 150
Republican Party, 210
Revolution, The, 210, 212, 214, 215, 220, 221
Rhode Island, early lecturers in, 81, 82
Rhode Island Freeman, The, 81
Robinson, Ex-Governor, of Kansas, 206, 208
Rose, Mrs. Ernestine L., 94, 99
Roosevelt, President, 289
Rudd, Mary Caroline, 43
Rush Medical School, 141
Russia, pogroms in, 289
Russian Freedom, American Friends of, 288

Sachs, Emanie, 222
Salem, Abby Kelley, 148, 149
Sampson, Deacon L., 87
Santo Domingo, 268
Savin Hill Park secured, 268
School vote, is barred from, 173 to 177
Seattle Convention, 292, 293
Seneca Falls Convention, 75, 99, 266
Servants, beloved by her, 256, 257

Severance, Mrs. Caroline M., 119, 215
Sewall, Judge, 5
Sewall, Samuel E., Appendix 300
Shaw, Dr. Anna Howard, Appendix 300
Shays' Rebellion, 8, and Appendix 299
Sherborn Reformatory for Women, 260
Shipherd, Rev. John, 42, 118
Shurtleff Public School, 274
Sixteenth Amendment, 224
Smith, Abby, 253
Smith, Gerrit, 96, 103, 105, 113, Appendix 299
Smith, Mrs. Judith W., 273
Smith, Julia, 253
Smith, Lettice, 117
Smith, Dr. Stephen S., 139
Spaulding, Eliza, 101
Spectator, The New England, 28 to 30
Spencer, Rev. Anna Garlin, 290
Spinner, General, 44
Spofford, Jane H., Appendix 300
Spofford, Ainsworth R., 150
Spooner, Thomas, 180
Springfield Republican, 93
Stewart, P. P., 42
Stanton, Henry B., 41
Stanton, Elizabeth Cady, 41, 94, 103, 106, 107, 111, 112, 171, 197, 199, 203, 208, 210, 211, 213, 214, 217, 219, 221 to 225, 230, Appendix 300
Starret, Mrs. Helen Ekin, 207
State Regulation of Vice, 241
Stone, Eliza, 11, 13
Stone, Francis, 8
Stone, Francis (Second), 7 to 10, 13, 23, 52
Stone, Francis (Third), 13, 55, 64, 277
Stone, Gregory, 7, 8
Stone, Hannah (Matthews), 3, 8, 9, 10, 13, 14, 15, 16, 18, 19, 40, 44, 48, 64, 65, 66, 71, 75, 163, 165, 263
Stone, Lucy, birth, 3; ancestry, 7, 8; childhood, 9 to 21; love of nature, 7, 11, 277 to 279; courage, 14, 15; determines to work for women's rights, 15; discovers the text, "He shall rule over thee", 15; resolves to go to college, 16; wrestles with high temper, 18; overworks to save her mother, 19; picks berries and nuts to buy books, 20; personal appearance, 21; joins the church, 22; tries to vote in church meeting, 22; teaches school, 23, 24; listens to "Pastoral Letter", 24, 25; pays tribute to the Grimké sisters and Abby Kelley Foster, 34 to 36; preparation for college, 37; attends Quaboag Seminary and Wilbraham Academy, 37; letter to brother on the woman question, 37 to 40; goes to Mt. Holyoke Seminary, 40; journey to Oberlin, 43 to 46; life at Oberlin, 46 to 74; teaches in preparatory department and does housework in Ladies' Boarding Hall at three cents an hour, 49; clashes with Ladies' Board, 50, 60, 61, 63, 68, 70, 114, 117; teaches colored school, 51; outline of day's work, 53, 54; prevents a suicide, 56; forms friendship with Antoinette L. Brown, 56 to 60; organizes first debating club of college girls, 60 to 62; makes her first public speech, 65; discusses her intention to lecture with her family, 64 to 67; refuses to write Commencement essay because forbidden to read it, 67 to 73; takes first

diploma achieved by a Massachusetts woman, 72, 73; speaks at Oberlin semicentennial, 74; gives first woman's rights lecture, 75; lectures against slavery, 76 to 86; has great eloquence, 76; puts up her own posters, 78; has hymn-book hurled at her head and is drenched with water, 80; subdues mob on Cape Cod, 80, 81; lectures on temperance, 82, 131, 132; is opposed as a "Garrisonian", 82; synopsis of antislavery lecture, 83; is called an infidel, 84; is expelled from West Brookfield church, 86 to 88; mixes too much woman's rights with her antislavery lectures: "I was a woman before I was an abolitionist", 89, 90; lectures for woman's rights, 89 to 93; sleeps in garret, three in a bed, 91; denounced by press as "she-hyena", etc., 92, 93; has remarkably sweet voice, 93; is first speaker to make woman's rights her main theme, hence called the "morning star", 94; plans for First National Woman's Rights Convention, 95 to 97; heads the Call, 97; speaks at Convention, 98; converts Susan B. Anthony, 99; meets her future husband for first time, 97; gets up National Woman's Rights Conventions year after year, and publishes "Woman's Rights Tracts", 100; opens new occupations to women, 101; puts on Bloomer dress, 103; adventures in wearing it, 104 to 106; discusses its pros and cons, 106 to 110; gives it up, 112, 113; proposal to put her on committee at temperance meeting causes uproar; she helps to call Whole World's instead of Half World's Temperance Convention, 115, 116; subdues mob at Fourth National Woman's Rights Convention, 120, 121; addresses Massachusetts Constitutional Convention, 124; courtship, 124 to 131, 145, 147, 155 to 160; lectures in Middle West; amusing incidents, 131 to 135; makes acquaintance of Blackwell family, 136, 145; praises rescue of little slave girl, 152; marriage, 161 to 166; Marriage Protest, 166 to 170; keeps her own name, 171 to 173; is barred from school vote, 173 to 177; offers Margaret Garner a knife, 184; visits Wisconsin, 185 to 192; removes to New Jersey, 193; discusses surname for daughter, 195; lets her goods be sold for taxes, 195, 196; is called "a little dunce"; gives up lecturing, temporarily, for baby's sake, 199; Civil War work, 200; makes successful appeal to Jews, 200, 201; urges inclusion of women in Fourteenth and Fifteenth Amendments, 201, 202; does suffrage work in New Jersey, 202, 203; chosen President of New Jersey Woman Suffrage Association, 203; is wise and loving mother, 203; helps organize New England and Massachusetts Woman Suffrage Associations, 204, 205; removes to Boston, 205; takes part in Kansas campaign, 206 to 209; refuses to oppose Fifteenth Amendment, 214; helps organize American Woman Suffrage Association, 215, 216; is accused of not being legally married, 219; refuses to rake up the early misdeeds of the National Association in the Woman's Journal, 237; family life

Stone, Lucy (*continued*)
at Pope's Hill, 232, 233; personal characteristics, as mother and housekeeper, 232 to 235; raises money to found the Woman's Journal, 236; becomes the editor, 238; resists religious intolerance, 241; uses Eddy legacy for suffrage propaganda, 242; does vast and varied suffrage work, 244; secures passage of married women's property bill in Canada, and of improved laws in many States, 244, 245; campaigns in Vermont, Michigan, Nebraska, Colorado and Rhode Island, 246; is delegate to Massachusetts Republican Convention, 247; defends Mrs. Tilton in Beecher-Tilton scandal, 249 to 251; works in Association for the Advancement of Women, 251; secures exhibit of tax protests at the Centennial Exposition; views on the American flag, 254; beloved by her servants, 256, 257; strong in womanly qualities, 258, 259; love of poetry, 261; affection for Wendell Phillips, 262; modest and without vanity, 262 to 264; catches cold, crossing flooded river, and loses strength of her voice, 264; at International Council of Women, Susan B. Anthony and Julia Ward Howe ascribe their conversion to her, 266, 267; portrait bust by Anne Whitney, 273, 274; speaks at World's Fair in Chicago, 276; her last illness, 276 to 282; last words, "Make the world better", 282; funeral, 284; cremation, 285; tributes, 285, 286
Stone, Luther, 10, 13, 14, 18, 97
Stone, Rhoda, 13, 17, 18, 40
Stone, Sarah, 13, 17, 18, 51, 55, 64
Stone, William Bowman, 13, 37, 49, 51, 64, 75, 86, 164, 165
Storer, Judge, 154
Stowe, Harriet Beecher, 122, 129, 143, 169, 249, 297
Sugar-refining, 269
Suicide, prevents a, 56
Sumner, Charles, 201, 213, 268
Switzerland, longs to see, 270
Syracuse Standard, 101
Syracuse University, 139

Taft and Mallon, 149
Taft, Mrs. Dora, 95
Taft, Mrs. Eliza, 95
Tariff reform, 294
Taylor, Father, 95
Taylor, Harriet, 99
Tax protest, 195
Tax protest exhibit at Centennial, 253
Tax protest tablet, 196
Teaches school, 23, 24
Temper, wrestles with high, 18
Temperance Conventions, Whole World's and Half World's, 115, 116, 119, 120, 121
Temperance lecturing, 82, 131, 132, 161
Thome, Professor, 60, 69
Tilton, Elizabeth, 249, 250
Tilton, Theodore, 217 to 219, 223, 249, 251
Train, George Francis, 208 to 212, 214, 221, 226, 229
Trall, Dr., 116
Tribute to the Grimké sisters and Abby Kelley Foster, 34 to 36
Truth, Sojourner, 99
Twentieth Century Club, 269
Tyndall, Sarah, 99

Underground Railroad, 51
Union of American and National Woman Suffrage Associations, 228, 229

Union Woman Suffrage Association, 217 to 219, 221, 249
Unitarian, she becomes a, 59
Universalists first denomination to sanction ordaining of women, Appendix 299

Vanderbilt, Cornelius, 222
Vermont, early lectures in, 82 to 86
Vilbert, George H., 216
Victorian Club, 269
Villard, Oscar Garrison, 196
Voice, sweetness of, 21, 81, 93; loses strength of, 264

Wade, Benjamin F., 268
Walker, Judge, 180 to 183
Wall, Sarah E., 253
Ward, Eliza T., Appendix 300
Washington, Conn., meetings at, 32
Washington Union, 170
Weld, Angelina Grimké, 26 to 31, 34, 35, 37, 94, 103, 126, 254, 262
Weld, Theodore D., 31, 120, 127, 128, 129, 256
Western Anti-Slavery Association, 71, 147
West Indies, 268
Westminster Review, 99
Whipple, E. P., 199
Whipple, Mr., 68, 69
White, Andrew D., 268
Whitney, Anne, 261, 273, 284
Whittier, John Greenleaf, 25, 284, 285, 296
Wife-beating, 4, 5
Wife-beating forbidden in Massachusetts, 5
Wilbour, Mrs. Charlotte B., 251
Wilbraham Academy, 37
Willard, Frances E., 266, 273
Winnebago County Fair, 275
Wisconsin, picturesque experiences in, 184 to 192
Woman's Bible, 230
Woman Citizen, The, 243, Appendix 301
Woman's Column, 242
Woman's Congress, 251
Woman's Christian Temperance Union, 270
Woman's Journal, 216, 219, 220, 227, 231, 235, 236, 237, 239, 240, 242, 243, 244, 246, 250, 251, 263, 271, 281, 285, 294, Appendix 300, 301
Woman's Journal, becomes editor of, 238
Woman's Journal, raises money to start, 236
Woman's Rights, lectures on, 89 to 93
Woman's Rights Tracts, 100
Women, condition of, 3 to 7
Women's Medical College of the New York Infirmary, 141
Wood, Hon. Samuel N., 206, 207
Woodhull and Claflin's Weekly, 222, 224, 249
Woodhull, Victoria C., 217, 221 to 226, 228, 229, 249
Worcester Spy, 168
Worcester Woman's Rights Convention, 36, 97, 98, 266
Working Girls' Clubs, 270
World's Anti-Slavery Convention, 41
World's Congress of Representative Women, 276
World's Fair, Chicago, 273, 274, 275; Woman's Building at, 281
World's Parliament of Religions, 280
World's Temperance Conventions, 115, 116, 118, 119
Wright, Henry C., 83, 96
Wright, Frances, 94, 138

Youth's Companion, 16

Zakrzewska, Dr. Marie E., 141